"*Clear Thinking in a Messy World* ... us how to filter the obscurity of our times by clarifying the critical life of the mind plays. Samples and Perez offer an apologia for developing and nurturing a Christian-oriented life of the mind through logic and reason. I recommend this book to anyone who is bewildered by the intellectual obscurity of our times and who seeks to love our Creator through a God-glorifying life of the mind."

—Miguel Angel Endara, PhD
Professor of Philosophy and Religion
Veritas International University

"According to Scripture, our enemy is 'the great deceiver,' and no one is immune. The most alluring deceptions are those we want to believe. The 'belt of truth' is our defense against the forces of darkness, establishing a biblical imperative to think soundly and clearly. In an age where deception runs rampant not only outside but within the community of faith, Kenneth Samples and Mark Perez have risen to the cause of defending us from Satan's wiles. In their thorough, nonpartisan, nonsectarian, and eminently readable book, they assist the reader in learning to think soundly, logically, and therefore *biblically*. *Clear Thinking in a Messy World* can benefit the general reader but could well serve as a study curriculum for Bible studies, small groups, homeschoolers, and college-level apologetics and philosophy courses. I heartily endorse this latest contribution from Reasons to Believe."

—Steven J. Willing, MD, MBA
Adjunct Professor of Divinity, Regent University
Author, *Superbia: The Perils of Pride. The Power of Humility*

"Kenneth Samples and Mark Perez guide the reader in how to think clearly in the contemporary world. The authors demonstrate how spirituality, faith, and the life of the mind are more compatible than often portrayed. They present a compelling portrait of the need for logic and reasoning for the Christian community. They analyze and explain both formal logic and informal reasoning, fallacies to avoid, and the problem of cognitive biases that can hinder clear thinking. I highly recommend this book for every Christian, but especially for our youth who would benefit enormously from training in reasoning from an early age, well before their first years in college. I'm hopeful that were this book put into the curricula of our youth and young adults, we would see the next generation better equipped for the challenges of our increasingly secular society and less likely to stray from orthodox Christianity after high school."

—Mark T. Clark, PhD
Professor Emeritus, Political Science
National Security Studies, CSU San Bernardino
President, the Association for the Study of the Middle East and Africa

"Our Lord invites us, 'Come now, let us reason together' (Isaiah 1:18). In this handy volume, Kenneth Samples and Mark Perez teach us how to do exactly that. Sanctified reason, operating as the handmaid of faith, serves the Lord with its logical and analytical capabilities. *Clear Thinking in a Messy World* demonstrates that we really do have a reasonable faith."

—Kenneth Keathley
Senior Professor of Theology
Director of the L. Russ Bush Center for Faith and Culture
Southeastern Baptist Theological Seminary

"It's not easy to find a book on logic that doesn't quickly overwhelm the beginner or bore the more advanced. But Kenneth Samples and Mark Perez have created a superb book that I'm thrilled to read. It's highly accessible and strikes the perfect balance of logic and critical thinking, all with an apologetic flavor that trains you to think better. This is the book I wish I started with. Highly recommended!"

—Brian Auten
Founder, Apologetics 315
Host of the *Apologetics 315* podcast

"We observe in the New Testament how Jesus, Peter, and Paul employed logic and sound reasoning in their numerous sermons, letters, and dialogues with others. With the blessing of the Holy Spirit, their message converted millions to the truth. As we present God's Word to a skeptical culture, we must follow their example. Presenting the truth in love requires sound reasoning and clear thinking. Kenneth Samples explains principles of logic and critical thinking clearly and with detail, and Mark Perez complements these principles with a cogent analysis of the most common biases that we all have when evaluating information we receive. This well-documented book not only provides guidance but also motivates us to be honest, fair, and convincing as we engage with people, 'giving a reason for the hope that we have.' You'll be instructed, inspired, and challenged by this book!"

—John Battle, ThD
Professor of New Testament and Theology
Western Reformed Seminary

"The need for clear, logical thinking is more urgent than ever in the culture and church. Beliefs and perspectives considered unthinkable just several years ago are now accepted with little critical thinking. Apologists and scholars Kenneth Samples and Mark Perez in *Clear Thinking in a Messy World* equip readers with an invigorating exploration of critical thinking from a Christian perspective and a concise-yet-detailed guide for thinking logically so that we might better love God with our minds and be salt and light in this confused age."

—Bill Feltner
Program Director
*Pilgrim Radio*

"Kenneth Samples and Mark Perez have done a wonderful service for the church and the academy. *Clear Thinking in a Messy World* is a tool that will help Christ followers dispel the myth that our faith is not an intellectual faith. Samples and Perez demonstrate that nothing could be further from the truth. Students, pastors, laypeople, and scholars alike will find not only an argument for clear thinking but also tools for how to carry out that endeavor. I highly recommend this resource!"

—Jason Neill, PhD, LPC
Associate Professor of Psychology
Anderson University

"In a day when critical thinking is no longer encouraged, Kenneth Samples and Mark Perez have done a great service to the church by instructing us in the art of proper thinking. We live in a world that no longer loves the truth—a culture of fake news and lies. Only through logical thinking skills can we see through the messiness of the world and defend the truth."

—Phil Fernandes, PhD, DMin
Pastor of Trinity Bible Fellowship
President of the International Society of Christian Apologetics
Professor of Apologetics and Religion, Veritas International University

"All too often, Christianity and its followers are relegated to the irrational and irrelevant heap. Many people, including Christians, are simply unaware or ill-informed about the world-changing impact Christianity has had in philosophy, science, and law, to name a few. In fact, most of what is considered secular has been borrowed from the sacred. Cultivating the life of the mind is essential to faith. In *Clear Thinking in a Messy World*, Kenneth Samples and Mark Perez invite the reader to emulate Jesus by properly engaging not only the heart but also the mind in our daily witness.

The authors' thoughtful approach to logic and reason is not only intellectually stimulating but also deeply rooted in Scripture, making it a valuable resource for those seeking to reconcile their beliefs with a rational understanding of the world."

—Harry Edwards
Founder and Director
Apologetics.com, Inc.

"Our world today seems to be noisier and more threatening. Many Christians feel like they're stranded in the middle of a busy street as the speeding traffic of arguments and ideas increasingly swirl around them. It's becoming harder and harder to safely navigate the messages culture drives at us. However, authors Kenneth Samples and Mark Perez have provided us with just the right vehicle to escape these dangers with their important new book, *Clear Thinking in a Messy World*. Samples and Perez explain how necessary it is to express our love of Jesus through growing our minds. They teach essential critical thinking skills and how to distinguish education from propaganda.

Written in a light, approachable style, this book should be required reading for everyone. It's especially suited for high schoolers, small groups, and pastors. If you're looking to navigate the road to thoughtful living more confidently in this day and age, *Clear Thinking in a Messy World* is for you."

—Lenny Esposito
President, Come Reason Ministries

"*Clear Thinking in a Messy World* is a wonderfully integrative resource every Christian should have in their library. It's engaging and accessible, yet robust in its treatment of the subject matter: the biblical case for thinking well and how to do so. Samples and Perez explain why the pursuit of holiness—of Christlikeness in all aspects of life—includes the intentional cultivation of the intellect. In addition to providing a sound theological perspective on the life of the mind, they equip the reader with the philosophical tools necessary for thinking critically and logically in a culture plagued by incoherent, destructive worldviews and dialectical chaos."

—Melissa Cain Travis, PhD
Fellow, Center for Science and Culture at
Discovery Institute

"As someone who has taught critical thinking for high schoolers and college students for years, I am genuinely excited to see this book! It's a clear and engaging text for homeschoolers, teachers, and anyone who wants to be a learned Christian. It also offers very practical ways churches can integrate critical thinking into services and small groups. Further, *Clear Thinking in a Messy World* will inspire and motivate readers to regain the church's intellectual heritage and be thoughtful Christians in a world of thoughtlessness."

—J. Brian Huffling, PhD
Director of the PhD Program and Associate Professor
of Philosophy and Theology
Southern Evangelical Seminary

"Kenneth Samples and Mark Perez help place stones for us to step on that lead to logic, reasoning, and cognitive analysis for studying God's Word. You'll get on a path to confident, clearer thinking with this book. In the famous words from Isaiah 1:18, 'Come now, let us reason together.' You'll learn as you enjoy the reader-friendly pages and logical presentations. *Clear Thinking in a Messy World* is very clear and made me want to read it!"

—Bill Arnold
*Afternoons with Bill Arnold*
Faith Radio

"In *Clear Thinking in a Messy World*, Kenneth Samples and Mark Perez have produced a well-researched, but readable wake-up call the church needs today. Learning to discern truth from error is essential for people to be delivered from the domain of darkness and lies and transferred into the kingdom of Christ. Samples and Perez masterfully demonstrate to the reader how they can know the truth that can set them free (John 8:32). As such, this book should be in every Christian's library so they may be able to use logic and reason to know the truth and refute error (Titus 1:9) to further God's kingdom in teaching, apologetics, and evangelism."

—Kevin Lewis
Christian Theologian, Apologist, and Attorney
Institute for Theology and Law

# Dedication

To the memory of my brother Frank and my sister-in-law Angie.
May you rest in peace in Christ and then rise in glory.
—Kenneth R. Samples

To those with minds open to wisdom.
—Mark Perez

KENNETH R. SAMPLES AND MARK PEREZ

# CLEAR THINKING
## IN A MESSY WORLD

### A Christian Guide to
### Logic, Reason, and Cognitive Bias

rtb PRESS

© 2024 by Reasons to Believe

All rights reserved. No part of this publication may be reproduced in any form without written permission from Reasons to Believe, 818 S. Oak Park Rd., Covina, CA 91724. reasons.org

Cover design: Kim Hermosillo with Danielle Camorlinga
Interior layout: Christine Talley

Unless otherwise identified, all Scripture quotations taken from the Holy Bible, New International Version®, NIV®. Copyright © 1973, 1978, 1984, 2011 by Biblica, Inc.™ All rights reserved worldwide.

Names: Samples, Kenneth R., author. | Perez, Mark, author.
Title: Clear thinking in a messy world : a Christian guide to logic , reason , and cognitive bias / Kenneth R. Samples and Mark Perez.
Description: Includes bibliographical references and index. | Covina, CA: RTB Press, 2024.
Identifiers: ISBN: 978-1-956112-06-1
Subjects: LCSH Apologetics. | Religion--Philosophy. | Philosophy and religion. | Theology. | BISAC PHILOSOPHY / Religious | PHILOSOPHY / Logic | RELIGION / Philosophy | RELIGION / Christian Education / Adult | RELIGION / Christian Theology / Apologetics
Classification: LCC BT1212 .S36 2024 | DDC 239--dc23

Printed in the United States of America

First edition

1 2 3 4 5 6 7 8 9 10 / 28 27 26 25 24

For more information about Reasons to Believe, contact (855) REASONS / (855) 732-7667 or visit reasons.org.

# Contents

| | |
|---|---|
| List of Figures and Tables | 15 |
| Acknowledgments | 17 |
| Introduction: Why Christians Need to Think Clearly | 19 |

## Part 1: The Whats, Whys, Wheres, and Hows of Logic

| | |
|---|---|
| 1. Christianity and the Life of the Mind | 25 |
| 2. Why Study Logic? | 41 |
| 3. The Basic Elements of Logical Arguments | 55 |
| 4. The Laws of Logic | 67 |

## Part 2: Informal Reasoning

| | |
|---|---|
| 5. Three Types of Logical Reasoning | 85 |
| 6. Positive Steps to Reinforce Clear Thinking | 105 |
| 7. Overcoming Common Obstacles to Clear Thinking | 115 |
| 8. Evaluating Propaganda and Conspiracy Theories | 125 |
| 9. Twelve Precarious Informal Fallacies | 141 |
| 10. Fifteen More Common Informal Fallacies | 169 |

## Part 3: Cognitive Bias

| | |
|---|---|
| 11. Cognitive Biases and Critical Thinking | 195 |
| 12. Biases in Science | 211 |
| 13. Biases in Thinking with Numbers Big and Small | 221 |
| 14. Mitigating the Effects of Cognitive Biases | 231 |
| 15. Integrating Thoughts on Clear Thinking | 239 |

| | |
|---|---|
| Bibliography | 247 |
| Notes | 251 |
| Index | 269 |
| About the Authors | 279 |
| About Reasons to Believe | 281 |

# List of Figures and Tables

Figures
4.1  Traditional Square of Opposition                                      79

Tables
1.1  The Life of the Mind and Intellectual Ability                         34
1.2  12 Suggestions for Pursuing Knowledge and Wisdom in Daily Life        39
2.1  Human Exceptionalism and the *imago Dei*                              42
2.2  Major Branches of Philosophy                                          52
4.1  Four Logical Relationships                                            77
5.1  A Dozen Contrasts of Deductive and Inductive Reasoning                99
6.1  Actions and Virtues Conducive to Careful Thinking                    113
7.1  Lewis's Argument from Desire                                         122
8.1  Jim Lehrer's 16 Principles for Traditional Journalism                128
9.1  Clarifying Definitions                                               153
10.1 Distinguishing Fallacies                                             191

# Acknowledgments

English philosopher and statesmen Francis Bacon had this to say about the reading of books:

> Some books are to be tasted, others to be swallowed, and some few to be chewed and digested; that is, some books are to be read only in parts; others to be read, but not curiously; and some few are to be read wholly, and with diligence and attention.[1]

*Clear Thinking in a Messy World* is a work we've contemplated and planned for several years. Writing a good book takes great diligence and attention, and we hope you, the reader, will chew and digest this book.

As authors, we're fortunate to have had many people support and encourage us in this literary venture as well as skilled colleagues who worked diligently behind the scenes to improve the quality of this work. Whatever errors remain are the responsibility of the authors alone. Expressing gratitude begins with our wives, Joan and Kathleen, who patiently endured the hours we spent researching and writing and offered us encouragement when we needed it the most.

Several astute scholars helped review the book, either as a whole or in part, including Steven Willing, Winfried Corduan, Vern Poythress, David Rogstad, and Jacob Rodriguez. These men provided insights that helped refine and improve the work.

The Reasons to Believe (RTB) editorial staff worked skillfully to improve the style and clarity of our writing. Our sincere appreciation goes to Maureen

Moser, Sandra Dimas, Joe Aguirre, Helena Heredia, Jocelyn King, and Karrie Cano. Because we're fortunate to be members of the RTB scholar team, we enjoyed the collegial support of Fazale Rana, Jeff Zweerink, Hugh Ross, and George Haraksin.

Finally, we offer gratitude and praise to the triune God—Father, Son, and Holy Spirit.

Faith Seeking Understanding,<br>
Kenneth Samples and Mark Perez

Introduction

# Why Christians Need to Think Clearly

Christians can *never* genuinely value and utilize logic and critical thinking because their faith prohibits them from basing their beliefs on rational considerations. Thus, logic and critical thinking are at odds with the Christian conception of faith.

This was the gist of one skeptic's challenge to Christianity on Reasons to Believe's social media accounts. To say he was mistaken is an understatement. Biblical faith is not blind faith; it never has been. From its foundations, Christianity has promoted the acquisition of knowledge, wisdom, and understanding (Job 28:28; Psalm 111:10; Proverbs 1:7) and the pursuit of such intellectual virtues as source-checking, discernment, testing, reflection, and intellectual renewal (Acts 17:11; 1 Corinthians 14:29; Romans 12:2; Colossians 2:8; 1 Thessalonians 5:21). The Bible's very definition of *faith* includes a necessary rational component because, from a scriptural perspective, one does not place their trust in a source of which they know nothing. Both the Hebrew and Greek words for *faith* used in Scripture convey the chief idea of trust placed in a credible source or object—namely God, Christ, or the truth. Thus, biblical faith can be said to involve a reasonable step of trust or confidence in what a person has good reason to believe is actually true.

Church history bears out this deep intertwining of faith and reason. Historic Christianity has made significant contributions to many rational fields, including education, logic, and science. Building on its connection to Judaism, ancient Christianity was a bookish religion that produced a robust textual tradition. The era of the church fathers was a rich intellectual period with brilliant thinkers and prolific authors. Upon the collapse of the Roman Empire, medieval Catholic monasteries preserved learning and scholarship through teaching, recopying manuscripts, and building libraries. Later Christians founded or helped found many of Europe and America's most prestigious universities. Men and women with deep ties to historic Christianity continued to be at the forefront of scientific discovery, philosophy, literature, art, and music for centuries afterward.

And yet, sadly, it's not hard to see how that skeptic on social media came to his conclusion. Anti-intellectualism presents a serious problem for the church today. The issue has been festering for at least a century, particularly in evangelicalism where there has been increasing emphasis on emotion and spiritual experience *at the expense* of intellect and clear thinking. The recent rise of cultural hostility toward historic Christianity in the West and the advent of the Internet, with its cacophony of competing voices and insulated echo chambers, have exacerbated the situation. For decades, leading evangelical scholars have expressed concern about this problem.[1] Our own interactions with Christian intellectuals through our years of college teaching and working in apologetics also demonstrate that too many believers think they must choose between being spiritual (or devout) on one hand or intellectual on the other.

## The Call to Be a Clear-Thinking Christian

Scripture makes it plain that God does not intend his people to choose between spirituality and intellectualism. The idea that a person must be either a thinker *or* a feeler is a false dichotomy that should be rejected. In his public ministry, Jesus Christ exhibited signs of being a first-rate thinker and debater, yet he was also keenly compassionate to the genuine needs of humanity. This is the model set before Christians.

Scripture teaches that all human beings are created in the express image of God, meaning that in a finite and temporal way, the human mind resembles God's infinite and eternal mind (Genesis 1:26–27). Moreover, Christians are called to participate in loving God with all their mind to the best of their personal abilities (Mark 12:30). In his classic book *Mere Christianity*, C. S. Lewis puts it this way, "God is no fonder of intellectual slackers than of any other slackers." He warns that becoming a Christian requires "the whole of you, brains and all."[2]

Clear thinking is an indispensable aspect of the Christian life and a critically important part of a believer's overall devotion to God (Matthew 22:37). It equips believers to appreciate the fullness of the gospel more completely. The pursuit of knowledge and truth, rooted in the reverence of the Lord, always has spiritual *and* moral dimensions. Genuine knowledge of life and the world is grounded in the reality of God and in his revealed moral law. In other words, devotion and learning go hand-in-hand—there should be no bifurcation between faith and reason.

Not only is clear thinking essential to a healthy personal faith, but it is also vital in the individual Christian's witness to the world about God's truth. Imagine if that skeptic on social media learned to perceive followers of Christ as people who love and prize truth? Since truth comes from God, believers ought to handle it, in all its forms, as something sacred. Striving to be intellectually informed, careful, fair-minded, and honest prepares believers to handle God's precious truth in a reasonable and responsible way.

**Sharpening Christian Minds**
Where does one start to answer the call to be a clear-thinking Christian? We believe that a basic understanding of logic, informal reason, and cognitive bias is a great place to begin on this journey. The purpose of this book is to present Christians with strong biblical motives to pursue these dimensions of clear thinking and, to this end, we have divided our book into three sections. Part 1 addresses logic, without which arguments cannot be tested rationally. Part 2 deals with informal reasoning, within which most daily thinking takes place and where reasoning errors are common. Part 3 tackles cognitive bias, the universal mental process that unconsciously distorts our thinking and deceives us into believing what's false or missing what's true.

By presenting logic, informal reasoning, and cognitive bias together, our goal is to help you see how these three dimensions of thought integrate. Each section can be studied independently and in nonsequential order. We encourage you to start with the area that most interests you. Both of us reviewed and contributed to the other's work; however, we each focused on the dimensions for which we had the most experience teaching or studying. For Ken those are parts 1 and 2 (logic, reason, and the life of the mind); for Mark, part 3 (cognitive biases and critical thinking).

To Christians daunted by his warning in *Mere Christianity*, Lewis includes these reassuring words, "Anyone who is honestly trying to be a Christian will soon find his intelligence sharpened: one of the reasons why it needs no special education to be a Christian is that Christianity is an education itself."[3] It's our hope that our three-dimensional approach to clear thinking will sharpen your mind, helping you to navigate your faith (and any other topic) with grace, humility, and a clear conscience in today's intellectually messy world.

# Part I

## The Whats, Whys, Wheres, and Hows of Logic

Kenneth R. Samples

# Chapter 1

# Christianity and the Life of the Mind

> Even though most people who reject Christianity treat it as a refuge for enemies of reason, the truth is that there may be no worldview in the history of the human race that has a higher regard for the laws of logic.[1]
> —Ronald H. Nash, *Worldviews in Conflict*

The relationship between the Christian faith and the cerebral enterprises of logic, reason, and the life of the mind is vitally important. In this chapter we'll briefly explore historic Christianity's connection to these rational components of life. This content represents our strong case that historic Christianity has prized reason and that today's Christians need to think clearly.

We'll look first at Jesus Christ and his use of logic and reason. Second, we'll note ways in which Christianity connects faith and reason. Third, we'll discuss a Christian perspective on the life of the mind. Lastly, we'll offer suggestions on how the evangelical church can help Christians to love God more deeply with their intellect.

## Jesus: The Sage Logician

When historic Christians think about Jesus Christ, they rightly think of him in his central role of Lord and Savior. Yet Jesus is also an example to all Christians both in his moral actions and in his exhibition of reasoning and the practice of intellectual virtue. Jesus reflected the profound abilities of a sage logician in his teaching, storytelling, and reasoning.[2]

*Masterful Teacher*
When we think of humanity's greatest all-time teachers, both Western and Eastern, names like Socrates, Plato, Aristotle, Confucius, and Gautama immediately come to mind. Yet Jesus's skill as a teacher may equal or even surpass these ancient sages.[3]

The four gospels reveal that Jesus consistently astonished his audience both as a miracle worker *and* as a master teacher. His extraordinary knowledge and wisdom were evident even as an adolescent when he was separated from his parents in Jerusalem and was later found in the temple courts in dialogue with Israel's greatest teachers. Luke 2:46–48 reports, "Everyone who heard him was amazed at his understanding and his answers. When his parents saw him, they were astonished."

All Jewish males of Jesus's time would've studied the Hebrew Scriptures; however, as a carpenter, Jesus wasn't trained formally as a scholar or rabbi. And yet, the instruction he imparted exceeded that of specialists in the Hebrew Scriptures and law. For example, Matthew 7:28–29 describes the crowd's reaction to the Sermon on the Mount: "When Jesus had finished saying these things, the crowds were amazed at his teaching, because he taught as one who had authority, and not as their teachers of the law." Later, Jesus's teachings met with a similarly incredulous response in Nazareth:

> Coming to his hometown, he began teaching the people in their synagogue, and they were amazed. "Where did this man get this wisdom and these miraculous powers?" they asked. "Isn't this the carpenter's son? Isn't his mother's name Mary, and aren't his brothers James, Joseph, Simon and Judas? Aren't all his sisters with us? Where then did this man get all these things?" (Matthew 13:54–56)

At the Festival of Tabernacles in Galilee, the astounded Jews who heard Jesus teach at the temple courts wondered where he had gotten his knowledge without formal instruction. "Jesus answered, 'My teaching is not my own. It comes from the one who sent me'" (John 7:14–16). In an article for *Christian Scholar's Review*, philosopher Dallas Willard says of Christ, "When I speak of 'Jesus the logician' I refer to his use of logical insights: to his mastery and employment of logical principles in his work as a teacher and public figure."[4]

### Creative Storyteller

Jesus's ingenious use of well-crafted parables as teaching tools also evinces his great wisdom. Biblical scholar Grant B. Osborne characterizes the parables as reflecting such elements as "earthiness, conciseness, major and minor points, repetition, conclusion at the end, listener-relatedness, reversal of expectation, kingdom-centered eschatology, kingdom ethics, and God and salvation."[5]

Many of Jesus's parables remain famous for their moral and spiritual insights. The parable of the prodigal son (Luke 15:11–32) memorably illustrates God's love for his wayward children. The story of the good Samaritan (Luke 10:25–37) demonstrates that God's people should love and do good to *all* people, including one's enemies. Other prominent examples include humility before God in the parable of the Pharisee and the tax collector (Luke 18:9–14), evidence of genuine faith in the parable of the sheep and the goats (Matthew 25:31–46), and God's persistent pursuit of wayward sinners in the parable of the lost sheep (Matthew 18:12–14).

Christian philosopher Travis Dickinson notes, "Now, being a good storyteller does not necessarily make one brilliant. But Jesus was not merely a good storyteller. Jesus often, seemingly on the spot, had the ability to package profound truths in stories that perfectly applied to his hearers and brought insight and conviction."[6]

### The Reasoner

When Jesus made a case for his identity as the long-awaited Jewish Messiah, he appealed to evidence and presented a logical argument. For example, in Luke 7, John the Baptist—imprisoned and, no doubt, discouraged—sent word to Jesus asking for confirmation of his messianic identity.

> Jesus replied, "Go back and report to John what you hear and see: The blind receive sight, the lame walk, those who have leprosy are cleansed, the deaf hear, the dead are raised, and the good news is proclaimed to the poor. Blessed is anyone who does not stumble on account of me."

The Hebrew Scriptures predicted that the Messiah would be an extraordinary miracle worker and a great teacher (see Isaiah 29:18–19; 35:4–6; 61:1–2). Jesus was, thus, appealing to his public healings and teachings as evidence that he is indeed the Messiah.

This response can be set forth in the formal logical structure of the *modus ponens* (a deductive argument form and rule of inference that will be explained in chapter 5):

> If P, then Q.
> P.
> Therefore, Q.
>
> If one does the extraordinary acts of healing and teaching, then one is the Messiah.
> I do these extraordinary acts of healing and teaching.
> Therefore, I am the Messiah.

Philosopher Douglas Groothuis notes, "The acts he cites are meant to point out necessary and sufficient criteria for identifying the Messiah, 'the one who was to come.'"[7]

Jesus's wisdom and highly skilled reasoning are especially evident when engaged in controversies with people who challenged him. Consider his response to the challenge of paying Roman taxes recorded in Matthew 22. Desiring to trap Jesus with his own words, the Pharisees and others presented him with an intellectual and moral dilemma, acknowledging Jesus's integrity and wisdom and then asking if he thought it right to pay the imperial tax to Caesar.

In his book *Logic and the Way of Jesus*, philosopher Travis Dickinson explains why this challenge was so significant:

> They pressed Jesus about whether it is lawful to pay taxes to Caesar. . . . This is a serious intellectual trap because if he said yes, then he recognized Caesar as an authority when the Jews were not supposed to have any authority except for God. In this case, he could be accused religiously. But if he said no, he broke Roman law and could be accused legally.[8]

However, Jesus's reply was incisive. First, he called out his challengers for their "evil intent" to trap him. Then, he told them to show him a denarius, the Roman coin used to pay taxes:

> They brought him a denarius, and he asked them, "Whose image is this? And whose inscription?"
> "Caesar's," they replied. Then he said to them, "So give back to

Caesar what is Caesar's, and to God what is God's." When they heard this, they were amazed. So, they left him and went away. (Matthew 22:19b–22)

Right on the spot, Jesus cogently and courageously met the intellectual and moral dilemma presented to him. He did this numerous times in the gospels whenever the highly trained religious authorities confronted him with controversial issues. Considering this aspect of Jesus's public ministry, theologian R. C. Sproul comments:

> I think that part of the perfect humanity of our Lord was that He never made an illegitimate inference. He never jumped to a conclusion that was unwarranted by the premises. His thinking was crystal clear and coherent. We are called to imitate our Lord in all things, including His thinking. Therefore, make it a matter of chief and earnest business in your life to love Him with all of your mind.[9]

Jesus, without formal training, operated as a sage logician and a truly world-class orator, debater, and rhetorician. He clearly, consistently, and powerfully exhibited the qualities of razor-sharp reasoning and intellectual virtue. He is our Lord and Savior but also our moral and intellectual example. His entire life and ministry reflected the virtues of truth and love.

## Christianity Connects Faith with Reason
*Faith Presumes Knowledge*
Philosophers commonly define *knowledge* as "justified, true belief." This means a person possesses knowledge when they believe something that's true and accompanied with proper justification or warrant—for example: facts, evidence, or reasons.[10] Faith (being trust or belief) is a necessary component of knowledge because a person must *believe* something to *know* anything. So, in Scripture, faith involves knowledge. For example, saving *faith* involves knowing certain historical facts about Jesus Christ's life, death, and resurrection. Justification for believing the truth of Jesus's identity as the divine-human Messiah comes through details such as Christ's fulfillment of prophecy, his intellectual skill and virtue, his miracles, his moral perfection, and his bodily resurrection from the dead.

*Faith and Reason Are Interdependent*
In historic Christianity, reason and faith function in a complementary fashion. While reason in and of itself, apart from God's special saving grace, can't cause faith[11]—the use of reason is normally a part of a person's coming to faith and supports faith in various ways. As noted earlier, even the very faith that results in salvation involves knowledge (facts surrounding the life, death, and resurrection of Jesus Christ) and discursive reasoning (as to what those facts really mean). Saving faith then includes three things: (1) knowledge of the gospel, (2) assent to its truth, and (3) confident reliance on the Lord and Savior Jesus Christ. Saving faith incorporates a human being's full faculties—mind (knowledge), will (assent), and heart (trust).

*Faith Is Harmonious with Reason*
The scholarly consensus of historic Christianity concerning the relationship of faith and reason—as is reflected especially in such influential thinkers as Augustine, Anselm, and Aquinas—is conveyed in the phrase "faith seeking understanding" (Latin: *fides quaerens intellectum*). While historic Christianity considers faith a gift of divine grace, that given faith can and should seek rational understanding. Reason can be applied rightly to evaluate, confirm, and buttress faith. Thus, Christians should be interested in the rational foundations of their faith. And in conjunction, the Christian apologetics enterprise works to show that there are good reasons (facts, evidence, arguments, etc.) to believe in the truth claims of historic Christianity.

*Faith Doesn't Violate Reason*
Divine mysteries of Christianity—such as the Trinity, the incarnation, and the atonement—often transcend finite human comprehension. However, a lack of full apprehension on our part does not make Christian truths irrational or absurd. We can define mysterious doctrines in ways that avoid creating actual logical contradictions. For example, the triune God's *oneness* (essence) is in a different logical respect from his *threeness* (personhood). Thus, being defined as one essential *What* and three personal *Whos* avoids violating the law of noncontradiction—a thing (A) can't equal both A and non-A at the same time and in the same respect. Christian truths, though they often transcend finite human comprehension, aren't irrational or absurd.

In other words, faith does not damage or violate reason itself.

*God's Rational Mind in the Foundation for Human Reason*
The Christian worldview offers a plausible explanation for affirming an objective source for knowledge, reason, and rationality. Christian theism avows that an infinitely wise and all-knowing God created the universe to reflect a coherent order of laws and logic. He also created humankind in his image and endowed people with rational capacities to discover that reasonable organization, thus guaranteeing that humans have the capacities to reason and discover truth. In effect, God networked the ordered, comprehensible cosmos and rationally capable human beings together with himself to allow for a congruence of intelligibility. The infinite and eternal mind of the creator God provides a reliable metaphysical ground for the rationality of the universe.

*Christianity Encompasses a Reasonable Diversity of Perspectives*
While the branches of historic Christianity are generally united concerning the core truths of the faith (for example, as expressed ecumenically in the Apostles' and Nicene Creeds), the faith, as a whole, is a big tent that allows for rigorous rational debate and differing perspectives on secondary issues. It's often the case that Christian scholars provide a more thorough and vigorous treatment of controversial issues than do other religious traditions and secularism. This diversity of perspectives throughout history has sometimes proved to be divisive but other times been quite positive.

Christianity is far from arbitrary and blind. It's robustly grounded in knowledge and reason. Christian thinker Greg Koukl offers this assessment of the relationship between reason and faith:

> Reason assesses, faith trusts. No conflict. The opposite of faith is not reason; the opposite of faith is unbelief, or lack of trust. The opposite of reason is not faith; the opposite of reason is irrationality. So it certainly is possible to have reasonable faith, and it is also possible to have unreasonable unbelief.[12]

In historic Christianity, faith and reason are complementary and compatible. And this compatibility makes the life of the Christian mind all the more important.

**Life of the Christian Mind**
The motto of the United Negro College Fund that is frequently aired on television powerfully states: "A mind is a terrible thing to waste, but a wonderful

thing to invest in." An awful lot is at stake when it comes to the life of the human mind. Surely not everyone is an intellectual, but if a person wastes their mind (rather than investing in it), then have they not in some profound way wasted their very life? And think of how important the mind is in both defining a human person and allowing that person to flourish in life.

The stakes are exponentially higher in the historic Christian worldview. According to Scripture, human beings are created in the express image of an infinite, eternal, and triune God. Therefore, the mind takes on an eternal dimension. We have a divine obligation to use our mind to the glory of our Creator and to also use our mind in our all-important command to love God (Mark 12:30).

What do we mean specifically when we refer to the "life of the mind"? As we saw in the introduction, from a Judeo-Christian perspective, all people are made in the image of God (Latin: *imago Dei*; Genesis 1:26–27). Therefore, when people have healthy brains and minds then they possess profound conceptual and linguistic faculties. In a finite and temporal way, the human mind resembles God's infinite and eternal mind. God created the world according to laws (Greek: *nomos*) and logic (Greek: *logos*) and then networked the cosmos and human minds together with himself. This metaphorical wiring enables humanity to experience an amazing life of the mind and to be, in effect, seekers of truth. So, it's not surprising that the scientific enterprise itself was birthed and subsequently flourished at a time when the Christian worldview was preeminent.

Historic Christianity affirms the view that God reveals himself to us in two ways: (1) in the book of nature (general revelation) and (2) in the book of Scripture (special revelation). While nature is only a figurative book, it's nevertheless a kind of library or repository of knowledge. Again, because humans are made in the image of God, our mind has been formed to be able to read and interpret both of these revelatory books. (In fact, the reading and translating of the biblical text itself led to increased literacy wherever Judaism and Christianity spread.)

This "bookish" nature of Christian revelation means that believers are primed to be readers and learners by nature. In fact, being disciples of Jesus Christ carries with it the picture of attentive students listening to the teachings of the Master. Thus, for Christians, study and scholarship are a carryover from the very intellectual tradition of the Old Testament with its historic expressions of Judaism.

New Testament scholar and historian of early Christianity Larry Hurtado explains how primitive Christianity was uniquely a textual community and thus a bookish religion:

> From a very early point the reading of texts was a typical part of corporate worship gatherings. This was unusual in the Roman-era setting for a religious group. Indeed, the only analogy was the use of texts in synagogue gatherings.
>
> In the production of new texts, likewise, early Christianity was remarkable and unusual. By my count, there were at least some 200+ texts that we know of composed by ca. 250 AD.
>
> The efforts at copying and dissemination of texts comprise a further distinguishing feature. This trans-local dissemination of texts reflected and furthered the sense of early Christian circles being connected with other circles in a larger, trans-local fellowship.[13]

For the average Christian, pursuing the life of the mind means learning to recognize and prize the conceptual and intellectual side of life. When a Christian values and cultivates the life of the mind, he or she brings glory to God similar to how children honor their parents by using the gifts their parents give them. One way of growing intellectually is seeking information, knowledge, and wisdom daily. This involves staying informed and becoming critical in our thinking faculties. We become prepared to handle truth in a reasonable and responsible way. And since "all truth is God's truth," when we discover truth of any kind, we're on the track to our Creator-Savior God.

However, the life of the mind is not entirely confined to intellectual knowledge—it also impacts a Christian's devotional relationship with God. The attempt to love God with our mind isn't about smugness and pride, but about the pursuit of intellectual virtues to the glory of God. The intellectual capacities that make the life of the mind possible are, after all, a gift from God—humility and reverence are mandatory. A Christian can be a careful thinker and grow in the other important areas involved in Christian devotion such as humbleness and spiritual sensitivity.

The life of the mind is certainly not the most important aspect of the Christian life. That distinction belongs to the truth of knowing the triune God through the redemption that is initiated by the Father, accomplished by the Son on the cross, and applied by the work of the Holy Spirit. The gospel is the "good news" that we can be forgiven of our sins and be reconciled to God through

> **Table 1.1 The Life of the Mind and Intellectual Ability**
>
> I (Kenneth) must admit that, when it comes to the life of the mind, I'm probably obsessive-compulsive. Currently, my personal library collection stands at about 5,000 physical books. I sense that God has called me personally to pursue tenaciously the life of the mind to his glory. For me, it's a burning passion. It grows naturally out of the way God designed me to reflect his image and the degree to which I understand the Christian worldview.
>
> By no means does this same passion need to apply to all Christians. Nevertheless, for all the reasons we've laid out in this book, the life of the mind does remain an important aspect of Christian life.
>
> Some Christians I've interacted with have expressed concern that if they're not gifted cerebrally or intellectually driven, then they can't participate in loving God with their mind. This is false. When Scripture instructs *all* Christians to love God with their mind, the expectation is that each Christian love God to the best of their personal intellectual ability. All Christians, regardless of the level of intellectual gifting, can join in seeking and striving to love God with their mind.

faith. But the life of the mind is an *indispensable* aspect of the overall Christian life and worldview. In fact, when the life of the mind is ignored or devalued, the fullness of the Christian worldview can't be fully appreciated.

**Evangelicals and the Life of the Mind Challenge**
It's highly ironic given Christianity's strong intellectual history, but there is a growing crisis in much of evangelicalism today regarding the life of the mind. However, most evangelical Christians are seemingly unaware of the nature of the emergency or of its looming repercussions. The problem is that, despite historic Christianity's deep intellectual roots, many intellectually oriented Christian adults increasingly feel out of place, particularly in evangelical churches. They often say that the typical evangelical church has little to offer them in terms of the life of the mind. Some even feel that their insatiable hunger for thinking and learning has caused them to be viewed as unwelcome within their local church congregations.

This issue has been festering for at least a century now. We know this "faith-or-intellect" tension exists based on concerns expressed by leading evangelical scholars over the last 40 years.[14] But we also know of the growing problem from our own interaction with many Christian intellectuals through our years of college teaching and working in the field of Christian apologetics. Cerebrally oriented Christians often say to us that they feel frustrated with the lack of intellectual rigor that's reflected in their own churches. This problem is also evidenced by the fact that this topic received more attention than any other on our social media accounts.

One of the ironic consequences of this crisis is that these Christian intellectuals are and will be desperately needed by their own churches to help convince young people that Christianity is indeed a rationally based faith system and one worth sticking with. Studies indicate that college-age evangelicals are leaving the church and the faith at an unprecedented rate.[15] Unfortunately, the discomfort of the intellectually inclined adults and the exodus of the college-aged students is largely one and the same. That is, the form of Christianity expressed by many evangelical churches seems to have little place for the life of the mind.

Exactly what is it about mind-faith issues that makes many intellectually oriented Christian adults feel out of place in evangelical churches? We think two common church-related factors contribute to the problem.

First, the importance of the life of the mind often receives little attention in some evangelical churches. Church historian Jaroslav Pelikan argues, "The church is always more than a school. . . . But the church cannot be less than a school."[16] Unfortunately, many evangelical churches are often not a place of learning and development of the life of the mind. Bible study is often highly prized in the evangelical church, and rightfully so. Churches often serve many other functions for their congregants: as a place of fellowship, a counseling center, a concert hall, an athletic venue, and more. These are all good and valuable things, of course—but the church much less often functions as a school—meaning a place of rigorous thought and study for adults.

Second, some within the evangelical theological tradition have struggled with the idea that pursuing the life of the mind is somehow at odds with Christian spirituality. It's an unfortunate belief that dies hard. Some Christians even think that reason and education tend to undermine faith. Church history has shown this to be largely false. Many great minds in Western civilization have belonged to people of a vibrant Christian faith.[17] Nevertheless, some evangelical churches are uncomfortable with the pursuit of the life of the mind, particularly in such areas as science and philosophy. Maybe they'd be less intimidated if they knew it was the life of the mind properly dedicated to the glory of God.

*Encouragement to Intellectual Christians*
Here we'll offer three suggestions to encourage our fellow cerebral types who often feel out of place in their churches. We have also, at times, struggled with feeling like we didn't fit in with our church because of our insatiable appetite for learning and reflection. Adopting these three ideas significantly helped us find a sense of belonging and a way to encourage others in valuing intellectual pursuits.

1. Read the works of Christianity's greatest thinkers.
There are times when we've felt alone because we've sensed that other Christians weren't interested in what we find intellectually stimulating and fulfilling. In those times, we've reached out to some of the great Christian thinkers of the past for solace, encouragement, and inspiration. For example, when we read Augustine, Pascal, and C. S. Lewis, we gain the sense that we know them and that we're part of their great conversation about ideas such as truth, goodness, and beauty. These three Christian authors write in such a way that we often feel they somehow know us and are writing to us.

As typical bookish introverts we find it much easier to pick up a book than to introduce ourselves to someone we don't know at church. Reading the writings of some of Christianity's most reflective thinkers gives us a special sense of community that crosses the centuries. We invite you to consider the community of saints available through the writings of great Christian thinkers.

A good place to start your reading journey is with the book *Classic Christian Thinkers* by Kenneth Samples, which introduces nine leading Christian thinkers. The book also introduces these authors' most influential ideas and books in an accessible manner.

2. Find like-minded intellectuals within the church and build community.
If you feel like you are a cerebral loner in the church, then talk with the church leaders about introducing you to people who may share your passion for the life of the mind. Even if your circle is small, at least you will have others to discuss ideas with. You can encourage each other in pursuing the life of the intellect.

3. Don't give up on the evangelical church.
Being an idea-oriented, bookish, and cerebral-type of Christian can have its challenges. People sometimes feel uneasy around intellectuals, perhaps not knowing what to say. We want to strongly encourage thinkers to not give up on being part of a church. Be patient with other Christians. Evangelical churches need their intellectually oriented members, and we need the church, as well. As the author of Hebrews said to first-century Christians, "And let us consider how we may spur one another on toward love and good deeds, not giving up meeting together, as some are in the habit of doing, but encouraging one another" (Hebrews 10:24–25).

Part of being made in the image of God means that human beings are capable of being hunters and gatherers of truth. That task should be sacred among Christians. We want to encourage our Christian friends to keep caring about truth, knowledge, and wisdom by valuing and using the life of the mind to the honor of our Maker.

**Welcoming Intellectual Christians in the Evangelical Church**
As we noted, thinkers sometimes feel disconnected to the evangelical church. This disconnect can lead many educated evangelicals to turn to other sources for support in their cerebral and academic interests. Some have embraced other branches of Christendom like Catholicism or Eastern Orthodoxy because they view these theological traditions as possessing greater depth in terms of history, theology, philosophy, the arts, and science. Those we've talked with who have converted from evangelicalism to Catholicism or Eastern Orthodoxy have said they feel their newfound church tradition welcomes their commitment to the life of the mind, rather than viewing it with suspicion.

Another approach evangelicals might take to fulfill their intellectual needs is to join intellectually oriented parachurch organizations, such as Reasons to Believe, Reasonable Faith, and the C. S. Lewis Society. These Christian organizations sponsor chapter groups that include discussion groups about critical ideas relating to Christianity. They often work across denominational lines and emphasize the life of the mind especially in promoting missions, evangelism, and apologetics. They usually focus on integrating Christian theology with academic fields such as science, philosophy, literature, etc.

Our more than 30 years of involvement in the apologetics enterprise has convinced us that these approaches from intellectuals are not uncommon. Unsurprisingly, this trend of intellectuals having to find outside sources to fulfill the life of the mind is not healthy for the future of the evangelical church.

Churches, of course, are required to balance biblical priorities like preaching, discipleship, evangelism, etc. Additionally, pastors, staff, and volunteers often find themselves—and their resources—stretched thin. Our intent isn't to encourage intellectuals to have a habit of faultfinding but rather to emphasize that the evangelical church needs Christian intellectuals just as much as these intellectuals need the church. As we noted earlier, a number of leading Protestant scholars have expressed concern over evangelicalism's apparent failure to conjoin intellect with piety. For example, church historian Mark Noll has observed:

> If what we claim about Jesus Christ is true, then evangelicals should be among the most active, most serious, and most open-minded advocates of general human learning. Evangelical hesitation about scholarship in general or about pursuing learning wholeheartedly is, in other words, antithetical to the Christ-centered basis of evangelical faith.[18]

If evangelicals are going to spread the gospel, then they need to do their intellectual due diligence. By welcoming academically minded people in the church and, more importantly, by encouraging *all* congregants to value the life of the mind, church leadership can help fortify their people—the youth in particular—against false or misleading teachings and worldview ideas.

## Three Ways to Encourage Christian Scholarship in the Church

How, then, can church leaders and congregants help foster an environment of thinking and learning within the church? Here are three practical ways to promote intellectual pursuits to God's honor and glory.

1. Teach logic and critical thinking skills from the pulpit.
As bearers of God's image (Genesis 1:26–27), humans have been granted exceptional intellectual qualities that make it possible for humanity to search for truth. Pastors can help their congregants recognize and appreciate this aspect of God's image by routinely incorporating logic and critical thinking into their sermons. Christians today desperately need to learn about their own worldview and how to apply it in such controversial areas as popular culture, education, and politics.

### Table 1.2 12 Suggestions for Pursuing Knowledge and Wisdom in Daily Life

1. Take inventory of how much of your weekly time is spent on entertainment and recreation as compared to the pursuit of knowledge and wisdom.
2. Make the pursuit of knowledge and wisdom a daily priority.
3. Set short- and long-term reading goals.
4. Consider reading classics of Western civilization.
5. Consider reading Christian theological, philosophical, historical, and literary classics.
6. Consider reading contemporary Christian theological, philosophical, historical, scientific, and literary works.
7. Stay on top of current issues and evaluate them according to your Christian worldview.
8. Recognize the limits of TV, radio, Internet, and social media for gaining reliable information.
9. Expand your education in art, philosophy, literature, etc.
10. Learn a new language or brush up on languages you've studied previously.
11. Plan visits to libraries, museums, art galleries, zoos, aquariums, historical landmarks, etc.
12. Find a trusted Christian mentor who can help you grow in wisdom and knowledge.

2. Sponsor scholarly lectures at the church.
Inviting guest speakers well qualified in their academic fields to present lectures on how Christianity relates to and has influenced such fields as science, philosophy, and the arts can be a great way to encourage deep thinking and reflection without overtaxing a church's pastoral staff. Church members can be enriched by discovering Christianity's profound influence in the world of ideas.

3. Start a great books reading club.
Christians are known as "people of the book" because the reading of biblical texts has been a part of the faith since ancient Christian times. In light of this

noble scholarly past, why not inaugurate a church reading club where the great books of the Western world are read and discussed? Ideally, the reading selections should reflect the distilled intellectual wisdom of Western civilization, which participants would then be encouraged to compare and contrast with the Bible and the broader Christian worldview.

Christian parents also have a vital role to play in promoting the life of the mind among believers. The best way to help young people grow intellectually and to develop genuine critical thinking skills is for parents to model it for them. That is, the things we daily model as parents tend to stay with our children for a lifetime.

We close this chapter on Christianity's relationship to logic, reason, and the life of the mind with more words from C. S. Lewis:

> Christ never meant that we were to remain children in *intelligence*: on the contrary, He told us to be not only "as harmless as doves," but also "as wise as serpents." He wants a child's heart, but a grown-up's head. He wants us to be simple, single-minded, affectionate, and teachable, as good children are; but He also wants every bit of intelligence we have to be alert at its job, and in first-class fighting trim.[19]

With this introduction of how historic Christianity has prized reason and why today's followers of Christ need to reason well, let's now discuss where to begin with the study of logic.

**Questions for Reflection**
1. How does Christianity generally relate faith to reason?
2. Explain how the Christian faith influenced education.
3. What is Christianity's relationship to logic?
4. Discuss Jesus as the sage logician.
5. In your opinion, what is the importance of the life of the mind for the Christian?

Chapter 2

# Why Study Logic?

In a republican nation, whose citizens are to be led by reason and persuasion and not by force, the art of reasoning becomes of first importance.[1]
—Thomas Jefferson, letter to David Harding, April 20, 1824

The art and science of orderly thinking, logic is a profound phenomenon unique to the way God made human beings. Since God equipped us with a brain and a mind to learn ordered reasoning, a biblical case can be made that these amazing gifts are endowments of being made in his image[2] (see table 2.1).

Logic doesn't teach a person *to* think; people think naturally and intuitively. Without an innate reasoning capacity, we wouldn't even be able to discuss whether what we are saying is rational. Rather, logic invites us to reflect on our own thinking. Do our thoughts reflect reality? Do they follow an orderly pattern? Learning to think in a careful manner takes training, discipline, and practice. If you want your thoughts on any given subject to be clear and cogent, it usually requires engaging the topic multiple times. In fact, to reason well involves a significant investment in the conceptual world of logic and critical thinking.

**Clear Thinking**
Over the years, I (Kenneth) have taught courses in philosophy and religion at colleges throughout Southern California. The course students seem to appreciate most is Introduction to Logic. They often confess that while initially nervous and even intimidated about taking such abstract, conceptual courses,

> **Table 2.1 Human Exceptionalism and the *imago Dei***
>
> Genesis 1–2 describes the creation process, wherein God declares all his work—day and night, water cycle, landmasses, plants and animals—good. However, only human beings receive the distinction of being created in God's image (*imago Dei* in Latin) and given stewardship over the rest of creation (Genesis 1:26–28). Christians have proposed various ideas of what it means to be God's image-bearers. Among these is human exceptionalism. Humans are different from animals not merely in *degree* (where both have the same basic defining qualities, but one simply has more while one has less of the same quality)—but in *kind*[3] (that is a profound, radical, and irreducible difference).[4]
>
> From a Christian philosophical and theological perspective, humans show this difference in kind by possessing six qualities or endowments that the Bible grounds in the *imago Dei*:
>
> 1. spiritual and religious
> 2. personal, self-conscious, and rational
> 3. deliberative and volitional
> 4. relational
> 5. immortal (conscious existence after death)
> 6. powerful (having dominion over nature)
>
> Again, animals share some of these qualities in a *limited* degree. Take intraspecies communication as an example. Animals do communicate with one another via sound, body language, and scent. Such capabilities are sufficient for an animal's survival and procreation needs. However, humankind's capacity for symbolic thinking and robust language skills profoundly demonstrates the important category difference from the animals.[5] According to philosopher and educator Mortimer Adler (1902–2001), animals don't engage in language, per se, but rather send signals to one another.[6] Meanwhile, human beings speak, listen, read, and write. We blend the sounds of letters to form words that symbolize ideas, objects, or entities (abstract or concrete). Language and thinking go hand in hand.
>
> Science seems to increasingly support the idea that human beings are exceptional creatures. Reasons to Believe scientists Fazale Rana

> and Hugh Ross summarize human exceptionalism in this way:
>
>> A wealth of scientific evidence shows that humans alone, as distinct from Neanderthals, *Homo erectus*, and other species, possess the capacity for symbolic recognition, for complex language, art, and music, and for spiritual and philosophical engagement. Humans alone manifest awareness of God, sin, moral judgment, and life beyond death. Humans alone demonstrate technological advancement, including the development of agriculture and civilization. New evidence shows that even during episodes of extreme environmental instability, humans were able to maintain small mixed farms (with multiple species of crops and livestock) and to manufacture flour and clothing.[7]

they soon felt empowered by studying the principles of sound reasoning. My students are bright and eager to think clearly, but their thinking is often scattered, disordered, and somewhat careless.

When thinking is crooked, logic can serve to make it straight. Learning to think carefully and critically about life's most important questions and issues can impact lives. It brings order, consistency, and discipline to one's thinking. It provides a skill set that changes us on the inside. Philosopher Peter Kreeft put it this way, "You may be wondering, 'What can I do with logic?' The answer is that logic can do something with you. Logic builds the mental habit of thinking in an orderly way."[8] And the purpose of this book is to help you the reader and thinker to achieve that valuable goal.

## *The Language of Thinking*

Logic and the principles of rational inference provide a mental model by which a person can structure their thinking to become consistent and compelling. In the human mind thinking and language go together, but we can also speak of logic as a type of language for the mind. In fact, if the language of science is mathematics, then the language of thinking, in general, is surely logic. Philosopher Ed L. Miller explains, "The philosopher, and others who reason critically, can no more do without logic than the physicist can do without mathematics."[9]

Learning to reason rigorously for oneself is clearly one of life's most important intellectual duties. Clear thinking offers significant advantages, including the ability to solve challenging problems, to live fiercely independent lives, and to detect and pursue life's meaning. In their book *Thinking,* Gary Kirby and Jeffery R. Goodpaster describe the benefits of such a reflective journey:

> If we begin to think more actively, some stunning changes are possible: we can know ourselves better; we can have more options in life; we can distinguish fact from fiction and hype from hope; we can begin to think more decisively as we choose liferoads to walk down.[10]

From a Christian perspective, a life of reflection can lead us to discover the alluring transcendentals—*truth, goodness, and beauty.*[11] These transcendentals need to be pursued and apprehended by each and every individual person for themselves. And one of the great benefits of bearing God's image is that human beings have been given the faculties to, in effect, hunt and gather these profound realities.

The study of logic and critical thinking also offers immense benefits to Christians engaged in apologetics (the defense of the faith). In my years of teaching logic, I've heard from apologetics leaders and students who report that studying critical thinking influenced their educational and vocational pursuits, motivated them to grow further in their faith, and bolstered their vocation as defenders of Christianity.

*How, Not What*
Unfortunately, we are concerned that much of formal education today in our postmodern and post-Christian society, especially in the social sciences and humanities, involves ever-increasing doses of indoctrination and sometimes even full-blown propaganda. In a 2018 Twitter exchange, Princeton law professor Robert P. George offered these cautionary words:

> Why can't people understand the difference—and the importance of the difference—between education (good) and indoctrination (bad)? This is NOT hard. It is not a "fine line."

Teaching young people HOW to think (carefully, critically) is different from telling them WHAT to think.[12]

As George noted, a true education involves the vigorous pursuit and discovery of knowledge, truth, and wisdom through critical analysis. Lewis Vaughn agrees, "Critical thinking is not about *what* you think, but *how* you think."[13] In classical education, the goal has been for students to develop the ability to form *for themselves* an independent, reasonable judgment of the topics studied. Thus, learning *how* to think is essential to gaining a genuine education. Logician T. Edward Damer remarks, "One of the main goals of an education is to develop the ability to discover and to defend reliable ideas about ourselves and our world."[14]

Indoctrination can mean mere instruction in a given topic. Of course, no one can evaluate a topic unless it is first presented, explained, and to some degree advocated, but indoctrination often means the instilling of ideas in an uncritical manner without appropriate challenge and debate. Indoctrination, as it is often employed today, stands closer to propaganda than to genuine education (see chapter 8 for more about propaganda).

As George noted, real education teaches *students* how to think; the same must be true of the professors. Much of the debate in our culture today about identity politics (the controversial topics relating to race, sex, and class) stems from ideas coming out of college campuses. Are these colleges today *educating* or *indoctrinating* their students? We must be cautious lest we draw a hasty generalization, but it's difficult to deny that political correctness, "woke" ideology, and controlled speech permeate many, if not most, elite college campuses.[15] We agree with educator John Ellison of the University of Chicago when he said: "Our commitment to academic freedom means that we do not support so-called 'trigger warnings,' we do not cancel invited speakers because their topics might prove controversial."[16]

Commenting on the need for careful thinking in our present cultural milieu, Notre Dame philosopher-theologian Ulrich L. Lehner observes, "A world dominated by half-truths and fake news cries out for more reason."[17] Such a world includes especially present-day college campuses.

An acceptable approach to learning acknowledges the ever-present challenge of human prejudice and bias (see part 3) and seeks to promote a reasonable open-mindedness and evenhandedness when considering topics. Discovering genuine truth is seldom without controversy. When there are multiple viable positions of a given topic, a sound model of education exposes students to a fair-minded discussion of all sides (including pros and cons). Unfortunately, indoctrination and propaganda are manipulatively one-sided. Former president of the University of Chicago Hanna Holborn Gray notes the paramount connection between free thinking and an authentic education:

> Education should not be intended to make people comfortable, it is meant to make them think. Universities should be expected to provide the conditions within which hard thought, and therefore strong disagreement, independent judgment, and the questioning of stubborn assumptions, can flourish in an environment of the greatest freedom.[18]

Like Gray, we believe the best way to battle this growing ideological stronghold is to teach people to think for themselves. As logic instructors, we seldom, if ever, tell students what position to adopt as the conclusion of a specific argument. Instead, we attempt to help people learn how to organize their thinking according to principles of logic. Aristotle defined logic as "ordered thought"—that is, thinking and arguing in a manner consistent with the laws of logic and the rules of rational inference.

Studying logic and critical thinking is crucial for anyone preparing to pursue a genuine education because it empowers the learner to evaluate truth claims properly. Again, logic, of all academic disciplines, teaches a person to reason skillfully. It's analogous to teaching someone to fish, as opposed to merely giving them a fish. The best education provides valuable tools for students to become sufficient and independent when facing various questions and challenges.

Given today's increased political polarization, one of our purposes in writing this book is to help people, especially Christians, to sort through the instant information and misinformation they encounter. It's our hope that this instruction will continue forward into a deeper appreciation for the life of the mind and an examination of our core beliefs and life. Christians, like all other people, need to learn to think critically.

Scripture speaks about the importance of discernment, which is a type of critical thinking informed by the Holy Spirit speaking through God's revealed Word. The wisdom literature of the Old Testament informs God's people, "The fear of the LORD is the beginning of knowledge, but fools despise wisdom and instruction" (Proverbs 1:7).

The epistles of the apostles in the New Testament reveal the need for both testing and discernment when examining truth claims:

> Do not treat prophecies with contempt but test them all; hold on to what is good (1 Thessalonians 5:20–22).

> Dear friends, do not believe every spirit, but test the spirits to see whether they are from God, because many false prophets have gone out into the world (1 John 4:1).

**An Examined Life**
Logic is a branch of the discipline of philosophy. And the ideal prototype philosopher was Socrates (470–399 BCE). He was ancient Greece's "gadfly" who provoked people to think deeply about life. His "Socratic method" consisted of a question-and-answer philosophical approach, where he'd carry out a form of reflective interrogation intended to help him and others discover answers to life's big questions. Socrates considered human beings as naturally reflective creatures. Therefore, failing to ask the deep questions of life means living a shallow and unengaged existence. Fortunately, the study of logic and critical thinking provides a process to investigate our ideas, beliefs, and arguments. As Vaughn states, "To examine your beliefs is to examine your life."[19]

If you still have doubts about whether an investment in such a cerebral subject is worth your time and attention, let us then provide ten good reasons for studying logic and making it a critical tool to utilize in both your thought life and in your daily living.

The value of logic to human beings should be intuitively obvious, and yet it is not taught universally in American schools. Pastor and author of *Logic for Christians* Zach Lee observes that as of 2021, "Most students today are not taught logic until college and, even then, most do not study it as part of their degree program."[20] Because the discipline is neglected in education, we think it's important to lay out some of the significant benefits to be had by becoming well acquainted with logic and, through diligent practice, becoming skillful in its use.

*1. Recognizing the Universal Three Laws of Logic*
Traditionally, the laws of logic—also called the laws of thought—are as follows: (1) the law of identity, (2) the law of noncontradiction, and (3) the law of the excluded middle. (Chapter 4 delves into the details of each law.) Intellectuals have viewed these laws as being both necessary and inescapable because all

thought, speech, and action presuppose their truth and implementation. In other words, these three universal laws of logic make the world rationally intelligible. The laws reflect being and reality and serve to ground reasoning and in themselves stand as undeniable.[21]

Philosopher Peter A. Angeles explains, "All coherent thought, and all logical systems, rely on them [the three laws] for justification."[22] Knowing, appreciating, and applying these laws will help you become a more discerning thinker, making the intelligible world come alive for you.

*2. Engaging the Foundational Human Discipline*
Activities such as reading, writing, conversing, and listening—as well as engaging in math, science, philosophy, music, etc.—presuppose humankind's capacity to track and use logic's universal laws and validity. Rational and logical abilities stand at the very core of what it means to be *Homo sapiens* (a thinking man or person). Philosopher and educator Mortimer J. Adler believed "it is man's glory to be the only intellectual animal on earth" and that this exceptionalism "imposes upon human beings the moral obligation to lead intellectual lives."[23] To lead a vibrant intellectual life involves being conversant with the laws of logic and the rules of rational inference. Such diverse sources as Socrates, Siddhartha Gautama, and the Bible agree with the words of Stoic philosopher and Roman Emperor Marcus Aurelius (reign c. AD 161-180) when he said, "Our life is what our thoughts make it."[24] As humans we all think, but studying logic can help one to think *well*. We should then pursue a discipline that will help facilitate the unique feature of our humanness.

*3. Ordering One's Thinking*
While all of us think, we don't always think in a deliberate and systematic way. Rather our thinking can often be scattered and inconsistent. Because of this we can all benefit from studying logic in helping us to improve the areas of our thinking that are lazy, undisciplined, and careless. Ordered thinking means reasoning in a clear, careful, consistent, cogent, and compelling manner (see chapter 6). The laws and principles of logic provide a conceptual network to systematize reasoning and thus, through personal application and practice, can make order out of disorder and structure out of the unstructured. As philosopher Peter Kreeft notes, "Logic orders and clarifies your thinking."[25] Having the extraordinary gift of a sound mind and a healthy brain gives us the capacity to think and to think rigorously, but studying logic will help order one's thinking.

### 4. Empowering One's Mind and Reasoning

Careful reasoning carries with it a natural empowerment. To be able to differentiate good reasoning from bad and articulate that difference can impact a person's voting, work life, ethical choices, and ultimately even their worldview outlook. The ability to engage in rational argumentation carries the power of persuasion and influence. Developing discipline and skill in reasoning builds personal confidence and helps establish authority among others. Many students have shared with us that studying logic has equipped them in their thought life and that positive endowment carried over into their life. The discipline of logic is unique in offering an enablement that can then be applied to other academic fields and to all of life.

### 5. Thinking for Oneself

Logic is a powerful tool for learning and thinking robustly for oneself. In a January 2021 tweet, Princeton professor Robert P. George challenged students to make the following New Year's resolutions:

> 1) If you don't have a smart friend who disagrees with you about important things that you deeply care about, make one.
> 2) Resist groupthink and self-censorship. Think for yourself; seek the truth; speak your mind.[26]

As said earlier, a vibrant educational experience involves developing an intellectual sense of autonomy and learning to form one's own considered conclusions. Of course, from a Christian perspective, this judgment is always informed by both our rational faculties and God's revelation of truth and wisdom. Learning to think conscientiously for oneself is one of the most important intellectual responsibilities in life. Teachers at every level then need to encourage their students to grow in their intellectual maturity so that they can truly think for themselves. Remember, in this book our emphasis is to teach you *how* to think rather than telling you *what* to think.

Get into the practice of *questioning* things. Do it appropriately and according to God's Word, but do it. Christians are always dependent on God's revealed truth. We must carry out discerning independence with respect, humility, and grace. But much of today's education doesn't seem to involve interrogating all positions fairly. So, let your inner Socrates come out and seek to be fiercely intellectually independent. In other words, carefully listen and learn and then strive toward being a mature thinker and a well-adjusted and gracious person.

The study of logic combined with fair-minded questioning could help one develop a cogent perspective on such hotly debated topics as Israel and Palestine, the abortion debate, sexuality and gender identity, race and equality, etc.

## 6. Differentiate Good Reasoning from Bad

Logic is an indispensable tool for constructing and evaluating the merit of arguments that seek to prove, or offer evidence for, truth claims. Knowing what constitutes a good argument assists a person in discovering a rational and truthful perspective of life. Yet reasoning processes can break down in various ways and fail to support the claim being made in an argument. Informal fallacies and cognitive biases (addressed in parts 2 and 3 in this book) are defects or errors in the reasoning process that cause arguments to fail. Critical thinking serves to filter the constant dangers of propaganda, wishful thinking, cognitive biases, and the general blind acceptance of ideas. Consider how many people in the twentieth century adopted destructive totalitarian ideologies without careful logical analysis of those political systems. Some argue that new political ideologies related to postmodernism and identity politics are on the rise in this century as well and have similarly not received adequate critical analysis.[27]

The content of this book, therefore, will help you to distinguish correct reasoning from faulty reasoning and will also help you to identify patterns that move in either direction. To engage in a subject that can only help one to reason more carefully is priceless. Our book is intended to give you an intellectual starting place on what we hope will be a continuing journey of intellectual growth and challenge.

## 7. A Rational Compass for Making Life Decisions

Common sense dictates we ought to consider pros *and* cons before making big decisions in life. Imagine choosing a university to attend or deciding on a career path *without* weighing all or at least the best available evidence for and against your choices. The same concept applies to beliefs and intellectual pursuits—in order to maintain intellectual integrity, we should consider all the apparent evidence for and against our view. Studying logic and the principles of rational inference can help to provide reliable direction and guidance in making the big decisions in life. You might think of logic as being analogous to a GPS directional guide. Logical reasoning serves as a reliable directional tool in navigating life's many important choices and decisions. On this point T. Edward Damer argues that using critical thinking to make decisions even gives people "a better chance of success in achieving their goals."[28]

*8. A Check on Our Emotions*
Emotions are part of what makes us human; feeling things deeply is a good thing. Psychology concedes that there are five basic emotions (anger, fear, sadness, disgust, and enjoyment[29]). Our emotions and feelings can be powerful, fluid, and influenced by circumstances and situations. Given the potential volatility, emotion isn't always a reliable means for making decisions. In fact, people who allow their emotions to run away with them risk making unwise choices. Sometimes clear thinking is obscured by powerful emotional and psychological states. Knowing about these difficult areas can help in one's important goal to think carefully.

Logic brings clarity, perspective, and an equilibrium to our state of emotions and passions. Damer notes, "Good arguments are usually more effective in trying to convince others of a point of view than are methods such as fear, intimidation, social pressure, or emotional bribery."[30] Logic therefore can serve as a needed check when our emotions run deep. One can thus be both a deep thinker and an empathetic feeler. Scripture affirms the need for both.

*9. A Guiding Tool in the Love and Pursuit of Wisdom*
Philosophy (meaning the "love of wisdom") involves reflection, contemplation, and an abiding spirit of curiosity in search of wisdom and truth (a moral education). One of the philosopher's main skills or tools of the trade is logic. Kreeft explains:

> Logic is one of philosophy's main instruments. Logic is to philosophy what telescopes are to astronomy or microscopes to biology or math to physics. You can't be very good at physics if you're very bad at math, and you can't be very good at philosophy if you're very bad at logic.[31]

Philosophy then is a rational, critical approach to life and thought. At its best, philosophy attempts to discover a rational world-and-life view, thus promoting views that are well conceived, logically coherent, sensible, and well evidenced. Philosophers use logic (among other critical tools) to answer some of life's big questions. What is the origin and destiny of human beings? Is there objective meaning and purpose to life? Is there a God? Studying logic will help you to become skilled at asking questions as well as analyzing the answers.

> **Table 2.2 Major Branches of Philosophy**
>
> 1. Metaphysics: the study of the ultimate nature, structure, and characteristics of reality; asks what is real?
> 2. Epistemology: the study of the origin, nature, limits, and validity of knowledge; asks what is true?
> 3. Ethics: the study of moral goodness; asks what is good?
> 4. Aesthetics: the study of beauty, taste, and art; asks what is beautiful?
> 5. Logic: the study of the principles of sound reasoning; asks what is reasonable?
> 6. Value theory: the study of the value of things in general (other than moral values); asks what is valuable?
>
> Second order disciplines include philosophy of logic, science, religion, history, education, law, language, and politics.

Contemporary philosopher Ed L. Miller describes logic and reason's relationship to philosophy:

> Philosophy is, in this broad sense of the word, rationalistic: Its principle tool is reason and its business is reflection; it is both critical and constructive; it is analytic (it takes ideas apart) and synthetic (it puts them together).[32]

Just as logic is the handmaid to philosophy, so the great classical Christian thinkers viewed philosophy as a handmaid to theology. Christians who want to carry out the great commission and reach the world with the gospel of Christ will want to learn to be skillful with the tool of logic.

*10. Pursuit of Truth and Reality*
In the history of Western civilization, *truth* has been designated as that which corresponds to reality. Logic can show the conclusions that must flow from a set of statements that correspond to reality. Human beings can think, reflect, and

analyze—the very qualities needed to pursue logic, truth, and reality. Historic Christian theology has affirmed that being made in God's image gives us these essential cerebral capacities.

The Christian worldview overall highly values logic and rationality, which find their source and ground in God (Proverbs 1:7) and even proclaim Jesus Christ as the logic of God (Greek *logos*, John 1:1). When Christians discover truth of any kind, they encounter the fingerprint of ultimate Truth, namely God. As the only creatures made in the image of God (Genesis 1:26–27), human beings alone possess profound intellectual faculties. Only human beings philosophize about whether their belief systems best match reality. And since truth is sacred, and logic is a tool to help discover it, then Christians should value logic and be committed to becoming skilled in its usage.

So, we have seen good reasons for studying logic. We hope these incentives will help motivate you to pursue the principles of logic and rational inference with vigor.

### An Invitation to Lifelong Learning

Some of the things in life that make us fulfilled and satisfied as human beings (Aristotle called it *eudaemonia*) are thinking, reading, reflecting, and learning. The life of the mind offers a rich, deep, and full sense of inner fulfillment. "Unlocking the powers of reason offers a way out of such a standstill," Lehner writes, "because it empowers people to scrutinize texts, (and images), distinguish aspects of questions, identify hidden presuppositions, and reject fallacious conclusions."[33] We're glad you're joining us on a rational journey to a greater appreciation and application of logic and reason. We hope this book will serve to fulfill you by challenging you.

### Questions for Reflection
1. Define what "free thinking and free speech" should look like on a college campus.
2. Describe the "How, Not What" teaching focus distinction.
3. Elucidate the problem that indoctrination poses in terms of learning to think independently.
4. Explain how a life of thought may bring fulfillment.
5. Discuss why everyone should study logic.

Chapter 3

# The Basic Elements of Logical Arguments

> The basis for the science and art of logic is two facts: the fact that human beings think, and the fact that thought has a structure.[1]
>
> —Peter Kreeft, *Socratic Logic*

Logic focuses on the art and science of thinking and reasoning. It has been described as the principles of valid inference or right or correct reasoning. It refers collectively to that body of knowledge, methods, or science that assesses and evaluates arguments and systems of thought.

The laws of logic and formal rules of argumentation are intended to help a person structure their reasoning rationally and arrive at reasonable and truthful conclusions.

**An Argument Defined**
Logic is about showing that something is true, correct, or right through the proper use of arguments (Latin: *arguere*, to "make clear"[2]). The "arguments" of which we speak are not bitter quarrels, nor are they intended to go hand in hand with clenched fists and increased blood pressure readings. No, *logical* arguments are something quite different. Because it's critically important to understand just what an argument is, including its essential elements, let's consider three definitions for an argument that are all interrelated:

1. Philosopher Ed L. Miller: "A real argument is a carefully devised piece of reasoning involving premises (what is reasoned *from*), a conclusion

(what is reasoned *to*), and an inference (the connection which yields the conclusion from the premises)."[3]
2. Logician Patrick J. Hurley: "A group of statements, one or more of which (the premises) are claimed to provide support for, or reasons to believe, one of the others (the conclusion)."[4]
3. Professor T. Edward Damer: "An argument, by definition, is aimed at the goal of *demonstrating* the truth or falsity of a particular claim, by presenting evidence that may convince the hearer or reader to accept it."[5]

Based on these definitions, a logical argument consists of three essential elements: (1) a conclusion, (2) premises, and (3) an inference. The conclusion is also known as a central claim. This is the point you want to prove or persuade people to accept. Premises are the supportive statements that include reasons, evidence, or facts. The inference (also called the connection or entailment) is the reasoning process expressed by the argument by which the claim follows logically from the support.

Damer further notes that "an argument is a supported opinion."[6] On the flipside, an opinion *without* support is definitely not an argument. A claim without any rational backing to either necessitate or suggest its truth is just a mere opinion. There is nothing wrong with having and expressing one's opinions, but opinions simply convey the ideas, beliefs, or emotions that a speaker or writer believes to be true or correct. Because opinions do not attempt to prove or rationally show anything (again, lacking support), opinions by themselves do not constitute arguments. So, while the terms are often used interchangeably, opinions do not equate with arguments.

On the other hand, sometimes a series of facts, evidence, and reasons (prospective support) is set forth without an actual claim being presented. Without a definite assertion, the reader or hearer is left with a cluster of interesting information but no argument. (Often in informal conversation, the claim is frequently left unstated but is understood or implied in context.) However, to have a logical argument, a conclusion (or claim) must be set forth and buttressed with premises (rational support) that reflect an inferential relationship.

It's also possible for a claim to be made and support to be offered, but to still lack the key inferential process that marks an argument. The inference is the *reasoning process* that moves the mind of the reader or listener from the premises to the conclusion. That connection is made when the conclusion follows from the premises. To put it another way, the premises *entail* (require, demand, or call for) the conclusion.

A solid argument requires that the premises genuinely back or entail the conclusion. With this connection in place, an argument is considered *valid* or *strong* (well-supported *deductive* arguments are valid while well-supported *inductive* arguments are strong, see chapter 5). A breach in this inferential relationship results in a fundamental breakdown or failure of the argument to prove or genuinely support its conclusion. The argument would then be rendered as *invalid* or *weak* (deductively invalid and inductively weak). Various errors in reasoning (informal fallacies) describe malfunctions in the all-important premise(s)/conclusion relationship. Many of the most common fallacies are addressed later in the book (see chapters 9 and 10).

**An Argument Recognized**
To evaluate an argument properly, one must know the conclusion that represents the central claim. This requires distinguishing among several statements and locating the specific conclusion from the various premises. To find the conclusion, look for the position or view that the communicator is attempting to defend, prove, or claim follows from the evidence (inferential relationship). Let's examine two simple examples.

> **#1 Deductive Argument**
> All dogs are animals.
> Gracie is a dog.
> Therefore, Gracie is an animal.
>
> **#2 Inductive Argument**
> Given that:
> Tom is a ragdoll cat that purred loudly.
> Smokey is a ragdoll cat that purred loudly.
> Mittens is a ragdoll cat that purred loudly.
> Fluffy is a ragdoll cat that purred loudly.
> Oreo is a ragdoll cat that purred loudly.
> Thus, it is likely the next ragdoll cat I encounter will also purr loudly.

Both examples lead with the premises (evidence) and close with the conclusion that must be proven or defended. Notice that indicator words can function as signals for the conclusion and premises:

- conclusion indicators: *therefore, wherefore, thus, so, hence, we may conclude, entails that, accordingly, implies that, consequently, we may infer, as a result*
- premise indicators: *because, since, for, as, may be inferred from, given that, for the reason that, the reason being, inasmuch, in view of the fact that*

*Recognizing Nonarguments*
Not all statements constitute arguments. The flip side of recognizing a central claim is identifying noninferential passages or *nonarguments*. Typical nonarguments include opinions, beliefs, pieces of advice, warnings, and reports. A hallmark of these types of statements is a lack of either specific support or a claim.

- **Opinion**: A claim with no support. Example: JFK was the best American president ever.
- **Piece of advice**: Support with no specific claim. Example: Read, read, read!
- **Belief**: A claim with no support. Example: There is no God!
- **Warning**: A claim with no support. Example: Mind your head.
- **Report**: Support (information) with no specific claim. Example: The cosmos contains exquisite fine-tuning.

Some nonarguments can easily serve as part of an argument and, therefore, are harder to differentiate. Examples include explanations, illustrations, and expository passages. Of course, all these typical nonarguments can be reworked to make or form arguments.

Upon discovering the conclusion of an argument, a helpful step is to then structure the argument in standard logical form. This formal framing will help to organize, clarify, visualize, and weigh the logical inference that moves from premises to conclusion. See the basic argument form below:

For the reason that:
Premise #1
Premise #2
Premise #3
------------------------
Therefore, conclusion

In simple terms: ARGUMENT = SUPPORT + CLAIM + IMPLICATION
In formal terms: ARGUMENT = PREMISE(S) + CONCLUSION + INFERENCE

**An Argument Thought Through**
Philosopher and logician Ed L. Miller states that rational arguments are "well conceived, well evidenced, well stated, and persuasive."[7] Thinking through an argument involves evaluating it for these four qualities.

Is the argument well-conceived? In reflecting about a particular topic, a person should check to ensure that the very foundation of the argument is well-thought-out. Well-conceived arguments possess a logical coherence that is reflected in an internal harmony or consistency. Vibrant arguments avoid self-stultification or being self-defeating in nature (that is, contradictory by both affirming and denying the very contention of the argument itself).

Is the argument well-evidenced? An opinion becomes an argument when a person supports that opinion with facts, evidence, or reasons that truly entail the central claim or conclusion. Well-backed arguments possess genuine support for the claims they make by the premises leading directly to the conclusion. The evidentiary backing should be in the right amount, of the right type, and at the right depth.

Is the argument well-stated? Clarity, conciseness, cogency, and simplicity of thought and expression are hallmarks of good arguments. Every part of an argument should be unambiguous. Succinct arguments possess great potency; logical cogency appeals forcibly to the mind; uncomplicated and direct arguments carry power of persuasion.

Is the argument persuasive? Rhetoric (the persuasive use of language) is closely connected to logic. Arguments that are articulated in a clear, concise, and cogent (logically constructed) manner also tend to be forceful and compelling in terms of personal persuasion. When a person's thoughts are shaped and ordered according to the principles of logic, that person tends to convince others. People can intuitively sense the force of well-crafted arguments. As an example, let's think through this argument for the Trinity's biblical basis:

- Premise #1: There is only one God (Deuteronomy 6:4; Isaiah 43:10; 1 Timothy 1:17).
- Premise #2: The person of the Father is God (John 6:27; Ephesians 4:6; Colossians 1:2–3).
- Premise #3: The person of the Son is God (John 8:58; 10:30; Philippians 2:6).

- Premise #4: The person of the Holy Spirit is God (Genesis 1:2; John 14:26; Acts 5:3–4).
- Premise #5: The Father, the Son, and the Holy Spirit are distinct and simultaneously distinguishable persons (Matthew 28:19; Luke 3:22; 2 Corinthians 13:14).
- Premise #6: The three persons are frequently listed together in a triadic pattern of unity and equality (John 15:26; Galatians 4:6; Ephesians 2:18).
- Inferential Reasoning: Since there is only one God, and because the three persons are all called God, and inasmuch as the three persons are distinct from each other, and given that the three persons are all equal, then the three distinct and equal persons are the one God: Father, Son, and Holy Spirit (Tri-Unity).
- Conclusion: Thus, the Trinity doctrine is not formally and explicitly taught in the Bible but it is derived implicitly from the direct content of Scripture.

This argument for the Trinity stands *well-conceived* in that it reflects logical coherence and consistency. It stands *well-evidenced* in that the various claims of the Trinity are supported by a variety of biblical passages. It stands *well-stated* in that it reflects clarity, conciseness, and simplicity. And, finally, it stands *persuasive* in that all three branches of Christendom (Eastern Orthodox, Roman Catholic, and Protestantism) have affirmed the Trinity doctrine for centuries.

**An Argument Properly Constructed**
Before we examine how premises need to support the conclusion to produce good arguments, let's define what constitutes viable premises.

Premises can contain information taken from such things as basic facts, personal empirical observations, experiments, data pools and sets, common knowledge, expert testimony, rules, definitions, principles, and the conclusions of previous arguments.[8] For the conclusion of an argument to be supported properly, all premises must be true or acceptable, and the argument must employ proper reasoning in utilizing them. In a sound (deductive) or cogent (inductive) argument, the premises must support the conclusion in five distinct ways. Using these standards guides a person's reasoning on the proper logical tracks.[9]

In understanding the proper inferential relationship between premises and conclusion Damer states, "The premises of an argument are those statements that together constitute the grounds for affirming the conclusion."[10] We'll use the acrostic T-R-A-C-K-S to outline how premises should appropriately ground or justify conclusions.

## T – True Premises

While truth in our present time is often considered relative and subjective, the traditional commonsense and objective definition for truth is that which accurately corresponds to reality (called the realist or correspondence theory of truth). The false would then be the opposite—that which does not accurately correspond to reality. Peter Kreeft explains logic's exclusive connection to truth claims: "Logic does not deal with interrogative sentences (questions . . .), imperative sentences (commands or requests . . .), exclamatory sentences (like 'Oh! wow!' . . .), or performative sentences (like 'I dub thee knight'), but only with declarative sentences, that claim to state a truth."[11]

In an argument, all premises must then be factually true or otherwise intellectually acceptable, meaning they represent consensually *acceptable views* more than *demonstrable truths*. Even one false premise defeats the argument. In a valid (deductive) and strong (inductive) argument, premises can't all be true and yet the conclusion be false. Arguments are thus evaluated based on both their correct reasoning and their truthfulness.

## R – Relevant Premises

Only relevant premises can inferentially support and produce a logically acceptable conclusion. Thus, by definition, relevant premises are pertinent, applicable, and solidly linked to the conclusion. Damer further fleshes out how relevance applies to an argument: "A premise is relevant if its acceptance provides some reason to believe, counts in favor of, or makes a difference to the truth or falsity of the conclusion."[12] Consider this argument. The Los Angeles Dodgers are the best team in Major League Baseball (MLB). Why? Because they've got the highest rated pitching, hitting, and defense of any MLB team. Notice that the last statement functions as the premises or support of the argument and includes essential elements that directly relate to a baseball team being superior.

In contrast, irrelevant premises have no relation to, nor do they offer confirmation of, or make a genuine impact on the truth or falsity of the conclusion. Suppose one claimed the Dodgers were the best team because they wear pretty blue caps and stunning uniforms. The premise of the argument now includes nonessential elements that are irrelevant to a baseball team's superiority.

*A – Adequate Premises*
Adequate premises[13] provide abundant support—"sufficient in number, kind, and weight"[14]—to validate the central claim of an argument. This point applies especially to inductive arguments that deal with empirical facts and evidence, such as scientific, historical, or legal issues. In ensuring an argument is adequately grounded by its premises, one may prudently ask questions concerning issues such as: How much? What sort? How substantive? Genuine and ample support supplies all the various reasons necessary to fortify the conclusion with sufficient depth.

*C – Clear Premises*
All parts of the argument must be as clear as possible, including statements, premises, conclusions, and inferences. Good arguments reflect both a transparency of what one is arguing for (the claim) and the reasons why (the support). Legitimate premises possess essential clarity of thought and expression, thus avoiding ambiguity, vagueness, and syntactical mistakes. Thinking, speaking, and writing are at their most potent and persuasive when they reflect a logical unity.

*K – Knowledgeable Premises*
The premises must reflect genuine knowledge (justified or warranted, true belief), thus avoiding unwarranted presumption. Good premises are not based on easily challenged assumptions, but instead on those beliefs that supply legitimate proof or strong evidence for accepting the truth of the conclusion.

1. Let's consider the argument that Lee Harvey Oswald, acting on his own and alone, assassinated President John F. Kennedy. This claim requires premises that demonstrate genuine knowledge of the known facts. For example, Oswald's prints were found on the boxes in the sniper's nest and on the rifle left on the sixth floor of the Texas School Book Depository in Dealey Plaza. Three spent rifle shells were found in the sniper's nest and the bullet and bullet fragments found in Kennedy's limousine matched ballistically and exclusively to Oswald's rifle. An eyewitness sitting directly across the street from the Depository (Howard Brennan) had also seen Oswald in the sixth floor window at the time of the shooting and witnessed him fire his fatal shot at President Kennedy.

These facts (and others) demonstrate a relevant, viable knowledge of the evidence from the Kennedy case. Therefore, we can reasonably conclude that Lee Harvey Oswald alone assassinated President Kennedy.[15]

*S – Stave Off Premises*

The best arguments not only back their conclusions but also anticipate and are able to rebut alternative viewpoints and challenges head-on. Philosopher Louis Pojman says, "A position has not been seriously challenged unless the best arguments for it have been refuted."[16] Rebutting takes a broad familiarity with the topic at hand as well as a good knowledge of the potentially best argument on the alternative side. Knowing and assessing all the evidence, when possible, must include a knowledge of the contrary evidence. Frequently, arguers fail to account for viable rebuttals to their own arguments.[17]

Over the last 60 years, most Americans have believed there was a conspiracy behind JFK's assassination. Let's look at some popular alternative theories about the assassination and see how to rebut effectively. (For more about conspiracies see chapter 8.)

Theory #1: Oswald was a CIA operative.
Rebuttal: Lee Harvey Oswald's turbulent childhood indicates he had much more in common with a typical school shooter than superspy Jason Bourne. Like so many of the deeply disturbed shooters, Oswald grew up without a father. He attended 12 schools in his youth and, at the age of 12, was placed in juvenile detention where a psychiatrist assessed him as "emotionally disturbed." A teenage Oswald later pulled a knife on his half-brother and sister-in-law.[18]

Theory #2: Oswald didn't have enough time to do the shooting.
Rebuttal: For decades, it was believed that the three confirmed shots at President Kennedy occurred within six seconds. People wondered how Oswald was able to fire three shots that quickly with his World War II-era Italian bolt-action Mannlicher-Carcano rifle. But assassination researcher Max Holland makes an impressive case that the first shot came much earlier than initially thought (perhaps even prior to the Zapruder film). If Holland is correct, then Oswald had about eleven seconds to fire three shots. "Eleven seconds to fire three shots is akin to all the time in the world," Holland says. "There's no longer any question of how it was so difficult to do and how he pulled it off."[19]

Theory #3: The single-bullet theory is highly implausible.
Rebuttal: The single-bullet theory is the Warren Commission's thesis that one

bullet (CE 399) hit both President Kennedy and Texas Governor John Connally. Skeptics have derided this claim, labeling it the "magic-bullet theory." However, careful research provides support for the Warren Commission's conclusion. The single-bullet scenario has been duplicated using lasers. It has been reenacted with riflemen shooting into dummies made to resemble human flesh and body parts. Computer animation also supports the single-bullet theory.[20] We may now refer to the single-bullet theory as a fact supported by reliable testing.[21]

Theory 4: Jack Ruby shot Oswald to shut him up about the conspiracy.
Rebuttal: Oswald and the man who killed him, Jack Ruby, were both independent and deeply disturbed people. No organization (organized crime, CIA, KGB, pro- or anti-Castro Cubans, etc.) would reasonably select either man to carry out a professional assassination attempt or to silence the assassin. But again, like the many school shooters who are also deeply troubled, Oswald and Ruby were capable enough to act out violently, given the opportunity. Ruby stumbled upon the opportunity to get close to Oswald and shot him out of angered compulsion. Moreover, if Oswald had to be rubbed out to keep from revealing a conspiracy, then so did Ruby as well as the man who would have to kill Ruby, and so on. But where does this faulty chain reaction reasoning end?[22]

*Getting Back on TRACKS*
Logic is a necessary tool for evaluating truth claims; knowing what constitutes a good argument greatly assists a person in arriving at truth. An argument that fails one or more of the TRACKS criteria is a defective argument. However, a deficient argument can often be reconstructed to remedy its deficiencies. We offer 12 suggestions on reworking invalid (deductive) or weak (inductive) arguments.

1. Attempt to step outside of yourself and look honestly and objectively at the argument you're advocating.
2. Put on the mind of a critic and read through your argument several times slowly and carefully.
3. Consider which aspects of the argument seem weak and susceptible to fair criticism. Focus on strengthening those weak parts of your argument.
4. Examine all the key terms in the argument and, if needed, clarify their meaning.
5. Identify the key assumptions of the argument and consider formulating the unstated ones.

6. Carefully examine the premises (in terms of both reasoning and truth), the conclusion (stated and unstated), and the inferential link between the two. Are there any vulnerabilities? If so, work to improve them.
7. Seriously consider counterarguments and identify the best argument against your argument. How would you respond to that challenge?
8. Consider whether your argument can be recast in a more orderly logical form.
9. Look to eliminate and replace any irrelevant features in your argument.
10. Consider how your argument could be restated with greater clarity and economy.
11. Identify and fairly balance any controversial premises.
12. Check for and consider softening any overstated or unjustified absolute claims.

Strengthening a previously deficient argument requires patience and careful reflection. Don't hurry the process. We encourage you to get into the practice of using these 12 points as a practical checklist to assist in your evaluation.

## An Opponent's Argument Evaluated

Along with developing our own arguments, we also need to learn how to evaluate the arguments of others. As Christians, we need to treat the arguments of other people the way we want our arguments treated—accurately and fair-mindedly. Here are suggestions when considering and evaluating the arguments of others. Some are procedural in nature, but others encourage intellectual and/or epistemic virtues.

1. Always consider the strongest version of an opponent's argument.
2. Charitably clean up your opponent's argument by restating it in its most economical form.
3. If questions arise, give your opponent's argument the benefit of the doubt when possible.
4. If you restate an opponent's argument, check back with the other arguer for correctness.
5. Be motivated by discovering truth rather than just winning the argument.

The intellectual golden rule is to treat other people's arguments the way you want yours treated. And by helping to improve the arguments of others, you're engaging in an intellectual type of good Samaritanism.

Logic is all about arguments. The careful thinker needs to know what an argument is and how it differs from typical nonarguments. The analysis of arguments also includes recognizing their essential parts along with knowing how to place them into logical form. It also involves thinking arguments through, constructing them, and strengthening them.

In the next chapter we turn to the critical topic of logic's formal laws.

**Questions for Reflection**
1. Give a definition for the word *argument*.
2. Describe the process for discovering and evaluating the specific conclusion of an argument.
3. Discuss what goes into making good premises.
4. Explain how one can become more objective and self-aware of their arguments.
5. Explore the importance of *rebutting* criticism of an argument.

Chapter 4

# The Laws of Logic

> Nothing can both be and not be at the same time in the same respect. . . . Opposite assertions cannot be true at the same time.[1]
>
> —Aristotle, *Metaphysics*

It's a fact that human beings think and speak—but have you ever wondered what makes human thinking and speaking intelligible? Are there invisible, conceptual, universal, timeless, necessary, and self-evident rational principles that serve to underlie and order reality and thought? In the ancient Greek world, such a cosmic principle of intelligence was referred to as the *logos* and translates variously as "speech," "discourse," "word," "thought," "idea," or "argument." It is, of course, the source of the English word "logic."

Aristotle, considered by many as the father of logic, didn't invent the field, but he was the first to describe the three laws of thought that anchor human thought and discourse. We can't overstate the importance of these laws throughout the history and study of logic. From Aristotle's time through the Christian thinkers of the Middle Ages and virtually up to modern times, logicians and philosophers have traditionally recognized the three laws of thought as bedrock rational principles. The Wikipedia entry on the three laws acknowledges their significance: "Generally they are taken as laws that guide and underlie everyone's thinking, thoughts, expressions, discussions, etc."[2]

We introduced these laws in chapter 2; here we'll explore them in greater depth.

**Stating Logic's Laws**
To review, the three laws of thought are:[3] (1) the law of identity (LI), (2) the law of noncontradiction (LNC), and (3) the law of excluded middle (LEM). Each law can be stated to reflect either a metaphysical standpoint or an epistemological standpoint. Metaphysics relates to reality or being and is interested in discovering what can or cannot be. Epistemology relates to truth, specifically what can be known to be true or known to be not true. Here are the three logical laws concisely stated and explained,[4] along with brief explanatory quotes from Aristotle:

*The Law of Identity*
- Metaphysical standpoint: Something, A, *is* what it *is* (A is A). A thing is identical with itself and can't at the time it is what it is, be something other than itself. Whatever it is, it is that. For example, a cat is a cat.
- Epistemological standpoint: If X is true, then X is true, and if X is false, then X is false. For example, it is true that a cat is a cat.

In his work *Metaphysics*, Aristotle uses the law of identity to demonstrate why it's necessary for words to have specific, limited meanings: "To say that the word [*man*] has an infinite number of meanings, obviously reasoning would be impossible; for not to have one meaning is to have no meaning, and if words have no meaning our reasoning with one another, and indeed with ourselves, has been annihilated."[5]

*The Law of Noncontradiction*
- Metaphysical standpoint: Something, A, can't at once *be* and *not be* (A can't equal A *and* equal non-A at the same time and in the same way); they are mutually exclusive (not both true). A cat can't be a cat and be a non-cat (anything that is not a cat) at the same time and in the same way.
- Epistemological standpoint: A true statement can't be true and not be true at the same time and in the same respect (and vice versa with false statements). It is true that a cat is not a non-cat.

Continuing on the topic of the meaning of words, Aristotle observes, via the law of noncontradiction, "It is impossible, then, that 'being a man' should mean precisely 'not being a man'. . . . It will not be possible to be and not be the same thing, except in virtue of ambiguity."[6]

*The Law of Excluded Middle*
- Metaphysical standpoint: Something, A, *is* or it *is not*, but not both or neither (either A or non-A), they are jointly exhaustive—one of them must be the case. There is no middle ground or alternative between a cat and a non-cat.
- Epistemological standpoint: Either X is true or X is false; one or the other, but not both at the same time and in the same respect. It is true that there is no middle ground or alternative between a cat and a non-cat.

"On the other hand there cannot be an intermediate between contradictories," Aristotle explains, "but of one subject we must either affirm or deny any one predicate."[7] Notice it doesn't matter if we can identify what an object is. Logic doesn't give us an infallible epistemology (theory of knowledge). However, we do know that it is either something whatever or something not-whatever.

*Possible Fourth Law*
Sometimes a fourth law, called the law of rational inference (LRI), is mentioned in the company of the other three. The LRI, also known as the transitive property of equality, can be expressed as: If A equals B and B equals C, then A equals C. For example, if John is the same height as Paul and Paul is the same height as George, then John is the same height as George.

**Applying Logic's Laws**
To illustrate the importance of these laws in terms of truth claims, let's apply the laws of logic to an apologetics clash of ideas between two of the major world religions:

Statement A: Jesus Christ *is* God in human flesh (a central claim of Christianity).
Statement B: Jesus Christ *is not* God in human flesh (a central claim of Islam).

Applying the law of identity (LI) to statements A and B conveys that a thing or being is identical to itself and different from all other things or beings. The subject terms of both statements reference Jesus Christ and their predicate terms reference human flesh or incarnation; thus the two identities described can't be someone or something else (A is A).⁸ The law of noncontradiction (LNC) shows that statements A and B negate one another. In other words, if statement A is true, then statement B is false, and vice versa. Thus, logically, both statements can't be true. Contradictory relationships reflect a "not both true" status. In this example, one of these religious views about Jesus Christ must be false. Philosopher Douglas Groothuis explains how the LNC necessarily functions in religious claims concerning the identity of Jesus Christ:

> Any truth claim negates every proposition that denies it. This is the logic of antithesis. . . . For instance, if Jesus is God incarnate, then he is not (1) a mere prophet of Allah (Islam), (2) a misguided reformer (Judaism), (3) an avatar of Brahman (Hinduism), (4) a manifestation of God (Baha'i Faith), (5) a God-realized guru (New Age), (6) an inspired but not divine social prophet (theological liberalism), and so on.⁹

The law of excluded middle (LEM) shows that truth can be found in only one statement or the other. While the LNC indicates that it's impossible for both to be true, the LEM trades on the LNC and subtly reveals that "either one or the other" must be true—no middle ground third alternative is possible. The LEM says either Jesus Christ is God in human flesh *or* he is not God in human flesh; one of those two statements must be true (and, therefore, the other one false). One can't reasonably claim that there is "some truth" in both statements. If the terms are used consistently and clearly, then a choice must be made—either Jesus Christ is, or he is not, God in human flesh.

**Challenges to Logic's Laws**
Traditionally, logicians have viewed the three laws as being both necessary and inescapable because all thought, discourse, and action presuppose their truth and application. Aristotle himself viewed the laws of logic as reflecting both reality and truth. Philosopher Ronald Nash explains that Aristotle believed the laws extended beyond grounding human thought to governing the intelligibility of the world at large. In other words, Aristotle considered these as "laws of being" that allow us to "grasp the logical structure of the world." As an example, Nash notes, "The law of noncontradiction is a necessary principle of thought because it is first a necessary principle of being."¹⁰

The laws are, therefore, said to be "ontologically real" (defining the ultimate aspects of reality), "cognitively necessary" (no coherent thinking is possible without their use), and "irrefutable" (their attempted refutation presupposes their use in seeking to invalidate them).[11] However, some modern logicians question and even reject the grand state that history has granted the three laws of thought. In the world of modern logic, the laws are at times referred to as three principles among many, or even considered mere conventional, definitional rules or social constructs. This movement away from the traditional view of logic's laws has led to many differing perspectives of logic.[12]

Let's now consider four challenges to the traditional view of the three laws of thought. These four challenges are called "logics"—however, they're not formal systems of thought but rather attempts to negate the law of noncontradiction in particular.

*Social Construct Challenge*
Our present postmodern culture has a deep concern for social injustice, especially concerning racism. Within this cultural climate has grown the view that concepts like the three laws of thought conceal a type of unjust power play. Groothuis explains that "some multiculturalists have claimed that basic logical principles are Western or male and thus not universally valid."[13] For example, the National Museum of African American History and Culture (NMAAHC) produced a chart entitled *Aspects & Assumptions of Whiteness & White Culture in the United States,* which stated that when it comes to an emphasis on scientific method, "objective, rational linear thinking" was the product of whiteness and white culture.[14] For those promoting the social construct view (multiculturalism), insisting on the universality of logic's laws "is to engage in a kind of intellectual imperialism or cognitive colonialism." Moreover, it's "wrong and narrow-minded."[15]

However, it's simply not the case that the three laws were constructed arbitrarily by Western or Caucasian men. Yes, Aristotle was the first to systematize the laws, but he certainly didn't invent them[16]—rather, they are conceptual and universal anchors that govern all reality and human thought, known to be true because they are intuitively obvious and self-evident. In fact, if these logical laws are not accepted as universally applicable and true, then nothing anyone thinks or says makes any sense whatsoever. Because it would be impossible to make a claim about anything if any one of these laws were not in effect and operative.

A person cannot significantly *think, speak, or act* without these logical laws. How so? Let's say I wanted to convey the message: "Return the book to the library." Without the law of identity (A is A), a book would be a book while at the same time and in the same way it would also be a nonbook (that is, anything that is not a book). So, if a book can't be distinguished from everything that is not a book, then I couldn't think of a book because I couldn't distinguish it from all nonbooks. Nor could I say the word *book* because the word is indistinguishable from all other things. And you couldn't act in returning the book because *return* would have no distinct meaning either.

Thus, even in critiquing the three laws one must use the laws! This makes denying their universality fundamentally self-defeating. Even the claim that "Logic is a social construct" couldn't be made without already relying on the three laws. Though the zeitgeist of today's society is generally critical of what it perceives as intransigent traditional perspectives, the permanence of logic's truths is important. Philosopher Peter Kreeft puts it this way: "Though *people* should not usually be rigid and inflexible, *principles* have to be."[17]

And lest logic seem cold, critical, and cynical, it's important to encourage people, especially those concerned about societal injustice, to see the ways logic can actually benefit all peoples. Author Zachary Lee observes, "There is no such thing as 'old people's logic' or 'white people's logic' or 'tall people's logic' or 'poor people's logic.' Logic is not part of one culture. It is a part of reality for all cultures."[18] And this shared reality provides not only the very foundation necessary to discuss and debate issues of justice and injustice, but also common ground. This, as theologian Ulrich L. Lehner puts it, "has the power to bring people together and create unity" in ways that can "lead to *mutual* learning, tolerance, and empathy as well as undermine prejudices and false assumptions" (emphasis original).[19]

*Dialectic Challenge*
Dialectical thinking is a method of argument based on the triads of thesis, antithesis, and synthesis.[20] The method proposes that clashing contradictory statements in the form of a thesis and an antithesis can be positively resolved into a synthesis that reveals a higher truth. Some view this as a challenge to the law of noncontradiction (LNC), overthrowing Aristotle's definition that "opposite assertions cannot be true at the same time."[21] (Remember Aristotle's statement that it's impossible that "being a man" should mean precisely "not being a man.")

Logician Peter Angeles states that Karl Marx and Friedrich Engels accommodated the dialectical method and "attempted to refute the *Three Laws of Thought* and develop a logic of *becoming* that attempts to present the ever-changing processes of things."[22] Angeles says that for Marx and Engels "contradiction exists in reality. It is possible for the selfsame thing to be and not to be—the same thing is and is not. It is thought that this process can be seen in the polarities of change (thesis and antithesis) found in all activity."[23] Thesis versus antithesis equals synthesis. In a Marxist context, this could mean communal ownership poverty versus private ownership wealth equals communal ownership wealth.

Yet a careful analysis of the dialectic indicates that the triadic method may work for statements that stand in logical *contrast* (reflecting a not-both-true relationship, see later in this chapter) or as logical *subcontraries* (reflecting a not-both-false relationship) but not for genuine logical contradictions (opposite truth claims). For as Angeles concludes, "The concept of noncontradiction, together with the other two Laws of Thought, is definitionally and irrevocably true."[24]

*Eastern Challenge*
There are other proposed forms of logic or ways of thinking such as Buddhist or Eastern mystical logic. Eastern thought recognizes what a contradiction is but ends up rejecting the law of noncontradiction (LNC). Instead of an either-or differentiation, Eastern logic affirms a both-and synthesis.[25] In Buddhist and Indian philosophy, we see the *tetralemma*,[26] which states that for any given statement, X, there are four possibilities:

(1) Affirmation (X)
(2) Negation (not-X)
(3) Both (X and not-X)
(4) Neither (X nor not-X)

The yin-yang theory of Chinese philosophy also embraces contradiction by attempting to connect opposites.

Dr. Nishanth Arulappan explains that "due to their intellectual tendencies and commitments," Eastern thinkers "attempted to swallow a contradiction, while the West did not."[27] The result, as Arulappan correctly notes, is *"different philosophies, not different systems of logic"* (emphasis original).[28] After all, even to differentiate between the proposed Eastern and Western logic, in discourse oriented to traditional Western style discussion, requires the use of the universal law of noncontradiction.[29]

The problem with these presumed alternative ways of thinking (be it multicultural, dialectical, or Eastern) is that the three laws of thought are self-evident and necessary for all rational people and must be universal to all people, cultures, religions, and worldviews. A person can't think, speak, or act in a significant manner without relying on the traditional laws of logic. Reflecting on the LNC, Lehner notes, "Everything you come up with to back up the principle presupposes it already, and everything you write or think about it is only possible because of it! So, we can say that the principle is the foundation of all our knowledge and communication."[30]

*Secular Brute Fact Challenge*
Again, it's clearly self-defeating to argue that the three laws of thought could somehow be conventional in nature—that is, mere human inventions—because one would have to first assume them to even engage in any significant thought whatsoever. It also seems a category mistake to propose, as secular naturalism does, that a purely natural, material, and physical cosmos could somehow produce a reality like the three laws of thought that is independent of the human mind. A deterministic world of materialism and physicalism is at odds with self-evident rational laws that are invisible, conceptual, universal, timeless, and necessary.

Yet another possible secular option is to propose that the three laws exist as brute abstract realities outside of time and space similar to Plato's forms.[31] In what might be called atheistic Platonism, the laws of logic would exist as eternal, transcendental, and nonnatural realities without the existence of God. In such a case, the laws of logic would stand as brute realities and no further explanation as to their grounding could be legitimately offered. But this is an odd form of naturalism because it includes nonnatural abstract entities. It also seems clearly ad hoc—that is, forced or conveniently formed to solve a problem.

Christian philosopher Travis Dickinson offers this argument against a secular case for the laws of logic:

1. If God does not exist, then either logical principles do not exist (naturalism) or they exist as brute abstract objects (Platonism).
2. It's not the case that logical principles do not exist because this is self-defeating.
3. It's not the case that they exist as brute abstract objects since this is ad hoc.
4. Therefore, God exists.[32]

For Dickinson, the only rational explanation for the three laws of thought is that they flow from God's nature and mind. This appears a cogent position.

## Historic Christianity's View of Logic

Classical Christianity views the three laws of thought as timeless, necessary, and self-evident universals, similar to mathematics.[33] These laws govern reality and thought (being and truth). Their truth and application are assumed within the biblical text—but they are not uncreated, brute realities. The consensus among Christian philosophers is that God is the only uncreated being. Thus, all things are either created by God (e.g., the laws of nature) or flow from his mind, character, or nature (e.g., the laws of logic).[34] Philosopher William Lane Craig argues that as "God is the basis of necessary moral truths, so He is the basis for the laws of logic, like the rules of inference."[35]

There's an important difference between created laws and laws grounded in God's own nature. While God can violate the laws of nature (e.g., Christ's virgin birth), he can't violate the laws of logic.[36] The mystery of an infinite and eternal God may range above the human capability to comprehend fully, but God doesn't violate reason itself. Even God can't exist and not exist at the same time. In the same respect, nor can he make something that is both true and false at the same time and in the same way. Further God can't perform the logically impossible such as creating square circles or creating a stone so heavy that even he, God, can't lift it. Yes, the truths of mere Christianity (the Trinity, incarnation, atonement, resurrection, etc.) are mysterious to the finite and temporal mind of human beings, but they aren't logical absurdities.

Because the three laws are timeless, necessary, and self-evident universals, some Christian philosophers believe God's existence can be proved from the laws of logic. James N. Anderson and Greg Welty, for example, offer this argument:[37]

> The laws of logic are necessary truths about truths; they are necessarily true propositions. Propositions are real entities, but cannot be physical entities; they are essentially thoughts. So the laws of logic are necessarily true thoughts. Since they are true in every possible world, they must exist in every possible world. But if there are necessarily existent thoughts, there must be a necessarily existent mind; and if there is a necessarily existent mind, there must be a necessarily existent person. A necessarily existent person must be spiritual in nature, because no physical entity exists necessarily. Thus, if there are laws of logic, there must also be a necessarily existent, personal, spiritual being. The laws of logic imply the existence of God.

Not all Christian philosophers agree with Anderson and Welty, but it's well worth careful consideration. Their line of reasoning avoids the ad hoc problem that plagues the secular brute fact view. There are various reasons and arguments that can be offered for God's objective existence (ontological, moral, cosmological, teleological, the miracles of Jesus, cumulative case, etc.).

The Christian worldview, therefore, grounds the three laws of thought in the maximally perfect being of God. The prologue of John's gospel states, "In the beginning was the Word" (John 1:1). Because the apostle used the Greek term *logos*, Christian philosopher Gordon Clark suggests the verse should be translated as, "In the beginning was Logic."[38] For the incarnate person of Jesus Christ possesses a divine, rational mind that serves as the underlying cosmic principle for the rational intelligibility of the cosmos. God imbued his amazingly created cosmos with *nomos* (laws) and *logos* (logic). He also made human beings as image bearers to have the rational capacity to think and track the world's intelligibility and to reason among themselves. The Lord then networked himself together with his cosmos and with his divine image-bearing human beings, meaning that reason and rationality are not the unique possession of Christians but rather are shared by all people within the created order.

**Categorical Propositions and Logical Relations**
We have worked through the inescapable and necessary three laws of thought with an appreciation for the foundational principle of noncontradiction.[39] Now we'll explore four types of categorical propositions and the four logical relations among them: (1) contradictory, (2) contrary, (3) subcontrary, and (4) subalternation.[40] Categorical propositions are statements about categories or classes and are either true or false.

The ancient Greeks, including Aristotle, identified four primary distinct types of categorical propositions and gave them standard forms (now called A, E, I, and O). Categorical propositions show how members of one category relate logically to another. The four logical interrelations are reflected when statements fitting two or more of the following categorical propositions are compared with one another:

**A, E, I,** and **O** represent the exact standard form of the categorical propositions listed (in table 4.1). *S* is the subject term; *P* is the predicate term. The terms *all*, *no*, and *some* are called "quantifiers" and the verb *are* is called the "copula." The quantity of the **A** and **E** propositions is universal in that they reference *all* the subject term (*no* = none, or *all* are not). The quantity of the **I** and **O** propositions is particular in that they reference only *some* (at least one) of

| Table 4.1 Four Logical Relationships | | | |
|---|---|---|---|
| Name | Title | Form | Example |
| A | Universal Affirmative | All $S$ are $P$ | All sages are philosophers |
| E | Universal Negative | No $S$ are $P$ | No sages are philosophers |
| I | Particular affirmative | Some $S$ are $P$ | Some sages are philosophers |
| O | Particular negative | Some $S$ are not $P$ | Some sages are not philosophers |

the subject term. The quality of the **A** and **I** propositions are affirmative in that their subject terms are *included* in their predicate terms. Whereas the quality of the **E** and **O** propositions are negative in that their subject terms are *excluded* from their predicate terms.

Let us now see how the four logical relationships work utilizing ideas from Christian apologetics. Be sure to note just how these assertions can stand in different logical interrelations in terms of truth. (To visualize these four interrelations, see the Traditional Square of Opposition later in this chapter.)

*Contradictory Relation*
Contradictory relation pairs of propositions have the *opposite truth values*. One is true, the other is false. Propositions **A** and **O** have a contradictory relationship, as do **E** and **I**, meaning they negate or deny one another. To see how these relationships work, let's compare examples from Christian apologetics.

> **A:** All of the New Testament canonical books are inspired. (orthodox view)
> **O:** Some of the New Testament canonical books are not inspired. (unorthodox view)
> **E:** No gods are real (or all gods are not real). (atheism)

I: Some gods are real (or at least one God is real). (theism)

In both sets of propositions (**A** / **O** and **E** / **I**), the statements have opposite truth value. Only one can be true and the other false; they can't both be true and they can't both be false.

*Contrary Relation*
Contrary relation pairs of propositions *can't both be true*. If one is true then the other is false, but both can be false. The **A** and **E** propositions stand in a contrary logical relationship. For instance, a set of religious truth claims could be stated as follows:

**A:** All religions of the world are true. (pluralism)
**E:** No religions of the world are true. (atheism)

While these **A** and **E** propositions can't both be true, the **I** proposition below shows how both **A** and **E** could be false.

**I:** Some (at least one) religions of the world are true. (historic Christianity)

A contrary relation differs from a contradictory relation in that the two *universal* statements (**A** and **E**) can both be false if the *particular* statement (**I**) is true. The two universal statements are said to be contrary, not contradictory, because although they can't both be true, it is possible for both to be false. On the other hand, statements **E** and **I** are contradictory: either no religion is true, or at least one religion is true.

*Subcontrary Relation*
Subcontrary relation pairs of propositions *can't both be false*. If one is false then the other is true, but both can be true. Propositions **I** and **O** stand in a subcontrary logical relationship. Let's take a set of Christological truth claims as an example:

**I:** Some of Jesus Christ's characteristics are divine.
**O:** Some of Jesus Christ's characteristics are not divine (but human).

As a subcontrary relation, the **I** and **O** propositions can't both be false, but they could both be true—and, according to historic Christian orthodox

Christology (the study of the person and nature of Christ), both are true. This example illustrates that, logically stated, Jesus Christ can have both divine and human characteristics (or attributes) without directly defying reason.

*Subalternation Relation*
Subalternation relation pairs have a more complicated relationship. If the universal is true, then so is the particular of the same *quality*. This is the relationship of the **A** to the **I** and the **E** to the **O**. If the particular is false, then so is the universal of the same *quality*. This is the relationship of the **I** to the **A** and the **O** to the **E**. In other words, the truth in the universal statements (**A, E**) guarantees truth in the corresponding particular statements (**I, O**) but not vice versa. Also, falsity in the particular statements (**I, O**) guarantees falsity in the corresponding universal statements (**A, E**), but not vice versa. To make these connections clear and simple, logicians formulated the Traditional Square of Opposition.

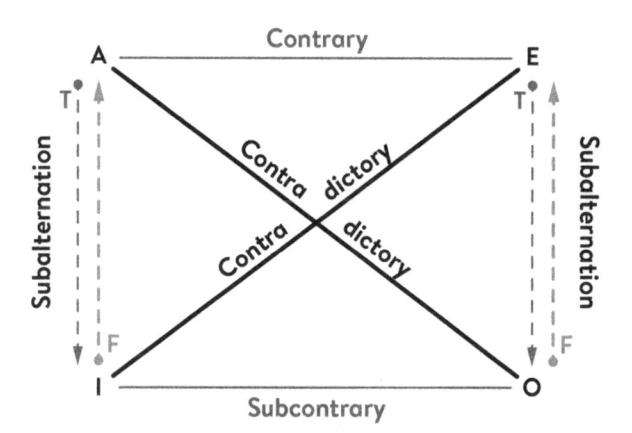

**Figure 4.1 Traditional Square of Opposition**

Notice the truth arrow starts with the top universal statements and flows down to the corresponding particular propositions. In contrast, the falsity arrow starts at the bottom with the particular propositions and rises up to the corresponding universal propositions. To practice performing the Traditional Square of Opposition, until it becomes second nature, start with a true **A** and then discern the logical relations for the **E, I,** and **O**. Then start with a true **E** and so on. Then start with a false **A** and then discern the logical relations for **E**,

**I**, and **O**, and so on from there. Logical relations that can't be shown to be true or false are designated as **U** for undetermined.[41]

To demonstrate, let's look at how a set of statements concerning the New Testament authors' testimony about Jesus of Nazareth illustrates the subalternation relations. Suppose it is true that:

**A:** All the canonical Gospels were written by eyewitnesses or close associates of eyewitnesses about the life of Jesus of Nazareth.

Then it must also be true that:

**I:** Some (at least one, the Gospel of Mark,[42] for example) of the canonical Gospels were written by eyewitnesses or close associates of eyewitnesses about the life of Jesus of Nazareth.

In this example, since the universal affirmative proposition (**A**) is true, then it follows in accord with the subalternation relation that the corresponding particular affirmative proposition (**I**) is also true. Based on the Traditional Square of Opposition, truth then flows from the top universal proposition down to its corresponding particular proposition (both **A** and **I** are affirmative or inclusive statements). Falsity flows only from the particular to its corresponding universal proposition. For example, suppose it is false that:

**O:** Some canonical Gospels are not divinely inspired.

Then it is also false that:

**E:** No canonical Gospels are divinely inspired.

In this example, a bottom false particular negative proposition (**O**) makes its corresponding upper universal negative proposition (**E**) false as well (both **O** and **E** are negative or exclusive statements).

The three laws of thought serve as anchors that make thinking possible and, in turn, make the world intelligible. These logical laws are invisible, conceptual, universal, timeless, necessary, and self-evident rational principles that flow from the mind of God and serve to underlie and order reality and thought. Along with appreciating the three laws of thought, it is crucial to know just how statements and propositions relate to one another, whether they be contradictory, contrary, subcontrary, or subalternation.

Next, we turn to part 2 of the book to explore informal reasoning.

**Questions for Reflection**
1. Discuss Douglas Groothuis's explanation of how the law of noncontradiction impacts the Christian perspective on Jesus Christ in comparison with the world religions alternatives.
2. Explain social construct logic.
3. Describe dialectic logic.
4. Evaluate Eastern logic.
5. Explain the historic Christian view of the three laws of thought.

# Part 2

## Informal Reasoning

Kenneth R. Samples

Chapter 5

# Three Types of Logical Reasoning

Reasoning is the process of using existing knowledge to draw conclusions, make predictions, or construct explanations. Three methods of reasoning are the deductive, inductive, and abductive approaches.[1]

—Butte College, Deductive, Inductive, and Abductive Reasoning

As we begin this chapter about the three basic types of reasoning, let's recall that a logical argument consists of three essential parts: (1) a central claim (conclusion); (2) support for the claim (premises) in the form of reasons, evidence, or facts; and (3) a connecting link (inference) that the claim follows logically from the support. Furthermore, a *good argument*, one that's valid or cogent, requires all your premises to be pertinent to your central claim, sufficient to justify that conclusion, and true.

There are three important forms of reasoning or arguments that students of logic should be quite familiar with: (1) deductive, (2) inductive, and (3) abductive.[2] Let's start with the formal reasoning known as deduction, which involves various types of specific deductive arguments.

**Deductive Reasoning**
Philosopher Peter A. Angeles defines deduction formally as "the process of inference from statements (premises) in which a necessary true conclusion is arrived at by rules of logic."[3] Deductive arguments are intentionally constructed in such a manner as to produce conclusions that follow from their premises with logical necessity or certainty. In other words, the conclusion can't be

reasonably denied. In a valid deductive argument, the *reasoning process* (inferential link) between the premises and conclusion is so well-established that it serves to ensure or guarantee the conclusion. So, with this tight inferential connectedness in place, if the premises are true, then the conclusion must also be conclusively true.

A deductive argument is logically *valid* if, upon inspection, its conclusion follows certainly or necessarily from the premises, and *invalid* if it doesn't meet this conclusive standard. Another way of putting it is that an inference or reasoning process is said to be deductively valid if there is no possible way in which all the premises are true and yet the conclusion is false. On the other hand, if the logical structure of a deductive argument fails to *preserve* the truth of the conclusion, then the argument is invalid. An invalid argument is a failed argument and either needs to be set aside or reconstructed.

So, deductive arguments, if constructed properly (that is, if valid), produce necessary or certain conclusions. And if the argument is valid with true premises, the argument is considered sound. The conclusion of a sound argument, therefore, is *certainly* or *necessarily true*. This is an obvious benefit of sound deductive arguments, but their shortcoming is that they apply to a very limited number of areas in life, principally formal logic.

The following serves as a classic example of a deductive argument:

1. All humans are mortal.
2. Socrates is human.
3. Therefore, Socrates is mortal.

What follows is the argument explained in terms of its parts, form, and terms:

| **Argument** | **Part** | **Form** | **Term** |
| --- | --- | --- | --- |
| All humans are mortal | Major Premise | All A are B | Subject term: Socrates |
| Socrates is human | Minor Premise | C is A | Predicate term: mortal |
| Therefore, Socrates is mortal | Conclusion | Therefore, C is B | Middle term: human(s) |

Typically, deductive arguments move from the general to the particular or from the universal to the individual. This is called a top-down approach to reasoning. Notice in the argument on the previous page the major premise makes a general statement about all human beings. Then the minor premise moves to a specific human being—namely Socrates. We can also add that deductive reasoning is usually more logically intuitive than empirically experimental and, thus, more theoretical than practical.

In evaluating a deductive argument, the certainty or necessity of the conclusion rests on the fact that there is nothing in the conclusion that is not already in the premises. Notice in the Socrates-mortality argument that the content of the conclusion (Socrates is mortal) appears in the premises. So, the conclusion of a deductive argument only states what is already contained or implied in the premises.

**Valid Forms of Deductive Reasoning**
There are three general areas of reasoning that typically fall under deduction.[4] The first is the argument based on mathematics, which includes arguments that use purely arithmetic and geometric computation. The second is the argument from definition, which is reasoning that involves appeal to the mere definition of a word.

The third, syllogistic reasoning, is the most common form of deductive arguments. A syllogism refers to the *form* of an argument that has exactly two premises followed by the conclusion. Form or pattern is critical in deductive arguments, particularly so with syllogisms. There are three basic types of syllogisms: hypothetical (conditional: if/then), disjunctive (alternatives: either/or), and categorical (classes: all, no, some) syllogisms.

Moving from the general areas of deductive reasoning, let's examine the specific forms. There are five popular deductive forms—*modus ponens, modus tollens,* hypothetical syllogisms, disjunctive syllogisms, and *reductio ad absurdum.*[5]

Throughout this chapter, we'll review the valid form (patterns) for each argument and the modern abbreviated symbolic form, as well as view examples. (There are invalid forms, too, but we'll cover these later.) In all forms, the first term (P) is called the antecedent and the second term (Q) is called the consequent. Think through these arguments and commit the valid forms to memory. In each case, you should see that the form produces an argument that follows logically, making it a valid deductive form.

*Modus Ponens* (Latin: mode of affirming)
*Modus ponens* argues by affirming the antecedent. In its classic form, *modus*

*ponens* proceeds as follows:

> If P, then Q.
> P.
> Therefore, Q.

Modern logic uses symbols to abbreviate arguments. Here, the arrow (→) symbolizes the conditional (if/then) and the three dots (∴) symbolize "therefore."

> p → q
> p
> ∴ q

For example:
1. If Lucy and Gracie bark, then there is an intruder in the house.
2. Lucy and Gracie are barking.
3. Therefore, there is an intruder in the house.

Theological example:
1. If you affirm Nicene theology (the Son as God incarnate and through his divine nature equal to the Father and the Spirit[6]), then you are theologically orthodox.
2. You do affirm Nicene theology.
3. Therefore, you are theologically orthodox.

*Modus Tollens* (Latin: mode of denying)
The *modus tollens* argues by denying the consequent. In its classic form, *modus tollens* proceeds as follows:

> If P, then Q.
> Not Q.
> Therefore not P.

Using modern logic's abbreviations, the arrow (→) symbolizes the conditional (if/then), the tilde (~) symbolizes negation, and the three dots (∴) symbolize "therefore."

p → q
~ q
∴ ~ p

For example:
1. If it rains severely, then the Dodger game will be cancelled.
2. The Dodger game was not cancelled.
3. Therefore, it didn't rain severely.

Theological example:
1. If you have genuine saving faith in Christ, then you will strive to express that faith through works of loving obedience.[7]
2. You do not strive to express that faith through works of loving obedience.
3. Therefore, you do not have genuine saving faith in Christ.

*Pure Hypothetical Syllogism (HS)*
A hypothetical refers to a conditional (if/then relationship). These sentences present situations (antecedent) and their outcomes (consequent). In its classic form, a *hypothetical syllogism* proceeds as follows:

If P, then Q.
If Q, then R.
Therefore, if P, then R.

Using modern logic's abbreviations, the arrow (→) symbolizes the conditional (if/then) and the three dots (∴) symbolize "therefore."

p → q
q → r
∴ p → r

For example:
1. If David doesn't study, then he will not graduate from high school.
2. If David does not graduate from high school, then his career options will be limited.
3. Therefore, if David doesn't study, then his career options will be limited.

Theological example:
1. If Jesus Christ is not the God-man, then he cannot truly represent God and man.
2. If Jesus Christ cannot represent God and man, then he cannot reconcile God and man in redemption.
3. Therefore, if Jesus is not the God-man, then he cannot reconcile God and man in redemption.[8]

*Disjunctive Syllogism*
In a *disjunctive syllogism* (either/or relationship), one argues by denying the disjunct. A disjunct refers to mutually exclusive choices in an either/or statement. In its classic form, a disjunctive syllogism proceeds as follows:

Either P or Q.
Not Q.
Therefore P.

Using modern logic's abbreviations, the letter *v* symbolizes the disjunctive (either/or), the tilde (~) symbolizes the negation, and the three dots (∴) symbolizes "therefore."

p v q
~ p
∴ q

For example:
1. Either Pat drove to school or walked to school.
2. Pat did not walk to school.
3. Therefore, Pat drove to school.

Philosophical example:
1. The cosmos is either contingent or necessary.
2. But it is not necessary.
3. Therefore, the cosmos is contingent.[9]

*Reductio ad Absurdum* (RAA)
A *reductio ad absurdum* (Latin: to reduce to absurdity) argument attempts to prove a given proposition (statement) P by showing that its denial, not-P,

entails a contradiction (or some other kind of absurdity) and is, therefore, false. Put another way, *reductio ad absurdum* is a mode of argumentation that seeks to determine a contention by deriving an absurdity from its denial, thus arguing that a proposition must be accepted because its rejection would be logically untenable. This argumentation has been employed throughout the history of mathematics and philosophy from classical antiquity onwards.[10]

The *reductio ad absurdum* can proceed as follows:
1. Assume not-$p$.
2. Provide argumentation that derives $p$ from this assumption.
3. Maintain $p$ on this basis.

The following offers two examples of *reductio ad absurdum*:
*Example 1:* Let's assume that a necessary being doesn't exist. But if a necessary being doesn't exist, then nothing would exist, not even contingent beings. Since something exists (contingent beings), then it is false that a necessary being does not exist. Therefore, a necessary being does exist.[11]

*Example 2:* A maximally perfect being can't be triune (premise 1). God is a maximally perfect being (premise 2). Only a triune being can demonstrate perfect love (premise 3). God demonstrates perfect love (premise 4). Therefore, God is triune (5 from 3 & 4). Therefore, a maximally perfect being can be triune (from 2 & 5, contradicts 1). The intended conclusion stands.

**Invalid Deductive Forms**
Having reviewed the valid deductive forms, let's now consider two common *invalid* deductive forms. First is denying the antecedent, which contrasts with the *modus ponens* (affirming the antecedent); and second is affirming the consequent, which contrasts with the *modus tollens* (denying the consequent). As invalid forms, these arguments violate reason.

Let's look at the classic forms of these common invalid deductive forms, along with some examples. As before, the first term (P) is the antecedent and the second term (Q) is the consequent. The classic form of *denying the antecedent* proceeds as follows:

If P, then Q.
Not P.
Therefore, not Q.

An example of *denying the antecedent* would be: If William is a father, then he is a man (premise). William is not a father (premise). Therefore, William is not a man (conclusion).

The classic form of *affirming the consequent* proceeds as follows:

If P, then Q.
Q.
Therefore, P.

An example of *affirming the consequent* would be: If William is a father, then he is a man (premise). William is a man (premise). Therefore, William is a father (conclusion).

In both cases, the form (whether denying the antecedent or affirming the consequent), produces an argument that doesn't follow logically. Thus, both are an *invalid* deductive form. Proper form is *critical* in deductive arguments as these failed syllogisms illustrate.

## Necessary and Sufficient Conditions

Another critical distinction in logic involves differentiating between *necessary* conditions and *sufficient* conditions. A necessary condition is one that *must* be met. Y is said to be a necessary condition for Z whenever Z can't occur without the occurrence of Y.

*Example 1*: Being an animal is a necessary condition for being a lion.
*Example 2*: Being a woman is a necessary condition for being a mother.

Being a lion *can't occur* without being an animal. Likewise, being a mother *can't occur* without being a woman. Thus, these are necessary conditions.

A sufficient condition guarantees the occurrence. So, Y is said to be a sufficient condition for Z whenever the occurrence of Y is all that is needed for the occurrence of Z. In other words, A is a sufficient condition for B if A is a condition that is enough to bring about the truth of B.

*Example 1:* Being a lion is a sufficient condition for being an animal.
*Example 2:* Being a woman is a sufficient condition for being a human being.

Being a lion is *all that's needed* (enough) to guarantee you have an animal. Being a woman is *all that's needed* (enough) to guarantee you have a human being. The conditions are sufficient.

Deduction is an essential type of reasoning and its logical form is critical to maintain. Yet because it's characterized by logical necessity or certainty, its propositions must be positively sure in nature (as opposed to probable or likely). But it's just that certainty that limits deduction's application. Most things in life seem to carry, at best, probability.

Let's now move to a discussion of the second type of reasoning known as induction, which focuses on probability.

**Inductive Reasoning**

Logic writer Lewis Vaughn states, "An inductive argument is intended to provide probable support for its conclusion."[12] The primary distinction of inductive arguments is that they are constructed in such a manner as to produce conclusions that *likely* or *probably* follow from the premises. Unlike deductive arguments, inductive arguments can't ensure or guarantee the truth of a conclusion. Since in inductive reasoning the conclusion isn't logically entailed by the premises, we can say inductive arguments can be *compelling*, but they can't be *conclusive*. A strong inductive argument then offers substantial evidence to support or confirm the conclusion. If the premises prove insufficient to suggest or favor the conclusion, then the inductive argument is considered weak (inadequately supported and unacceptable).

The strength of an inductive argument, in contrast to the validity of a deductive argument, can fluctuate from strong to stronger, but also in the other direction from weak to weaker. While inductive arguments, by definition, lack necessity or certainty, in most actual situations, *probability* is the best a person can hope for. Therefore, most arguments end up being inductive. Though these arguments have limitations in terms of fully substantiating the conclusion, they nevertheless remain a very common and invaluable form of reasoning. The following serves as a classic example of an inductive argument:

Premise 1: Socrates is mortal.
Premise 2: Plato is mortal.
Premise 3: Aristotle is mortal.
Premise 4: I'm mortal.
Premise 5: You're mortal.
Conclusion: Therefore, all humans are probably mortal.

Typically, inductive arguments progress from the particular to the general or from the individual to the universal. Deriving reliable generalizations from instances of experience or observation is called bottom-up reasoning. Notice in the argument directly above that the premises mention specific individual persons (Socrates, Plato, etc.), but then in the conclusion the logical direction is to a general statement about all human beings. In contrast to what we said about deductive reasoning, inductive reasoning is usually more empirically experimental than logically intuitive and, thus, one can say more practical than theoretical.

Philosopher Louis Pojman describes inductive reasoning thus, "We learn from experience, that is, by induction. We observe resemblances and regularities in life and generalizations from them."[13] There are eight areas of reasoning that typically fall under induction:[14]

1. Generalizations: Arguments that move from the knowledge or awareness of a selected sample set to a claim about the whole group.
2. Statistics: The collection, analysis, and interpretation of numerical data, especially in terms of inferring proportions or shares in a whole from those in a representative sample.
3. Bayesian: An application of probability theory (the analysis of chance events) to inductive reasoning.
4. Analogical: A comparison of things based on ways they are alike to make some sort of explanatory point.
5. Prediction: An argument that moves from one's knowledge of the past to a claim about a future state.
6. Causal inference: An argument that moves from knowledge of a cause to a claim about an effect and vice versa.
7. Authority: An argument that draws the conclusion that something is true because a presumed expert or witness testifies that it is true.
8. Signs: An argument that moves from the knowledge of a sign to a claim about the thing or situation that the sign is said to symbolize.

All these areas reflect an inductive or probability-based type of reasoning. In evaluating an inductive argument, the probability of the conclusion rests on the fact that the conclusion expresses something that extends beyond what is said in the premises. In other words, the conclusion makes a claim that moves beyond the limited evidence in the premises. While it's quite reasonable to conclude that all humans are probably mortal, the five specific examples listed in the previous argument can't guarantee a certainty about universal human mortality. There are, at least conceivably, exceptions to the generally perceived instances given only the premises listed in the argument. While inductive reasoning can't guarantee the truth of a conclusion, nevertheless substantial evidence can make for a strong inductive argument. In other words, more support can increase probability (if X1, X2, X3, X4, X5, and X6 are all Y [premise], then it's probable that the next X encountered, X7, will also be Y [conclusion]).

In contrast to deduction, induction has broad areas of application but carries something less than certainty. Again, probable truth is valuable especially when human decisions so often must be made without the advantage of having a complete data set. Pojman offers a cautionary word, "The wise person guides his or her life by the best evidence available, always realizing that one could be mistaken."[15] Following the evidence must be undertaken with prudence and humility. Despite induction's broad applicability, it does encounter some basic difficulties.

*The Problem of Induction*
Peter A. Angeles defines what's called the problem of induction as "inferring a true statement about all members of a class on the basis of observing only some members of that class."[16] As an example, let's consider the premise that all the swans I've ever seen are white. If I conclude, therefore, that *all* swans are white, my conclusion constitutes a reasonable and yet false (weak) conclusion because, in reality, some swans are black. So, let's restate the argument.

>Premise: All the swans I've ever seen are white.
>Conclusion: Therefore, most swans are probably white.

This restatement constitutes both a reasonable and a more carefully considered conclusion.

There are three basic deficiencies possible in inductive generalizations.[17] The first is forgetful generalization in which a sample is too uniform, as in the case of the white swans. As another example, let's say you survey one hundred people at 1060 W. Addison St., Chicago, Illinois, and decide that an overwhelming majority of Americans are baseball fans. Your data is immensely skewed because that address happens to be the professional baseball park Wrigley Field.

The second is hasty generalization, where the amount of data considered is insufficient. For example, if 7 out of 10 people say they believe in God, you can't conclude that probably most people believe in God because the data set is insufficient. Along that line, if you asked 10 people whether they believe in a "higher being," you can't conclude that probably most people believe in the biblical God. (See chapter 9 for more on the fallacy of hasty generalization.)

Third is slothful generalization, in which the conclusion is weaker than the data demonstrates. Imagine you take a statistically correct poll that shows that most people in Wheaton, Illinois (the location of the Christian school Wheaton College), believe in God. You conclude that the people in Wheaton are probably not totally inclined to doubt the existence of a higher being. Reasoning from the specific to the general (or generalizing) is an important characteristic in induction, but as we've observed there are challenges that accompany it.

*Analogical Induction*
An important element of inductive reasoning involves the use of analogies, which (as we defined previously) comprise a comparison between two things, typically for the purpose of explanation or clarification. Lewis Vaughn describes analogical induction this way: "Because two or more things are similar in several respects, they must be similar in some further respect."[18] The form for analogical induction follows this pattern:

Entity X has qualities (or properties) A1, A2, A3, as well as A4.
Entity Y has qualities A1, A2, and A3.
Therefore, entity Y likely has quality A4.

Careful appraisal of analogical arguments involves forming judgments based on several factors. To begin, one must weigh the relevance of similarities and dissimilarities. When the topics of an analogy share more genuinely relevant similarities, the more likely the conclusion. Conversely, the number of genuine dissimilarities makes the conclusion less likely. One must also evaluate the number of instances being compared. Generally, the greater number compared makes the conclusion stronger. Finally, one must consider the diversity of cases compared. Generally, the more diversity compared, the stronger the conclusion.[19]

*Positive analogy* is opposite from inductive generalization. Here the more similarity you have, the stronger your argument becomes. Also, inductive analogy shows that induction doesn't always move from individual to universal. It can move from an individual or a class to another individual or class.

According to logician Patrick Hurley, "Analogical reasoning may be the most fundamental and the most common of all rational processes."[20] And Vaughn summarizes its near universal use in stating: "Arguments by analogy are probably used (and misused) in every area of human endeavor—but especially in law, science, medicine, ethics, archeology, and forensics."[21]

*Induction in Science*
Inductive reasoning is the foundation for the scientific method. Thinking inductively takes empirical observation of the real world seriously. First, a problem or question is identified. Second, scientists gather data through observation and experimentation. Third, based on that data and through careful inductive inference, hypotheses are developed. Fourth, appropriate predictions are made. Fifth, the hypotheses are then tested. Sixth, based on the tests the hypothesis is subsequently accepted or rejected. Seventh, theories are then developed.[22]

Judging scientific theories involves the following (see also chapter 12):[23]

- Testability: Determining how a theory can be appropriately tested for correspondence or truth
- Fruitfulness: Weighing the number of novel predictions projected
- Scope: Assessing the number of phenomena potentially explained
- Simplicity: Evaluating the number of assumptions involved
- Conservationism: Understanding how well a theory fits with present existing knowledge

The scientific enterprise seeks knowledge and understanding of physical reality through positing, testing, and assessing theories. Within its appropriate limits, science is a critical search for truth about reality. Vaughn offers a fair assessment of what science is and its value:

> Science is not a worldview, and we can't identify it with a particular ideology. Science is also not scientism—it is not the only way to acquire knowledge. It is, however, a highly reliable way of acquiring knowledge of empirical facts.[24]

Having introduced deductive and inductive reasoning, let's now distinguish them from one another.[25]

**Contrasting Deduction and Induction**
When evaluating both deductive and inductive arguments, follow a three-step evaluation process: (1) make sure all terms are clear and unambiguous, (2) check the inferential link between the premises and conclusion, and (3) confirm the truth of the premises. In determining whether an argument is deductive or inductive, examine the form of the argument and see which way it leans. See if the argument fits the category of typical deductive or typical inductive arguments, or if the argument indicates whether the conclusion is intended to follow with certainty or probability from its premises.

The following flow chart illustrates and explains the process for evaluating deductive and inductive arguments:

```
                           ┌─ Sound
                  ┌─ Valid ─┤
Deductive Argument ─┤        └─ Unsound
                  └─ Invalid
```

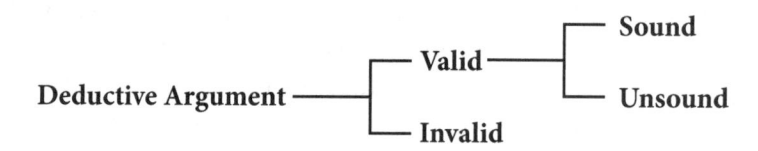

The conclusion of a valid deductive argument does, in fact, follow with certainty from the premises and a solid inferential connection exists between the premises and conclusion.[26] Building on validity, all the premises of a sound argument must be true or acceptable, ensuring a necessarily true conclusion.

**A Sound Argument = A Valid Argument + All True Premises**

```
                            ┌─ Cogent
                   ┌─ Strong ─┤
Inductive Argument ─┤         └─ Uncogent
                   └─ Weak
```

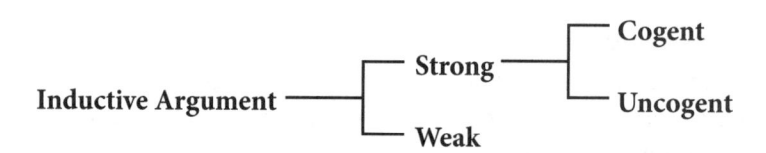

The conclusion of a strong inductive argument follows probably or likely from the premises, meaning the premises provide sufficient evidence to support the conclusion. Building on strength, all the premises of a cogent argument must be true or acceptable, producing a likely true conclusion.

**A Cogent Argument = A Strong Argument + All True Premises**

| **Table 5.1 A Dozen Contrasts of Deductive and Inductive Reasoning**[27] | |
|---|---|
| **Deductive Arguments** | **Inductive Arguments** |
| Certainty or necessity of conclusions (primary distinction) | Probability or likeliness of conclusions (primary distinction) |
| Conclusive support for the conclusion | Compelling support for the conclusion |
| No new information in the conclusion | Possible new information in the conclusion |
| From general to particular (usually) | From particular to general (usually) |
| From universal to individual (usually) | From individual to universal (usually) |
| From whole to parts (usually) | From parts to whole (usually) |
| From cause to effect (usually) | From effect to cause (usually) |
| Top-down approach | Bottom-up approach |
| *A priori* reasoning (prior to experience) | *A posteriori* reasoning (from experience) |
| Philosophical reasoning (typically) | Scientific reasoning (typically) |
| Arguments are valid or invalid | Arguments are strong or weak |
| Argument forms are sound or unsound | Argument forms are cogent or uncogent |

Inductive reasoning is primarily characterized by logical probability or likelihood. Yet inductive reasoning has broad application. Let's now move to a discussion of the third type of reasoning known as abduction.

**Abductive Reasoning**
In a viable abductive argument, the conclusion or hypothesis provides the best explanation of the data.[28] Lesser known than either deductive or inductive reasoning, abductive arguments attempt to arrive at the best explanation for an event or a given situation. Unlike deduction, abduction can't provide certainty in its conclusions. Many logicians view abduction as a subcategory of induction. However, abduction doesn't generally seek to predict the probability of future states of affairs like scientific inductive reasoning does, though scientists do use abduction to form hypotheses.

*Testing Explanations*
The quality of explanations needs to be weighed or evaluated. Abduction provides a general criteria for testing alternative explanations. Good explanations generally possess certain characteristics.

The best explanations exhibit such qualities as:

- coherence (reflects logical consistency)
- simplicity (balances simplicity and complexity)
- explanatory power and scope (explains the facts of reality and its range)
- correspondence (meshes with well-established truth)
- competition (adjusts to new data, responds to reasonable challenges, stands superior to alternative theories)

An explanation that scores poorly in these qualifications is considered inadequate.

So, who uses abductive reasoning? The answer is everyone who offers a *diagnosis* (an investigation or analysis of the cause or nature of a condition, situation, or problem). Scientist and philosopher John and Susan Josephson describe abduction as "a pattern of reasoning that occurs in such diverse places as medical diagnosis, scientific theory formation, accident investigation, language understanding, and jury deliberation."[29] For example, symptoms lead to a diagnosis for a physician and evidence leads to theory for crime scene detectives.

*Abductive Form*
In seeking to provide the most plausible explanation an abductive argument may be framed accordingly:

Form 1
1. The extraordinary experience, X, is recognized.
2. But if A is true, X would be an expected matter of course.
3. Thus, there is plausible reason to conclude A is true.

Example
1. The extraordinary human experience of longing for God and eternity is universally recognized.
2. But if Christian theism is true, then longing for God and eternity would be an expected matter of course.
3. Thus, there is plausible reason to conclude Christian theism is true.

Form 2
1. There are multiple explanations.
2. Explanation X has the highest explanatory power or probability.
3. Explanation X is the best explanation, given the current state of evidence.

When used by scientists in hypothesis formation, abduction may be framed this way:

1. Multiple hypotheses exist.
2. Hypothesis #1 would explain the data.
3. Hypothesis #1 would offer the best explanation of the data.
4. Therefore, hypothesis #1 is the best explanation.

Example
1. Human desire and longing for God and eternity exists.
2. Christian theism would explain the data.
3. Christian theism would offer the best explanation of the data (over evolutionary naturalism and mystical pantheism).
4. Therefore, plausibly, Christian theism is confirmed.

An abductive argument provides an inference to the best explanation. It also seems to be the approach to reasoning that is most natural and intuitive for human beings. For example, when we wake up in the morning and peek through the blinds and see that the street is damp, we naturally search our minds for the most plausible explanation (for example, rain, the street sweeper, or possibly an illusion). This type of abductive reasoning is so common that some have even described human beings as explanation-seeking creatures.

*Applying Abduction to Christian Apologetics*
An abductive approach to Christian apologetics can be set forth. Abductive reasoning is often associated with the apologetics methodology known as a cumulative case approach. Christian philosopher Richard Swinburne makes the case for God's existence providing the best explanation for an array of data:

> Scientists, historians, and detectives observe data and proceed thence to some theory about what best explains the occurrence of these data. . . . We find that the view that there is a God explains *everything* we observe, not just some narrow range of data. It explains the fact that there is a universe at all, that scientific laws operate within it, that it contains conscious animals and humans with very complex intricately organized bodies, that we have abundant opportunities for developing ourselves and the world, as well as the more particular data that humans report miracles and have religious experiences. . . . The very same criteria which scientists use to reach their own theories lead us to move beyond those theories to a creator God who sustains everything in existence.[30]

In accord with Swinburne's reasoning, the Christian theistic worldview is compared to the worldviews of secular naturalism or Eastern mysticism. It's then proposed that Christian theism provides the best explanation for the vast array of life's most meaningful realities. I (Kenneth) use the acronym CLEAR to demonstrate the power and sheer scope of Christianity's explanatory power. Each letter denotes an aspect of reality that all worldviews must account for:

**C**osmos (e.g., singular beginning, order, complex fine-tuning, intelligibility)
**L**ife (e.g., human consciousness, intentionality, free agency, meaning, humanity's enigmatic nature)
**E**thics (e.g., prescriptive, objective morality, ethical duties and values)
**A**bstractions (e.g., numbers, propositions, logic, universals, theoretical models)
**R**eligion (e.g., sense of the divine, religious experience, miracles)

Here is the logical pattern reflected in the Christian theistic inference to the best explanation for the world and life's meaningful realities:

**Premise 1**: The universe and life exhibit diverse, complex, and meaningful realities (see CLEAR on previous page).
**Premise 2**: The Christian theistic God and worldview (revealed in the Bible) best explains these realities individually and cumulatively better than naturalism or mysticism.
**Conclusion**: Therefore, the Christian theistic God and worldview is the most plausible explanation.

Apologetically speaking, this abductive approach could also be used in seeking the best explanation for the origin of humanity (naturalistic evolution versus biblical creation). An abductive approach may also be used in determining the best explanation for the life of Jesus of Nazareth (divine Messiah, legendary figure, etc.).[31]

What are reasonable criticisms of this abductive approach to thinking? Well, the calculus in assessing and weighing can be extremely complex. None of the explanations may be clearly compelling. Even with those challenges abductive reasoning is employed every day in many critical fields (logic, philosophy, law enforcement, history, medicine, etc.), making abduction a viable and valued form of reasoning.

The abductive form of reasoning isn't as common as deduction and induction. It's possible that abduction is underused in Christian apologetics reasoning. However, when it comes to evaluating competing explanatory hypotheses, abductive arguments can be both preferable and invaluable. Being able to draw an inference to the best explanation is often crucial in evaluating competing worldview claims.

To summarize, remember that sound deductive arguments produce certainly true conclusions, cogent inductive arguments produce probably true conclusions, and viable abductive arguments produce most-plausible conclusions. Logic is all about constructing and evaluating arguments. The three standard ways these arguments take shape are through deductive, inductive, and abductive reasoning. Becoming aware and skillful in their use can lead a person to rational and truthful conclusions.

In the next chapter we'll explore constructive steps to buttress careful thinking.

**Questions for Reflection**
1. Explain the three basic types of reasoning.
2. Contrast deductive and inductive reasoning.
3. Distinguish between necessary and sufficient conditions.
4. Discuss Christian theism's CLEAR explanation.
5. Of the three basic types of reasoning, explain which type you find most interesting and why.

Chapter 6

# Positive Steps to Reinforce Clear Thinking

> Critical thinking is also first and foremost an *active* endeavor. It is never *passive*.[1]
> —Ulrich L. Lehner, *Think Better*

We often assume our arguments are well-thought-out. However, there are well known obstacles to thinking carefully and critically. Things like irrelevance (logical unrelatedness), ambiguity (multiple uses of a term), vagueness (blurred or fuzzy meaning), and superficiality (a lack of logical depth) can pose big problems in arguments. In this chapter we will underscore some positive, practical principles and tips that can help you promote a logical connectedness, clarity, substance, and persuasion in your thinking and reasoning. The content of this chapter will intentionally overlap with some of the principles discussed earlier but will serve to reinforce them by applying them in hopefully more practical and memorable ways.

**Think Again: *Point, Point, Point!***
*What's the point?* That's the critical question to ask and keep on asking when examining arguments of all varieties. In a logical argument, the point is always what the argument's conclusion dictates having been inferred directly from the premises. Thus, the conclusion is also called the *central point* of the argument. It's what the arguer is attempting to prove or is endeavoring to persuade others to accept. The sooner you clearly identify the point of the argument, or make the conclusion known to others if it's your argument, then the better off you are in your critical thinking endeavor.

Since knowing the point is crucial in thinking through an argument, losing sight of the point is logically disastrous. In fact, one of the biggest obstacles to careful thinking is distraction. Any premises that are logically irrelevant to the central point of the argument provide no support for that conclusion whatsoever. The problem of *irrelevance* is that it tends to throw the reader or listener off track, and thus the point is concealed or lost. Relevancy is defined by the reality that the conclusion does indeed follow from the premises.[2]

*Relevancy*
There's a group of informal errors in reasoning called fallacies of relevance (we will discuss fallacies in greater depth in chapters 9 and 10). Fallacies of relevance include such common errors in reasoning as straw man, red herring, and missing the point. All three of these errors involve diversion and cause huge logical problems with an argument. Here's how these three informal fallacies of relevance come forth:

- *Straw man:* This fallacy involves misrepresenting the argument of another, usually by distorting the argument and making it seem more extreme.
- *Red herring:* This fallacy misleads the reader or listener by appealing to secondary or extraneous issues (changing the subject).
- *Missing the point:* This fallacy is committed when a person draws a conclusion other than the specific one in which the premises support (drawing a conclusion "out of left field" so to speak).

All three of these fallacies are especially common and can be detected and corrected by diligently pursuing the genuine point of the argument. Thus, again be conscientious in focusing on the central point of the argument and then examine the inference to see if the premises really do support it.

Do a *relevancy check* on your own argument. Ask yourself, What is the central point of my argument? How do each of my premises connect to, relate to, bear upon, and remain pertinent to the conclusion? Are there areas of my argument that divert attention away from the central point?

Remember to get into the constant habit of asking that critical question, What's the point? This short but direct question is truly golden in logic. Ask the question and keep on asking it as you evaluate the logical claims that both you and others make. Be relentless about it. Be active, not passive. Don't ever lose sight of the point. If so, your ability to evaluate the argument is lost, or at least negatively affected. Also, keep checking to see that the support is relevant to the argument's point. Arm yourself with this powerful question and you'll see your thinking become more active, ordered, and disciplined.

**Think Again:** *Clear, Clear, Clear!*
*Is your argument crystal clear?* Clarity is so important in logic that it deserves a more extended discussion in this chapter. Jewish scholar and popular radio talk show host Dennis Prager often says, "I prefer clarity over agreement."[3] And philosopher and educator Mortimer J. Adler says, "You must be able to *say*, with reasonable certainty, 'I understand,' before you can say any one of the following things: 'I *agree*,' or 'I *disagree*,' or 'I *suspend judgment*.'"[4] Logically speaking, I can't evaluate an argument that I can't understand. And I can't understand an argument that isn't clear. Thus, clarity in an argument is truly crucial.

Moreover, when it comes to reasoning, clarity carries its own persuasive power. Clutter and excessive complexity in an argument frequently stand in the way of the argument's understandability and, thus, its ultimate persuasiveness. Consider the master communicator C. S. Lewis's advice in terms of presenting things simply and clearly:

> I have come to the conviction that if you cannot translate your thoughts into uneducated language, then your thoughts were confused. Power to translate is the test of having really understood one's own meaning.[5]

Surely it isn't easy to take truly substantial issues and topics and make them broadly accessible to a wide audience. It takes knowledge, understanding, insight, effort, discipline, and practice—and even then, we may come up short of our goal. When it's done well, however, it can carry a great breadth of logical persuasion. So, cojoining substance and accessibility is a task worthy of our best efforts even if we're only partially successful.

Lack of clarity can cause at least two common informal fallacies: equivocation and amphiboly. Equivocation occurs when an argument's conclusion depends on an ambiguous meaning of a term (see chapter 9). Amphiboly (am-FIB-o-lee; Greek: "irregular speech") is where the conclusion depends on an ambiguous statement (improper grammar or syntax) that causes the reader or listener to draw an erroneous conclusion (see chapter 10). The amphiboly fallacy shouldn't be confused with tautology, which is a phrase or expression in which the same thing is said twice in different words.

Since being clear in one's reasoning process is so advantageous, keep clarity in the forefront of your mind as you begin to construct your argument. A logical argument is really a simple thing: you first make a *claim*, then seek to *support* that claim, and then check to ensure that the inferential *link* between the claim (conclusion) and the support (premises) is genuinely connected. Because you want people to embrace and accept your conclusion based on the premises, the statement that constitutes the conclusion should be quite apparent in the overall argument. As T. Edward Damer notes, "The first step in the construction of an argument is to make very clear just what claim is being defended."[6]

This type of clarity can often be achieved by making the specific conclusion the first or last statement in the argument. And, as we saw in chapter 3, another way of clearly identifying one's conclusion is by using conclusion indicator words such as *thus*, *therefore*, and *accordingly*. For added visibility, consider beginning your conclusion statement with the words, "In conclusion."

You can also bring clarity by making evident which sentences in the argument serve as supporting premises. If you have multiple premises, then you might want to enumerate them so people can more easily recognize and remember them. There are also premise indicator words—such as *so*, *because*, and *since*—that let listeners know you're providing support. You never want the conclusion or premises of your argument to be unclear to those who are considering and evaluating its viability and acceptability.

Do a *clarity check* on your argument. Ask yourself, Are the key terms I'm using in my argument clear and unambiguous? Is my conclusion properly distinguished from its supporting premises? Is the inferential reasoning process reflected in the argument straightforward and understandable? Are there aspects of my argument that are verbose, overly technical, or excessively complicated?

People tend to appreciate clarity, especially when it's contrasted by its opposite in a dialogue or debate, whether written or spoken. Readers and listeners are usually more open to, and even inclined toward, accepting the clearest position. So, work to legitimately give them what they want, *clear and careful reasoning*, and gain the benefits of logical persuasion.

However, bear an important point in mind: being clear doesn't mean being simplistic, unsophisticated, or insubstantial. When presenting your strongest evidence in support of your conclusion, deliver the ideas in the clearest terms possible *without* compromising the substantive integrity of your argument. Remember that whenever clarity meets with ambiguity, clarity wins—especially when the clear arguments are also substantial.

**Think Again: *Reflect, Reflect, Reflect!***
*Have you thought the argument through?* In thinking about a logical argument, it's important to ask whether the very foundation of the argument has been adequately reflected on. In other words, the argument needs to be thought through from the bottom up. This foundational thinking can produce solid logical results. Well-thought-out arguments tend to reflect a potent rationality, which means they're logically coherent and possess an internal harmony and consistency. Such carefully considered arguments also avoid self-stultification or being self-defeating (that is, being contradictory by both affirming and denying the very same central point of the argument). These deliberate arguments are also well-grounded in terms of corroborative evidence, facts, and reasons. These reasoned reflections can be well expressed and, thus, in totality tend to be convincing.

Damer notes the benefits to be had from genuinely thinking our own arguments through:

> If we demand good arguments of ourselves, that demand will lead us to new and better ideas, reinforce the strength of our present beliefs, and expose weaknesses that might lead to qualification or abandonment of those beliefs.[7]

So, before presenting an argument, take the time to think deeply, introspectively, and especially critically about it.

Do a *coherence check* on your argument. Ask yourself, Does the argument make sense as a whole? Is it logically well-structured? Is it well-grounded evidentially? The crucial inferential reasoning process expressed by a skillfully conceived argument has premises that contain information derived from facts, observations, and data and then passed along to the conclusion.[8]

**Think Again: *Rebut, Rebut, Rebut!***
*What's the best argument on the other side?* Many arguments, especially those about controversial topics (ethics, religion, science, etc.), are presented within the context of there being at least two sides to the story. Get in the habit of anticipating that there will be challenges to your argument. Along with making a cogent argument in favor of your view, it's important to respond to the best alternative view that challenges your position. You can be prepared to do so by carefully examining all the available evidence that runs contrary to your view.

Ultimately the argument that is cogent and can best answer the other side's chief challenge will emerge as the most viable and plausible argument. Become diligent in anticipating counterevidence.

Do a *rebuttal check* on your argument. Ask yourself, What's the very best argument against my position? Can I frame that alternative position fairly and accurately and in its strongest form? How can I effectively respond to the alternative view? Does my argument need to be adjusted considering the alternate perspective?

Ulrich L. Lehner makes an important point: "It is easy to think of ideas we disagree with, but hard to imagine arguing against ideas that are dear to us."[9] Rigorously examining our own arguments and positions isn't easy. We often have deep emotional attachments to our views and a natural inclination to avoid that which challenges beloved beliefs. However, if we want to strengthen our arguments, then we need to willingly consider the best rebuttals to them.

**Think Again:** *Compel, Compel, Compel!*
*What are the legitimate rhetorical means by which I may maximize my reason in order to make the most persuasive case?* Aristotle not only wrote Western civilization's first great book on logic (titled the *Organon*, meaning "tool"), he also wrote the first great book on rhetoric. In the *Art of Rhetoric*, Aristotle affirmed that persuasion comes by the proper use of *logos, ethos,* and *pathos*—reason, character, and feeling. Rhetoricians would later come to refer to this trio as "the rhetorical triangle." Think of the alluring appeal that often takes place in literature, television, and film when a credible character (*ethos*) combines reason (*logos*) and the passion (*pathos*) of storytelling. These can be marshalled as legitimate tools of persuasion.

Consider this example. During World War II, California coastline communities (such as Santa Barbara) found themselves in danger of Japanese attacks and the wildfires that could result from them. With the usual firefighters in short supply due to the war, the US Forest Service made efforts to educate the public on fire safety techniques in wild land areas. They found that the use of cartoon animals, such as those from Walt Disney's 1942 film *Bambi*, made their communications much more effective. Fire safety education provided reason (*logos*), but the innocent animal characters (*ethos*) added a powerfully emotional appeal (*pathos*) that made the education memorable and enduring. This led to the creation of the iconic Smokey Bear in 1943, who is still used as the US Forest Service mascot today.[10]

Do a *compelling check* on your argument. Ask yourself, Is there a place in my argument to combine reason with the two other tools of persuasion? How can I be more creative in the presentation of my argument? What legitimately attracts people's attention and acceptance? Have I considered different styles such as storytelling and powerful metaphors?

Consider Mortimer J. Adler's description of Aristotle's approach to persuasion:

> In Aristotelian terms, the good leader must have ethos, pathos and logos. The ethos is his moral character, the source of his ability to persuade. The pathos is his ability to touch feelings to move people emotionally. The logos is his ability to give solid reasons for an action, to move people intellectually.[11]

Logical argument and rhetorical usage can cojoin to produce persuasion in the mind and heart of the reader or listener (see table 6.1).

## Christian Apologetics and Persuasion in Action

Participating in Christian apologetics means entering the enterprise of personal *persuasion*. When apologists defend the faith, it's for the purpose of convincing people of the truth of historic Christianity. But what's involved in making a good case of persuasion in general and for Christian apologetics in particular?[12]

*Rhetoric* is the field of discourse aimed at persuasion. And persuasion is involved in many critical areas of life such as education, law, politics, and religion. However, too often people associate rhetoric with disingenuous attempts to sway people through manipulation—but abuse doesn't rule out the proper use of rhetoric. Pre-Christian Greek philosophers first systematized these basic elements of persuasion. But the principles are generally evidenced in Scripture and have been used by Christian thinkers such as St. Augustine of Hippo and St. Thomas Aquinas.

*Ethos – Persuasion of Character:* The Greek word *ethos* means *character*. Credibility is critical to persuasion. Many people won't listen to an argument until they know the person giving it can be trusted. Inviting, trustworthy, and reliable people convey believability. Apologists can build credibility by handling competing positions with accuracy and fairness, maintaining a respectful tone, avoiding inflammatory language, and appealing to credible sources. Candidly identifying the weaknesses in one's own position shows that the person presenting the case cares more about truth than merely winning an argument.

*Pathos – Persuasion of Feeling:* The Greek word *pathos* refers to feelings and emotions. This is the root of words like *empathy* and *sympathy*. Human beings are both thinkers and feelers. An appeal to emotions illustrates why the reader or listener should care about the topic at hand. Persuasive writers and speakers often use vivid imagery (metaphors, storytelling, etc.) to provoke feeling. Shared values, beliefs, and needs can ground emotional appeals. However, it's best to avoid manipulative emotional appeals. These can backfire and turn people off.

*Logos – Persuasion of Reason:* From the Greek word *logos* we get the English word *logic*. Logic persuades through reason and argument. Credibility and passion are powerful, but ultimately a person must ground his or her case in solid reason. Coherence and sound evidence are essential. Logical appeal alone may not persuade all people, but its absence will certainly persuade none.

Two other elements of persuasion are structure (*taxis*) and style (*lexis*). Structure refers to a presentation's organization, from style to its delivery. Both elements assist a writer or speaker in presenting a clear, concise, and believable argument.

In Scripture, we generally see these five principles linked to apologetics. Peter instructs Christians to be ready to give reasons for their faith but to do so with gentleness, respect, and a clear conscience (1 Peter 3:15–17). Paul is described as reasoning about the faith and seeking to persuade non-Christians of its truth (Acts 18:4). He rebutted challenges (2 Corinthians 10:5) and appealed to the collective beliefs, values, and needs (Acts 17:22–31). Like Peter, Paul insists that a Christian's conduct and speech reflect grace and wisdom (Colossians 4:5–6). And in Jude 3, the author speaks of the need for Christians to contend for the faith.[13]

## Think Again: *Check, Check, Check!*

*What's on your handy checklist when evaluating your argument?* When you give a speech, write an article, or engage in an informal dialogue or discussion that includes a logical argument, get in the habit of consciously asking yourself five key questions. These interrogatives summarize the points we've covered in this chapter and can serve as your checklist to ensure that you're on the proper logical track. We refer to these questions as the "five Cs of logical persuasion."

1. *Is my argument adequately* **concise**? Long-winded arguments often lose both focus and force. Keep your points as succinct and crisp as possible to keep the argument on target. Remember, stating a substantive argument in its simplest form is often quite powerful and persuasive.

2. *Is the claim that I'm defending sufficiently* **clear**? The conclusion of our argument is what we're trying to prove or justify and, therefore, what we want

| Table 6.1 Actions and Virtues Conducive to Careful Thinking ||
|---|---|
| **Actions of a Careful Thinker** | **Virtues of a Careful Thinker** |
| Formulation | Curiosity |
| Consideration | Humility |
| Definition | Honesty |
| Identification | Generosity |
| Analysis | Courage |
| Questioning | Carefulness |
| Judgment | Fair-mindedness |

people to be persuaded by and to embrace. Thus, we try to be crystal clear in setting forth this important central claim. Make your claim so transparent that others will not mistake it for anything besides your conclusion.

3. *Is my argument logically **cogent**?* Good arguments are conceived carefully and exhibit a solid logical structure. Proper support for the conclusion is abundant and logically relevant. A cogent argument reflects well-ordered and potent thinking.

4. *What possible counterevidence have I **considered**?* Most arguments have both strengths and weaknesses, and pros and cons. Some counterevidence could serve to weaken or falsify an argument. Careful thinkers consider their argument's potential limitations and weaknesses. Anticipation of criticisms helps you develop a complete argument.

5. *Have I used skillful language and powerful metaphors to make my argument **compelling**?* Even with the formidable force of reason, persuasion often involves more than mere logical argument. Captivating rhetoric and imaginative stories can also serve to help induce the human will to conviction. It is crucial, however, that one's rhetoric and narrative remain consistent with sound logical reasoning.

Asking the five Cs of persuasion helps ensure order and consistency. When constructing your arguments verbally or in writing, give careful consideration to such things as relevance, clarity, coherence, rebuttal, and the compelling nature of your reasoning.

In table 6.1, we offer a list of thinking actions and intellectual virtues that can help promote robust careful thinking. These intellectual virtues are relevant to the epistemic evaluation of a person's beliefs and belief revision.[14]

A great benefit of studying logic is that it serves to order a person's thinking. Order helps protect a person from crooked or fallacious thinking and arguments. Logic is also a tool that can help people discover truth. And since truth is a sacred thing, logic is a valuable tool indeed.

We've briefly examined positive steps that can serve to reinforce clear thinking. In the next chapter, we'll identify common obstacles to clear thinking and illustrate how to overcome them.

**Questions for Reflection**
1. Describe a relevancy check.
2. Explain a clarity check.
3. Elaborate on a coherence check.
4. Discuss a rebuttal check.
5. Explore a compelling check.

Chapter 7

# Overcoming Common Obstacles to Clear Thinking

> Critical thinking is more about helping others than attacking them; and to the extent we are able to think critically about our own ideas, it is about helping ourselves. Our goal is knowledge and understanding, not winning or coming out on top.[1]
> —Brooke Noel Moore and Richard Parker, *Critical Thinking*

There are many well-known obstacles that clearly stand in the way of thinking critically and carefully. Logical thought can be disrupted by various cognitive biases, some of which will be addressed later in the book (see chapters 11–15). In this chapter, we'll address such impediments to clear thinking as preference, passion, popularity, presumption, and enculturation.

**Think Again: The Challenge of Preferential Reasoning**
*What role does preference play in our thinking process?* Human beings seem disposed to gravitate toward whichever logical conclusion each one *prefers* to be true. When it comes to assessing arguments for reasonableness and truth, preference can weigh heavily on our final evaluation. Preference can even, at times, override solid evidence that points to the truth of a different conclusion.

As careful and conscientious students of logic, we should always attempt to be fair-minded and objective in our reasoning—but the sway of personal preference is powerful. Let's look at an example from my (Kenneth's) world as a sports fan.

*Sports Preference*
As a sports fan, I eat, drink, and sleep in Lakerland, so to speak. I've been a die-hard Los Angeles Lakers fan since the 1969–1970 NBA (National Basketball Association) season. I watch a lot of Lakers games on television, and I avidly read articles and books about the sports franchise and its many famous players, coaches, and owners. I even have a collection of Lakers championship hats. When I think about the Lakers, I think about them with both my head and my heart, but maybe especially the latter. More than once, I've been told that I can be somewhat temperamental about purple and gold, the famous Lakers uniform colors.

In light of my strong attachment to the Lakers, let's ask a question: Are the Los Angeles Lakers the most successful basketball franchise in NBA history?

Well, as a dyed-in-the-wool Lakers fan with a love of sports history, my strong *preference* is that the Lakers be viewed as the finest basketball franchise. And I have some good reasons to think my preference is objectively correct. For example, out of 75 total NBA seasons, the Lakers have made it to the NBA finals 32 times and won 17 individual titles. So, as of the end of the 2022–2023 season, the Lakers, on average, make it to the championship round 43% of the time and win the title 23% of the time. Those are some great historical winning percentages in any professional sport. Many teams in various sports go decades without appearing in the championship round, let alone winning the title.

Yet the Lakers' major competition in NBA history is clearly the Boston Celtics. In 75 NBA seasons, the Celtics have played for the title 23 times, while also winning 17 titles. On average, the Celtics make it to the championship round 31% of the time and win the title 23% of the time. While the Celtics haven't been to the finals as often as the Lakers, when they do get to the championship series they usually win. The Celtics also had a dynasty streak, winning eight straight NBA titles (1958–1966) and ten titles in 11 seasons. Moreover, the two teams have met in 12 head-to-head finals series matchups. The Celtics defeated the Lakers in nine of those meetings. In the 1960s, the Lakers lost the finals to the Celtics six straight times. Even so, three of those series were extremely competitive, with the Lakers losing two seventh games to the Celtics by just two points and a third seventh game by a mere three points. These intense matchups even extended to the last moments of the seventh games.

While my clear preference is to think the Lakers are the NBA's winningest and, therefore, most successful franchise, the evidence is far from clear-cut. In fact, Boston fans can make a strong case for the reverse. I must think with my head and not just with my heart. For as Lewis Vaughn rightly states, "Watch out when things get personal and you become emotionally vested in an issue."[2]

### *Beware of the Genetic Fallacy*

We'll address the genetic fallacy in chapter 10, but let's examine it briefly here and relate it to the Lakers and Celtics rivalry. A fallacy occurs in logic when an argument contains a specific *defect* that causes the argument to flounder and, thus, fail to produce genuine support for its central claim (conclusion). In this case, the genetic fallacy is easy to commit because it can appeal to either personal preference or aversion.

The genetic fallacy takes place when a person appraises a position (idea, person, practice, etc.) in terms of the thing's beginning and ignores developmental changes relevant to the position's present importance or value. In summary, one argues against a point of view simply because it has questionable origins. The point to remember is that a belief's truth or verifiability is more important than how the belief originated.

To put it mildly, there is no love lost between the Lakers and the Celtics or their respective fans. One might even say that in Lakerland, nothing good can come from Boston.

However, a book by NBA historian Charley Rosen makes a potent case that the most prominent basketball mind in developing the Los Angeles Lakers into an NBA dynasty belongs to a man who played his entire career as a Celtic—NBA Hall of Fame player and coach Bill Sharman.[3] It seems that when Sharman coached the Lakers and later served as the team's general manager (1971–1991), he integrated many positive elements he had learned from the championship Celtics teams of the 1950s and 1960s. Sharman, in effect, brought some of the Celtic mojo to the Lakers.

Here lies my difficulty with the genetic fallacy. Nothing good can come from Boston, right? (Except for maybe American independence.) Can anything possibly be good for the Lakers when it came from the Celtics? I surely don't want to give any credit to the Celtics for the Lakers' ultimate success. But if Rosen is right, then I must logically separate the value of Sharman's basketball genius from where it was originally shaped.

Despite my personal preference, I must acknowledge that the Lakers and their fans have benefited from the coaching of a former Celtic. One might say that this personal epiphany was made possible by allowing truth to triumph over origin.

Watch out for preference because it is a very strong force in influencing one's thinking.

Yet it needs to be properly understood that one's preference in selecting an argument can also be reasonable. How so?

*Beliefs and Rational Considerations*
Beliefs can be based on rational, nonrational, or irrational considerations (or even a combination thereof). *Rational* considerations involve things like arguments, facts, evidence, reasons, explanations, and so forth. *Irrational* considerations arise when a person forms a belief that violates the necessary and irrefutable laws of logic or standard principles of reasoning (fallacies, biases, unsubstantiated conspiracies, ignorance, etc.). Lesser known *nonrational* considerations include things like intuition, presuppositions, poetic vision, mystery, etc. Thus, various factors influence a person's beliefs about reality and truth—some of the factors are consistent with reason (rational), some in conflict with reason (irrational), and some not based on reason (nonrational).[4]

Of course, rational factors should be given appropriate priority. However, nonrational factors may be quite consistent with what is first supported by reason. For example, to focus on religious beliefs, a person may *prefer* historic Christianity to be true (perhaps due to the attraction of an infinitely loving and forgiving God) over other religious and nonreligious belief systems, but there are still viable, cogent reasons for believing Christianity is, in fact, rationally true (e.g., the resurrection of Jesus Christ and his extraordinary life).

So, do a *preference check* on your argument. Ask yourself, Do I have a vested interest in the argument I am evaluating? Can I set aside my preference and be fair-minded and judicious? Should I give the alternative perspective a special evaluation? Should I ask someone who has no such preference to assess my argument? Be especially cautious about leading with your personal preferences when it comes to evaluating arguments, but remember that some beliefs, while not directly based on reason, nevertheless can still be consistent with reason.

## Think Again: The Challenge of the Passions
*Are logic and passion enemies?* Remember in logic, an argument isn't a spat or a fight that you might have with your spouse or with a sibling. As we noted in chapter 3, it's possible to engage in a rigorous argument without your face turning flushed red, your jugular vein protruding, and your voice cracking. Especially when it comes to emotion, lots of people think of arguments solely in terms of verbal spats, but this book is about logical arguments.

It's quite easy to feel passionate about the central point of your argument—especially when the person you're talking with feels equally passionate about an opposite point. Strong emotions, while a natural and normal part of being human, can color one's logical analysis. It may not be easy to engage in a dispassionate analysis of one's deeply held conclusion. However, it's important to make the endeavor. Admitting that one's passions exist is the first step in controlling their influence.

*Psychological Obstacles*
There are two emotional states that have especially significant ability to cloud clear thinking. One is anger. Sometimes anger is an appropriate response and can even be constructive in thinking through issues in a clear and cogent manner. Philosophers Plato and Aristotle were of the mind that anger could be an ally of careful reasoning. Christian theologian Martin Luther even once asserted that he believed he thought most clearly when he was in a rage.

Though Luther was a great and deeply influential Christian theologian, we think some of his public comments may have shown him to have been mistaken about his relationship to anger.[5] Angry feelings easily muddle thinking, causing a person to lose perspective and even their self-control. A livid person needs time to calm down and regain intellectual composure before he or she can regain the ability to engage in dispassionate logical analysis. If that is the case, admit it and step away from your logical analysis until you can gather your composure.

The second powerful emotion is depression. Dubbed "the common cold of mental illness," depression erodes one's outlook and capacity to think clearly and carefully. Being in such a psychological condition can, among other effects, cause a person to exaggerate the negative and fail to properly recognize the positive.

Depression has many causes (negative thought patterns, experiencing a loss, biochemical factors, stress, etc.). Most people experience only moderate cases and can regain their logical concentration once the melancholy mood lifts. Others who suffer from clinical depression, however, may require medical treatment to effectively confront this common mental health illness. Of course, this doesn't mean that people who struggle with mental health issues can't also be clear thinkers. It just means that psychological factors can be potential obstacles to thinking carefully.

Sometimes careful thinking is obscured by the uncritical acceptance of various beliefs and at other times by powerful emotional and psychological conditions. But, again, knowing about these challenging areas can help in one's important goal to think carefully and attempt to be fair-minded.

Another related issue to watch out for in verbal debates is caring too much about winning the argument as well as possibly caring too much about what other people think of you. Discovering truth through argument is more important than one's ego. Unfortunately, some of us polemical types like to keep score of our debate wins and losses. It would be more preferable to take a hit to one's pride and lose the debate, as well as even suffer in the eyes of others, if the result was that you were corrected and discovered an important truth. The importance of truth always trumps the fragile needs of our ego. Lewis Vaughn warns: "Beware of the urge to distort your thinking to save face."[6]

Next time you engage in a verbal formal argument, see if you can present your argument in the most winsome way possible.

Do a *passion check* on your argument. Ask yourself: Are my feelings playing a strong role in my evaluation of this argument? Would I benefit from taking a fresh look at this argument once my mood has changed? How can I work at being objective about a topic that seems very subjective to me? Would I benefit from fresh eyes that are not passionately predisposed?

*Leading with Head and Heart*
As a youngster, I (Kenneth Samples) was a huge fan of the original *Star Trek* television series. In high school, I watched the series in perpetual reruns even when I was supposed to be doing my homework. I've also seen the original series movies numerous times. Rewatching one of my favorite episodes entitled "The Galileo Seven" led me to think about human nature, specifically when it comes to the head and heart in relationship to leadership roles.

In the original series, Captain James T. Kirk (William Shatner) regularly receives advice from two confidantes and subordinate officers: science officer Mr. Spock (Leonard Nimoy) and starship physician Dr. Leonard "Bones" McCoy (DeForest Kelley). Spock and McCoy are clear contrasts in personality, life philosophy, and career motivation. Mr. Spock is half human and half Vulcan with a stoic, pensive personality and a relentless devotion to logic. Dr. McCoy is passionate, cantankerous, and emotional. Both are men of science, yet they often clash with one another over issues facing the *Enterprise*'s space mission. You might say that Kirk appeals to Spock's razor-sharp mind on one hand but to McCoy's compassionate and developed conscience on the other.

During "The Galileo Seven," Mr. Spock oversees a shuttlecraft that lands on a planet populated by warlike creatures. He deliberately and skillfully follows the logical path in each decision he reaches, yet he encounters great difficulty and failure. In the end, faced with what appears to be inevitable death for him and his crew, Spock employs a rather desperate act that ultimately leads to their rescue. In rewatching the episode, I wondered whether *Star Trek* creator and screenwriter Gene Roddenberry wasn't making a powerful philosophical point about human nature and the requirements for effective leadership. It seems what makes Captain Kirk such a capable starship commander is his ability to combine logic and compassion. In effect, Kirk relies on and balances *both* Spock's reason and McCoy's emotion.

Effective leaders possess strong intellectual qualities and virtues. They are critical thinkers, learned and committed to the cogent ways of reason. Yet they are also people of moral conscience. They display genuine compassion toward others. As both a Christian and an instructor of logic, I desire to be a compassionate feeler (employing Aristotle's *pathos*) as well as a critical thinker (employing Aristotle's *logos*). I want to be a man of the head and of the heart. Like my Lord and Savior (as well as my ethical example and teacher) Jesus Christ, I want to be driven by both truth and love.

May our political, educational, and spiritual leaders be people of both extraordinary head and heart. Human beings who have been created in the *imago Dei* (image of God) stand to benefit greatly from such needed character traits.

**Think Again: The Challenge of Presumption**

To revise a famous line from the movie *The Godfather*: "Keep your friends close, but the laws of logic closer!"

*All of us have presumptions.* Since logic is about proving (or verifying) things using arguments, presumption can be a big problem. The truth of an argument's conclusion shouldn't be merely presumed. Rather, a good and viable argument offers evidence, facts, or reasons to support the conclusion being drawn. Several informal fallacies fall under the presumption category. We will examine fallacies more closely in chapters 9 and 10, but let's briefly look at two fallacies of presumption.

*Question Begging:* This fallacy engages in circular reasoning. Question begging occurs when an argument either (a) conceals an essential premise, or (b) bases a premise on the truth of the as-yet unproved conclusion. In the first form, the supporting premise is assumed rather than backed by reason. In the second, the conclusion supports the premise instead of the other way around.

Do a *question begging* check on your argument. Ask yourself if you're so deeply attached to your conclusion that you, even without knowing it, smuggle it in without giving a rational basis for accepting it. Always be on guard concerning the obstacle of presumption.

| **Table 7.1 Lewis's Argument from Desire** |
|---|
| Christian author C. S. Lewis has presented an "argument from desire" in his apologetic writings but that argument is an attempt to provide the best explanation for why human beings have basic desires to begin with. In other words, Lewis is explaining, by appeal to God, why we have desires, not attempting to justify any presumptive desires. Thus, Lewis's argument doesn't involve the wishful thinking fallacy.[7] |

*Wishful Thinking:* The logical fallacy of wishful thinking consists in assuming that because we *want* a particular thing to be true, it *must* be true. Conversely, we can assume that because we *do not* want something to be true, it is false. The problem occurs when the "wishing" is treated as support for the desired conclusion. However, of course, mere wishing doesn't make something either true or false. This fallacy is very easy to commit because people often desire a specified outcome. Wanting something in and of itself isn't necessarily evidence. Good arguments must have genuine evidence that supports the conclusion. (See also chapter 10.)

Everyone is susceptible to wishful thinking. Contemporary secular philosopher Thomas Nagel, a brilliant and influential thinker, admits that he hopes there is no God. He writes, "I don't want there to be a God; I don't want the universe to be like that. . . . [I]t is just as irrational to be influenced in one's beliefs by the hope that God does not exist as by the hope that God does exist."[8] Nagel's candor is deeply refreshing. In contrast to Nagel, not only do I *think* God exists, but also I *want* God to exist. I don't want the physical cosmos to be all there is. But as Nagel says, believers and nonbelievers in God need more than just wishes and hopes. We also need good reasons.

Do a *presumption check* on your argument. Ask yourself, What assumptions am I starting with that may impact my evaluation of this argument? What leads me to affirm the truth of this argument's conclusion—evidence or my starting point? Do my assumptions need a rational evaluation? How many of my beliefs are based on presumption rather than on arguments?

When it comes to the reasoning process, no one stands in a completely neutral position without assumptions already in place. Since logic is about verifying things with arguments, unwarranted presumption and assumptions present a big challenge. The truth of an argument's conclusion shouldn't be presumed without justification. Rather, one should seek to acknowledge and to properly justify their presuppositions, and then offer evidence, facts, or reasons to support the conclusion being drawn. Knowing we aren't naturally neutral is the first step in working toward greater objectivity.

**Think Again: The Challenge of Enculturation**
*How strong a role does tradition play in your thinking?* Merriam-Webster defines *enculturation* as "the process by which an individual learns the traditional content of a culture and assimilates its practices and values."[9] People inevitably accept and accommodate ideas, beliefs, and practices that are passed down from family, peers, culture, tradition, religion, and general worldview orientation. These concepts provide context for life and usually deeply enrich our lives. However, the viewpoints to which a person is exposed will also contain gaps, prejudices, and blind spots that need to be critically analyzed. As Lewis Vaughn notes: "Some of your beliefs truly inform you, and some blind you."[10]

One's place of birth plays a significant role in determining one's initial religious beliefs. This is true of nonreligious people, too. A child born in the US or the UK has a much higher chance of being raised in an atheist household than does a child born in Saudi Arabia or India. Circumstances of birth and childhood are beyond our control. The power of these circumstances should remind us how limited our knowledge and perspective can be. Thus, the reflective person will want to learn to think independently. We need to think outside of our own worldview and look broadly at how different people make sense of the world. When positions conflict, logically testing truth claims becomes crucial. Whether a belief is true is more important than when and where a belief was encountered.[11]

Do an *enculturation check* on your argument. Ask yourself: How does my exposure to tradition or culture affect my argument? What is the origin and justification of my important ideas, beliefs, and practices? Which of my most cherished ideas, beliefs, and practices have avoided rational scrutiny? Are there areas of my life that are given to bias, prejudice, and narrowmindedness?

A person needs to be able to challenge accepted opinion and think for oneself, so to speak. Logical scrutiny serves to purify the ideas, beliefs, and practices we receive as part of our enculturation. As we noted in chapter 2, the study of logic can help us be more fiercely independent in our thinking.

Would such independence conflict with being people of faith? Unique among the world's religious traditions, Christianity exhorts believers to approach religious claims deliberately (1 John 4:1–3) in order to evaluate them carefully (Acts 17:11) and test them appropriately (1 Thessalonians 5:21). Thus, historic Christianity encourages a healthy intellectual life that includes a modest but crucial form of skepticism and independence.

Circumstances and conditions, such as preference, passion, presumption, and enculturation, can stand in the way of clear and cogent reasoning. Knowing about these potential logical potholes can help one avoid them in an appropriate and rational manner.

Two challenging conditions we face today in our society are propaganda and conspiracy theories. The next chapter will address these issues.

**Questions for Reflection**
1. Describe a preference check.
2. Explain a passion check.
3. Elaborate on a presumption check.
4. Discuss an enculturation check.
5. Discuss psychological obstacles to clear thinking.

Chapter 8

# Evaluating Propaganda and Conspiracy Theories

> We do not condone the creation of intellectual "safe spaces" where individuals can retreat from ideas and perspectives at odds with their own.[1]
> —John "Jay" Ellison, Dean of Students, The University of Chicago

In 1945, as Allied troops gained ground in Nazi territories, they uncovered the atrocities of the Holocaust. Reports of the grisly discoveries motivated General Dwight D. Eisenhower to go to the camps himself. He explained, "I made the visit deliberately, in order to be in position to give first-hand evidence of these things if ever, in the future, there develops a tendency to charge these allegations merely to 'propaganda.'"[2]

Often troubling and all-too-common, propaganda and conspiracy theories present serious challenges to critical thinking. In this chapter, we will explore these issues and offer logical tools to help you think through these perplexing scenarios.

Let's first address the topic of propaganda.

## Propaganda

We are all susceptible and even vulnerable to propaganda. If you think not, listen carefully to the words of architect Albert Speer, the brilliant man whom Winston Churchill called the most crucial Nazi because his competent managing of the German war machine (as minister of armaments and war production) likely lengthened World War II by two years. Yet Speer apparently joined the Nazi Party without applying critical thinking. In his postwar memoirs, Speer laments being taken in by the propaganda:

> My decision to enter Hitler's party was no less frivolous. Why, for example, was I willing to abide by the almost hypnotic impression Hitler's speech had made upon me? Why did I not undertake a thorough, systematic investigation of, say, the value or worthlessness of the ideologies of *all* the parties? Why did I not read the various party programs, or at least Hitler's *Mein Kampf* and Rosenberg's *Myth of the Twentieth Century*? As an intellectual I might have been expected to collect documentation with the same thoroughness and to examine various points of view with the same lack of bias that I had learned to apply to my preliminary architectural studies. . . . As a result, I remained uncritical.[3]

Of course, some may think Speer was simply looking for an excuse to avoid his share of moral responsibility for the regime's crimes against humanity. Nevertheless, it's certainly the case that the biased and misleading dissemination of Nazi arguments, rumors, half-truths, and lies manipulated millions of both average and highly educated people. Public opinion can be powerfully influenced by such irrational things as propaganda, conspiracy thinking, cognitive biases, and informal logical fallacies.

*What Is Propaganda?*
Propaganda involves the dissemination of information—including biased and misleading information—to get someone to accept a particular agenda, often of a political nature. Propaganda is worse than well-intended indoctrination: where some teach a particular viewpoint uncritically and without regard for teaching how to think, propaganda intentionally seeks to manipulate a person into accepting a specific viewpoint or ideology.

*Journalism and Propaganda*
America of the 2010s and 2020s has seen a great deal of discussion about topics like yellow journalism, fake news, and political propaganda. People consistently raise questions about whether the media in general are fair and objective in carrying out their important task.

Traditionally, journalism has been understood as the daily gathering and disseminating of factual reports about events, people, and ideas. The goal of these efforts was to inform society "to at least some degree of accuracy."[4] In a 2022 article for *Writer's Digest*, journalist Alison Hill further defines traditional journalism as "the legacy or mainstream media . . . regulated by media law and press ethics" and "once highly regarded as the bastions of reliable news."[5]

Veteran journalist Jim Lehrer (former executive editor and anchor of *The NewsHour with Jim Lehrer* on PBS) conducted his brand of traditional journalism according to principles that, in many respects, reflect both the logical and intellectual integrity we have discussed in this book (see table 8.1).[6] For example, Lehrer carefully separated opinion and analysis from straight news stories and clearly labeled them as such. He believed that though *total* objectivity may be impossible, fairness never is.

There are, however, other approaches to journalism that do not prioritize objectivity or fairness. Some journalists and reporters have admittedly adopted advocacy journalism or adversarial journalism over traditional journalism.

1. Advocacy journalism: "Advocacy journalism is a genre of journalism that intentionally and transparently adopts a non-objective viewpoint, usually for some social or political purpose. Because it is intended to be factual, it is distinguished from propaganda."[7]

2. Adversarial journalism: "Adversarial journalism refers to a kind of journalism or a journalistic role where the journalist adopts an oppositional and combative style of reporting and interviewing. The goal of adversarial journalism is to reveal supposed wrongdoings of actors under investigation."[8]

The adoption of a traditional approach to journalism, as Lehrer outlines it, would seem to significantly reform the field, and would largely eliminate propaganda from the news business. Lehrer's principles could easily apply to many other fields including Christian apologetics.

**Education, Indoctrination, and Propaganda**
There is also increasing attention and debate given to whether public schools and colleges in our time *educate* or *indoctrinate* their students. What's the difference between education and propaganda? One of the best ways of avoiding propaganda is knowing what it is and how it functions differently from a classical liberal education. First, it's necessary to define three key terms.

### Table 8.1 Jim Lehrer's 16 Principles for Traditional Journalism

- Do nothing I cannot defend.
- Do not distort, lie, slant, or hype.
- Do not falsify facts or make up quotes.
- Cover, write, and present every story with the care I would want if the story were about me.
- Assume there is at least one other side or version to every story.
- Assume the viewer is as smart and caring and good a person as I am.
- Assume the same about all people on whom I report.
- Assume everyone is innocent until proven guilty.
- Assume personal lives are a private matter until a legitimate turn in the story mandates otherwise.
- Carefully separate opinion and analysis from straight news stories and clearly label them as such.
- Do not use anonymous sources or blind quotes except on rare and monumental occasions. No one should ever be allowed to attack another anonymously.
- Do not broadcast profanity or the end result of violence unless it is an integral and necessary part of the story and/or crucial to understanding the story.
- Acknowledge that objectivity may be impossible but fairness never is.
- Journalists who are reckless with facts and reputations should be disciplined by their employers.
- My viewers have a right to know what principles guide my work and the process I use in their practice.
- I am not in the entertainment business.

*Education* is the pursuit and discovery of information, knowledge, truth, and wisdom (and the skills to do so) through critical analysis. That challenging process of discovery can be unaided (self-study) or aided (teachers). The prized goal of education is for the student to develop the ability to form an independent, reasonable judgment of the topics studied. Thus, the goal of the tutelage is to equip the student to think both analytically and independently.

A modern or classical liberal education prioritizes competency development over knowledge accumulation and general education over specialized education. Learning to learn and self-directed, life-long learning are also key concepts. The goal is to guide students to become critical-thinking adults with civil competency. Tools for achieving these goals include: academic freedom, practice and experience, effort, political neutrality, and interaction and Socratic dialogue.[9]

*Indoctrination*, as we saw in chapter 2, can refer to mere instruction in a topic. To some extent education involves a level of indoctrination. However, indoctrination often carries the negative meaning of inculcating ideas in an *uncritical* manner. It often lacks the necessary critical analysis, as such, it undercuts the goals of modern liberal education. Indoctrination then to some degree is closer to propaganda than to education.

*Propaganda* involves the spreading of information—including slanted and deceptive information—to get someone to accept a particular agenda, usually of a political nature. Propaganda is then worse than well-intentioned indoctrination because it seeks to control a person and maneuver them into adopting a specific ideology or viewpoint.

Intellectual historian and political philosopher Richard M. Weaver contrasts education with propaganda:

> It is of primary importance to distinguish propaganda from education. These two are confused in the minds of many people because both are concerned with communication. Education imparts information and also seeks to inculcate attitudes. Propaganda frequently contains information, and it is always interested in affecting attitudes. A good part of modern propaganda, furthermore, tries to parade as education. The critical difference appears only when one considers the object of each.[10]

The lack of freedom of speech on American university campuses and thus the legitimate concern of encroaching propaganda in education has intensified over the last quarter century. The University of Chicago, in response to this growing concern, developed guiding principles to attempt to secure academic freedom and return to a classical liberal education standard. This Wikipedia article explains:

> The Chicago principles, also known as the Chicago Statement, are a set of guiding principles intended to demonstrate a commitment to freedom of speech and freedom of expression on college campuses in the United States. Initially adopted by the University of Chicago following a report issued by a designated Committee on Freedom of Expression in 2014, they came to be known as the "Chicago Statement" or "Chicago principles" as the Foundation for Individual Rights in Education (FIRE) led a campaign to encourage other universities across the country to sign up to the principles or model their own based on similar goals. . . . As of April 2022, FIRE reported that 84 U.S. colleges and universities had "adopted or endorsed the Chicago Statement or a substantially similar statement."[11]

In this chapter we quote extensively and affirmatively from statements made about education and freedom of speech and expression from the University of Chicago.

Let's now look at seven specific ways true education differs from propaganda.

**7 Ways Education Differs from Propaganda**
A classical liberal education (analytical discovery) strives to incorporate the following seven ideals, practices, and virtues, whereas propaganda (manipulative persuasion) in turn denies, ignores, or limits them.

1. Education emphasizes how to think instead of what to think. Genuine learning requires developing critical thinking skills that can aid the student in analysis and evaluation in order to form a reasonable judgment on a given topic. A good education prepares students to develop the necessary skills to learn to think for themselves. And logic is a discipline of careful thinking.

Propaganda tells a person exactly what to think, even specifically what conclusion to draw from an argument. Propaganda is interested, not in developing rational judgment in the mind of the student, but in the pure persuasion of the student's mind toward its specified ends. It prescribes what the *propagandist* wants you to think, while discouraging what *you* think.

2. Education pursues objectivity instead of subjectivity. A solid approach to learning acknowledges the challenge of human bias and prejudice and seeks to promote a reasonable open-mindedness, an evenhandedness, and a basic fairness when considering issues. Education usually serves to broaden one's perspective and to seek the objective if it can indeed be found.

Propaganda appeals to human bias and prejudice if it serves its purpose. Rather than an open, evenhanded, and fair mind, propaganda wants a mind that is fully subjected to its aims. Propaganda is agenda driven. It focuses on the subjective goal of persuasion and significantly narrows one's perspective of the issues. Weaver, again, contrasts education with propaganda:

> The true educator is endeavoring to shape his audience for the audience's own good according to the fullest enlightenment available. In doing so he erects and strives to follow a standard of objective truth. The propagandist, on the contrary, is trying to shape his audience according to the propagandist's interest, whether that be economic, political, social, or personal.[12]

3. Education introduces disagreements instead of shielding them. Discovering genuine knowledge and truth about life and the world is seldom without controversy and disagreement among people. A good learning environment exposes students to the general and important differences concerning topics and perspectives. Education presupposes an intellectual free market of ideas. Even if the school has a particular worldview focus (religious or secular), alternative views are presented accurately and given a thoughtful discussion and comparison. People who hold opposing views are even invited on campus for dialogue and debate.

Propaganda selectively shields people from controversies and disagreements. It doesn't want its ideas to be openly inspected and challenged. There's no free market of ideas debate. People who hold opposing views are shouted down or not given a place at the table of discussion, while free speech and open debate are constrained in favor of ideological safe spaces.

In contrast, the University of Chicago, a beacon for free speech and a free market of ideas, describes their approach to education:

> We teach students how to think, not what to think, in an independent, flexible, and creative way. We foster a skeptical approach and a demand for data balanced by optimistic belief that the greatest challenges provide the richest rewards.[13]

4. Education examines both sides instead of just one side. When topics are divided between viable positions, a good model of education exposes students to a fair-minded discussion of both sides of a controversial issue. The

perspective of a classical liberal education is to expose students to the differing positions and arguments and let the student develop the capacity to form an independent judgment on the matter.

Propaganda tends to be manipulatively one-sided in perspective because it has a lot to lose by allowing both sides to be compared and contrasted. Propaganda's goal is to win acceptance and protect its perspective at nearly any cost.

In 2014, the University of Chicago appointed a Committee on Freedom of Expression to evaluate and express the institution's responsibilities toward its students. The committee concluded that a conflict of ideas is inevitable, even natural, and that it is not the school's place to help students avoid such conflicts: "But it is not the proper role of the University to attempt to shield individuals from ideas and opinions they find unwelcome, disagreeable, or even deeply offensive . . . concerns about civility and mutual respect can never be used as a justification for closing off discussion of ideas."[14]

5. Education reviews both pros and cons. Proposed solutions to problems can be controversial and usually involve potential strengths and weaknesses. A fair-minded approach to learning gets into the practice of examining both the pros and cons of a position. Genuine learning involves knowing a viewpoint's strengths and weaknesses.

Such knowledge is a serious threat to propaganda. If people examine the pros and cons, then they may begin to think for themselves and take differing positions. Propaganda is all about persuasion; thus, the focus is exclusively on either the strengths or the weaknesses, the pros or the cons, depending on how it relates to the agenda.

A fair-minded approach to learning examines both the pros and cons of a position. The University of Chicago argues that they have a "solemn responsibility not only to promote a lively and fearless freedom of debate and deliberation, but also to protect that freedom when others attempt to restrict it."[15]

6. Education promotes honest intellectual inquiry, not deception. A proper education stresses the critical importance of honesty at every stage of the learning process. Because ideas, evidence, and arguments are prized, they should be treated with integrity. Reality and truth can't be separated from moral virtue.

Unfortunately, manipulation and intellectual deception are the hallmarks of propaganda. Persuasion means winning—and, for propaganda, if winning comes at the cost of truth, honesty, and rationality, then so be it. Intellectual honesty is always the casualty of propaganda.

Richard M. Weaver maintains that propaganda often employs four informal logical fallacies that manipulate thinking:[16] *ad hominem* (character attacks), false cause (confusing cause-effect relationships), weak analogy (faulty analogies), and unqualified authority (inappropriate appeals to authority). All four of these fallacies are addressed in detail in chapter 9.

7. Education encourages dialogue over monologue. Respectful discussion, dialogue, and interaction enhances learning. In fact, learning under multiple voices is often superior to learning under one especially authoritarian voice. Propaganda, on the other hand, permits no other voices to be heard. It is a monologue where other voices are drowned out intentionally, lest they challenge the agenda. Christian theologian Tim Keller illustrates the benefits of dialogue this way:

> When you listen to and read one thinker, you become a clone; Two different thinkers, you become confused; Ten thinkers, you'll begin developing your own voice; Two or three hundred thinkers, you become wise.[17]

A good education (unaided or aided) can provide the critical tools to help students gain genuine knowledge, truth, and wisdom. Robert M. Hutchins, former president of the University of Chicago, who along with Mortimer J. Adler introduced the university to the study of the great books, believes student discussion should not be restricted. He insisted that the "cure" for ideas we oppose "lies through open discussion rather than through inhibition."[18] Hutchins also added that "free inquiry is indispensable to the good life, that universities exist for the sake of such inquiry . . . without it they cease to be universities."[19]

A noble learning experience illumines the human condition and greatly enhances the human experience in life and in the world. A genuine education would, by its very nature, be the solution to the deep problem with propaganda. Which of education's seven ideals, practices, and virtues do you find the noblest? How prevalent is propaganda today? How would your education experience stack up?

Next, let's apply the principles of logic to the controversial topic of conspiracy theories.

**Applying Logic to Conspiracy Theories**
Merriam-Webster defines *conspiracy theory* as "a theory that explains an event or set of circumstances as the result of a secret plot by usually powerful conspirators."[20]

Conspiracy theories never seem to go away. This seems especially true of the ones that involve clandestine plots by the United States government. Like all perspectives, conspiracy theories need to be thought through critically and dispassionately. As Christians, we have a duty to pursue truth. However, in a fallen world, truth is not always easy to discern. Nevertheless, as creatures made in God's image, we possess the ability to reason through explanations carefully and discover truth. We hope to illustrate this idea in consideration of conspiracy theories.

*The Big Four Conspiracy Theories*
You have heard of these covert plots. It appears that a lot of Americans believe that high-level members of the US government are involved in assassinations, cover-ups, secret societies, etc. Here are four such conspiracy theories that have gained popular acceptance among many Americans over the decades.

*JFK assassination conspiracy theory:* The idea that there was a government plot behind the 1963 assassination of President John F. Kennedy in Dallas, Texas, is widely considered the greatest conspiracy theory of all time. A Gallup poll[21] taken in 2001 reported that 81% of Americans believed in one conspiracy theory or another. However, the number had dropped to 60% by 2018.[22] As the decades pass without verification of an actual conspiracy, we expect the numbers to continue to drop. (For rebuttals to conspiracy theories concerning the JFK assassination, see chapter 3.) Some of the most common highly speculative scenarios propose that top officials of the American government were engaged in a coup d'état to kill President Kennedy. (See note for more resources on the JFK assassination.)[23]

*UFO conspiracy theory:* Belief in extraterrestrial visitors to Earth is long standing and strong. A 2021 Gallup poll says 40% of US citizens believe that real spacecrafts are visiting Earth from distant places in the universe.[24] A 2023 poll shows that "a majority of voters believe the U.S. government knows more about UFOs than it says it does"[25] with "57% of people polled say government has more info about UFOs than public."[26]

The topic was further stirred up in 2023. In April, a spokesperson for the US military declared that they had "found no credible evidence thus far of extraterrestrial activity, off-world technology or objects that defy the known laws of physics."[27] But, in July, Air Force Major David Grusch testified before a congressional committee that the US military has been in possession of crashed unidentified aerial phenomena for decades and had recovered nonhuman remains of extraterrestrial "biologics."[28] Grusch's claims made headlines, but they are not novel. As of November 2023, no one connected to the US military has corroborated or proved the claims. (See note for resources on UFO conspiracies.)[29]

*9/11 conspiracy theory:* A 2016 article on LiveScience notes that half of Americans believe that the US government was involved in the events of 9/11.[30] Conspiracy theorists (called Truthers) claim that high-level members of the Bush administration either participated in or did nothing to stop the terrorist attacks on September 11, 2001. (See note for resources on 9/11 conspiracies.)[31]

*Secret society theory:* Many people around the world believe that clandestine societies control the world.[32] Allegedly these shadowy groups, whose members are wealthy and well-connected politically, control events around the world for their own benefit. In the 1930s, the Nazis set forth the conspiracy theory that Jewish people were the puppet masters behind communism and had manipulated the money markets of Europe to cause societal unrest. Popular author Dan Brown's 2009 novel, *The Lost Symbol*, weaves a story about secret fraternal organizations in early America and how their rituals and symbols have deeply influenced history. (See note for resources on secret society theories.)[33]

**Other Conspiracy Theories**

A 2016 LiveScience article[34] revealed the following percentages of Americans agreed or strongly agreed that the federal government is concealing what they know about several popular conspiracy theories:

- The 9/11 attacks: 54.3%
- The JFK assassination: 49.6%
- Alien encounters: 42.6%
- Global warming: 42.1%
- Plans for a one-world government: 32.9%
- Obama's birth certificate: 30.2%
- The origin of the AIDS virus: 30.1%
- The death of Supreme Court Justice Antonin Scalia: 27.8%
- The moon landing: 24.2%

In 2020, a Pew Research Report[35] showed 5% of Americans believed it is definitely true and 20% believed it is probably true that a powerful group of people intentionally planned the COVID-19 pandemic.

**Thinking through Conspiracy Theories**

There are many reasons why these provocative conspiracy theories remain popular.[36] Some conspiracy theories have proven to be true. History indicates that people have plotted to carry out illegal, subversive, or secret plans. For example, it was proven in a court of law that a small group of individuals conspired to assassinate President Abraham Lincoln in April 1865.[37] It's been proven members of the US government do sometimes engage in conspiracy. Former President Richard Nixon later acknowledged that he knew much more about the Watergate break-in than he initially expressed. So, conspiracy theories, even those involving the US government, should not be rejected prior to reasonable analysis (a priori).

Some conspiracies serve to even things out, so to speak. It's hard to balance how a person as inconsequential as Lee Harvey Oswald, acting alone, could murder someone as consequential as President John F. Kennedy who was the leader of the free world.[38] A clandestine conspiracy involving powerful figures would help even the odds in an otherwise seemingly implausible scenario (see chapter 3).

Additionally, weaving speculative narratives makes us feel like we know more than we really do. As finite human beings, our knowledge is limited. There are things we don't know and at times it troubles us. Conspiracies are popular because they easily fill that knowledge gap.

Conspiracy theories also appeal to humanity's sinful foibles. For example, they can serve to justify our biases and prejudices. They can also feed the tendency to gossip. People enjoy speculating about grand enigmas. Conspiracy theories give us that opportunity.

And unfortunately, there are bad actors out there who actively use conspiracy theories to deceive sometimes for political propaganda purposes. One fraudulent conspiracy theory claimed the Israeli government orchestrated the 9/11 attacks to force the US into attacking its regional enemy countries. The evidence offered for this conclusion was that no Jews died in the 9/11 attacks.[39] Antisemitic Nazi conspiracies of the 1930s also projected blame for social ills onto powerful Jewish elites, claiming that these shadowy figures influenced world events for their own nefarious purposes.

Moreover, the Internet and social media provide fertile soil to an unprecedented degree to postulate conspiracy theories. Scholar Steven Willing notes:

> A little knowledge can seem like a lot when you have no idea how much you don't know. It takes no real effort to blindly

accept a list of 20 or 30 assertions and repost them on Facebook.
. . . It takes an extraordinary amount of effort to track down
the source of each claim and spot the error.[40]

It requires much less intellectual effort to level a claim than to offer a refutation. Given that people do not often give conspiracy theories sufficient critical analysis, how do you evaluate such theories? Let's explore these seven logical questions to consider when thinking about such theories.

*Seven Logical Questions for Evaluating Conspiracy Theories*
1. How many people would have to be in on the plan to pull off the subversion? It just seems common sense to wonder if the silence of a large number of participants could be safeguarded. Could all the people be sufficiently coerced to guarantee nothing would ever leak out? There would always be the possibility of people having a crisis of conscience or simply being unguarded in their speech. Some may even stand to gain a great deal by being a whistleblower on one of the most remarkable conspiracies in history. So, it seems reasonable to conclude that the more people who know about the conspiracy, the greater chance someone is going to reveal the secret. As Benjamin Franklin once said, "Three may keep a secret, if two of them are dead."

Logical problems like this also apply to all the big government conspiracy theories that require the involvement of great numbers of people, like the JFK assassination and the 9/11 attacks.

2. Does the theory hold together foundationally? Well-conceived theories are logically sound and internally consistent. Viable explanatory theories avoid self-stultification or being self-defeating in nature (contradictory by both affirming and denying essential elements of the same theory). Genuine contradictories in a system are a sign the theory is wrong. An acceptable explanatory theory must possess logical coherence.

For example, in his 1991 film *JFK*, director Oliver Stone puts forward a smorgasbord of conspiracy theories. Essentially, the film claims everyone (organized crime, CIA, KGB, pro- or anti-Castro Cubans, etc.) *except* Oswald murdered President Kennedy. There is no logical coherence to be found in Stone's movie.

3. Does the theory comport with the facts? Good theories are closely connected to the facts. They not only correspond to the known facts but also make sense of the facts by tying them together in a coherent explanatory fashion. "Facts are stubborn things," as American founding father John Adams

said. Failing to account for the facts can show a theory to be unacceptable. Unfortunately, in many debates about conspiracy theories the parties can't agree as to the specific constituted facts.

4. Does the theory avoid unwarranted presumptions? There's a huge difference between *presuming* to know something and in fact *knowing* something. Good theories keep assumptions to a minimum. If assumptions are made, they are shown to be plausible. Genuine knowledge includes proper justification for one's true beliefs. Solid theories are based on that which can be proved or verified. Too many unwarranted assumptions can doom a theory.

5. How well does the theory handle counterevidence and viable challenges? Feasible theories are flexible enough to accommodate possible counterevidence. The most potent explanatory theories consider the best critiques from alternative perspectives and answer the challenges. Having a sufficient rebuttal is important in defending an argument and a broad theory (see chapter 3). Clear thinking, however, demands that a person fairly consider viable alternatives. Unfortunately, too many of the people who accept the four big conspiracies have not done so.

6. Is the theory at least theoretically open to falsification; if so, how? Viable explanatory theories largely make claims that can be tested and proven true or false (verified or falsified). Non-falsifiable claims that can't be investigated, evaluated, and critiqued tend to carry little rational weight. So, what would have to happen for the conspiracy theory to be shown false?

7. Is the theory the best explanation for the available data? Remember from chapter 6, the best explanation combines logical coherence, simplicity, explanatory power and scope, correspondence, *and* competitive success.

Conspiracy thinking is common in our culture, and that includes Christians who are sometimes taken in by fanciful conspiracy theories. Christians may be susceptible to big government conspiracy theories because they believe there is an invisible, malevolent hand at work behind the scenes. Also, many Christians affirm an eschatology that involves a one-world government in the end times, which tends to further erode their trust in government. Like all people, Christians need to be discerning when it comes to conspiracy theories.

Willing notes the high cost when Christians fail to do their due diligence and instead spread false rumors:

> Succumbing to such deceptions exacts a great cost for both individuals and the Church at large. They corrupt our character, demolish our credibility, lead us to sin against others, and

place us in alignment with malevolent spiritual forces.[41]

An important starting point when thinking about conspiracy claims is asking the appropriate questions.

Big government conspiracy theories run rampant and have only increased since the COVID-19 pandemic. Some conspiracies have been shown to be true, so we ought not reject them a priori. But alternative explanations need to be submitted to rigorous rational analysis. Part of that analysis—and our duty as Christians—involves investigating original sources. Propaganda and conspiracy theories must be thought through with toughness and fair-mindedness. For Christians, truth is sacred. We must work hard to discover it and then handle it with great care.

In the next two chapters, we'll look at the challenge of informal logical fallacies and how to avoid them.

**Questions for Reflection**
1. Discuss the approaches to journalism. Why does journalism have problems with propaganda?
2. Describe a classical liberal education. What are its strengths?
3. Why do you personally think conspiracy theories remain popular?
4. Of the four big conspiracy theories, which do you find the most intriguing? Why?
5. How has the pandemic impacted conspiracy theories?

Chapter 9

# Twelve Precarious Informal Fallacies

Fallacy: A defective (false, incorrect, erroneous, mistaken) argument in which the conclusion is not justified by the statements supporting it.[1]
—Peter A. Angeles, *The HarperCollins Dictionary of Philosophy*

In my (Kenneth's) many years of teaching logic, I've found that instruction in informal fallacies ranks as one of the most empowering topics for my students. Being able to spot faulty reasoning, give it a name, and explain why it is problematic is a critical part of thinking clearly and carefully. But cultivating this ability takes time and practice, so go over these fallacies thoroughly and examine the examples of the fallacies with great care. Remember, the study of logic serves to order your thinking.

A logical fallacy (Latin: *fallacia*, deceit, trick[2]) consists of a fundamental mistake or defect in the reasoning process that causes an argument to go wrong and thus fail to adequately support the conclusion.[3] Fallacies violate logic's rules of inference in various ways.[4] Because fallacies by their very nature can be deceptive or misleading, it isn't always easy to detect whether an argument actually contains a fallacy. Fallacious arguments tend to be common and can be easily and regrettably accepted by the uncritical listener or reader.

Fallacies can be divided into two broad groupings: *formal* and *informal*. Formal fallacies are violations of the rules of formal logic (see chapter 5). Informal fallacies, on the other hand, are mistakes in reasoning in the content of the argument itself. They reflect claims phrased in ways that distort, obscure, or distract from the point of the argument. Informal fallacies are then divided into categories; we'll use six of the most common:

1. Fallacies of relevance (premises with no bearing on the truth of the conclusion)
2. Fallacies of emotional appeal (irrelevance focused specifically on appealing to the emotions)
3. Fallacies of insufficient grounds (premises that inadequately support the conclusion)
4. Fallacies of obscurity and presumption (premises with problems of ambiguity, vagueness, improper grammar or syntax, and assumption)
5. Fallacies of illicit transference (an attribute is incorrectly transferred from part to whole or the reverse)
6. Fallacies of ineffectual rebuttal (serious challenges to the conclusion remain unaddressed)

Studying fallacies is a practical and critical part of one's overall logic studies. In doing so you'll learn both how arguments break down or fail and, conversely, how to avoid bad arguments by constructing good ones. You'll also be empowered by your developing skill to recognize and classify various fallacies.

The next two chapters will focus exclusively on 27 different fallacies.[5] You'll learn the specific names of the fallacies and be given their linguistic roots, meaning you'll learn some Latin along the way. Certain patterns of *faulty* reasoning have been used in arguments so often, some even over the centuries, that many of them have been given designated names. In fact, some of these popular and recurring fallacies were identified by ancient and medieval philosophers. However, a fallacy does *not* require a specific name to qualify as a fallacy.

We'll also look at the specific logical defect in each fallacy's reasoning and its fallacious logical forms, as well as varieties, examples, and exceptions for each fallacy. Finally, we'll offer advice on how to respond to these fallacies and how to self-check your own reasoning. So, let the study of informal fallacies begin.

**The Twelve Most Precarious Fallacies**
These first dozen fallacies are especially common in discourse. They're also tricky because they're easy to commit and difficult to detect. So, give them an especially careful examination.

## *Ad Hominem:* **Argument against the Person**

Logic is all about examining ideas and arguments. Any criticism should be focused on the idea and the argument—not on the person. There are times when the character of the person is appropriate to criticize, but for the most part learn to stick with the argument.

The *ad hominem* fallacy always involves two arguers. It takes place when the first arguer presents their argument, but the second arguer ignores the argument given and instead attacks their opponent's character for the specific purpose of discrediting the argument. The faulty thinking that stands behind the *ad hominem* is the idea that, by disparaging an opponent (their personality, character, motives, intentions, qualifications, etc.[6]), one undermines the argument of that person. Put another way, *ad hominem* attempts to reject an argument by criticizing the person presenting it rather than the given argument itself. So, the mistake in reasoning is that criticism is directed "against the person" or "man" (Latin: hominem) instead of the argument.

The *ad hominem* goes wrong on two specific counts. Firstly, a person has an intellectual responsibility to respond to the *content* of the argument given by one's opponent. Secondly, a person's character is generally *irrelevant* to whether his argument is acceptable. Morally flawed people can present good arguments. Even the devil himself is capable of cogent reasoning. When it comes to logical engagement, criticism must focus on the argument, not on the person who presented it.

To summarize, what makes the *ad hominem* logically erroneous is the second arguer irrelevantly attacks the person making the argument rather than addressing the argument itself. Thus, the *ad hominem* is a fallacy of relevance.

*Fallacy Varieties and Examples*
This common and problematic fallacy comes in three distinguishable varieties. The abusive variety involves ignoring the person's argument and directly denouncing a person's character. It often consists of simple old-fashioned name-calling or verbal abuse. Here are two hypothetical examples of abusive *ad hominem* from the American political scene.

*Example 1:* Former president Donald Trump has argued that it's in America's national interest to diligently control its borders and to become energy independent through developing domestic sources of oil and natural gas, but Trump is clearly self-centered, petty, childish, bigoted, and xenophobic. His arguments about immigration and energy independence should be dismissed.

*Example 2:* President Joe Biden has argued that America stands to benefit from expanding the Affordable Care Act to make health insurance less expensive and more readily available to the under-resourced. Also, he argues that the US must confront climate change by developing clean energy and eliminating carbon emissions. But Biden is a mean-spirited, narcissistic, greedy, and lazy person. We can't take his arguments about health care and climate change seriously.

Both examples illustrate the *ad hominem* abusive fallacy because the initial argument is set aside in favor of a personal assault on character.

The second *ad hominem* variety is called circumstantial (also referred to as "poisoning the well"). This variety seeks to raise special circumstances to discredit a person's motives and, thus, cast suspicion on the person's argument. It often takes the form of insisting that an arguer has a vested interest and/or an ulterior motive. Again, a person's alleged interests or motives are irrelevant to the soundness of the argument. Let's consider two examples of poisoning the well relating to the controversial bioethical topic of abortion.

*Example 1:* "Even though your arguments against abortion are shaped by your extensive training and experience as an obstetrician-gynecologist and as a philosopher of bioethics, you are still a male. And because you're not a woman, any argument you make about abortion carries no significance whatsoever."

*Example 2:* "While you base your pro-abortion argument on your previous careers as surgeon general and as a professor of bioethics, your current job as a politician from a predominately blue state (a US state that predominantly votes for or supports the Democratic Party), it's in your best interest politically to be pro-choice. Therefore, if truth be told, your arguments are shaped by your political calculations."

Both examples illustrate the *ad hominem* circumstantial fallacy because the initial argument is set aside in favor of a suspicious charge of having a vested interest or a hidden agenda.

The third variety is called *tu quoque* (Latin: "You [did it], too"). This type of *ad hominem* fallacy consists of accusing the other arguer of hypocrisy as an attempt to avoid your own ideas critiqued as hypocritical. In effect, accusing your opponent of engaging in similar behavior serves to sidestep rebutting the initial criticism of your ideas. Logically speaking, citing another's culpability can't abdicate one's own responsibility for the same fault.

*Example:* "Pope Francis often speaks and writes presenting arguments for the moral need to care for the powerless and the poor in society—widows, orphans, and immigrants. But his arguments should be rejected because he lives in ostentatious wealth and power in the Vatican. Why doesn't he practice what he preaches?"

In this example the pope's arguments are set aside in favor of a charge of personal hypocrisy.

In its basic logical form, the *ad hominem* fallacy proceeds as follows: X argues that a person should do or believe Y (premise). But X has a defective character, or an ulterior motive, or is a hypocrite (premise). Therefore, one should reject X's argument for doing or believing Y (conclusion).

*Exceptions, Considerations, and Advice*
There are legitimate occasions for criticizing a person's character, such as when a person's character is the issue under discussion or debate. The courtroom serves as a good example. Jurors in a legal case need to know if a witness has been found guilty of perjury in past testimony. In a case such as this, character traits relate to the reliability or believability of testimony in a way that they don't relate to the credibility of an argument. Nevertheless, unless character is directly relevant, personal attacks are not acceptable.

Unfortunately, when you strongly disagree with someone over an important issue it's easy to disregard your opponent's logical argument and instead impugn their character. This proclivity illustrates humankind's deep flaws of both mind and moral fiber.

As forgiven sinners, Christians are certainly not immune to engaging in name-calling or impugning the character, interests, or motives of others. However, steering clear of this fallacious practice during a rigorous debate involves intellectual concentration and moral discipline. When critiquing the position of an opponent, stay focused on the central argument under discussion. Realize that uncovering the truth of an issue is itself a noble task. And arguing cogently and fairly is certainly much more important than winning an argument or debate by appealing to illegitimate and/or dishonest tactics.

If you're the recipient of an *ad hominem* attack while engaged in a debate, resist the temptation to respond back in kind. Instead, clearly identify the irrelevant attack on the part of your challenger. Then you can refocus the discussion by getting the discourse back to the logically relevant issue. Often, attacks on character are actually a compliment to the quality of the other person's argument. They can't answer the argument and, therefore, feel compelled to attack the person.

Many times, those listening to the discussion will appreciate the care and fairness you have exhibited and will be more open to your viewpoint. Even your opponent may be impacted positively by your show of intellectual integrity.

Do an *ad hominem* check on your argument. Ask yourself, Have I focused on the central argument of my opponent? Is character the actual issue under discussion or debate? Does my response to this argument involve an irrelevant personal attack (personality, character, motives, intentions, qualifications, etc.)?

Remember, attitude and demeanor may carry as much weight toward ultimate persuasion as do the arguments themselves.

## *Ad Populum*: Appeal to the People

Logic appeals to a person's reason in setting forth arguments. Arguments must contain rational justification. So, the focus of logic is on the rational aspects of life. The *ad populum* fallacy ignores rationality in favor of playing on human psychological needs to get a conclusion accepted. And since all people have a need to be respected, accepted, and included, this appeal can be incredibly powerful. Yet the flaw of the *ad populum* fallacy lies in its attempt to evoke assent through appealing to feeling and emotion instead of supporting a conclusion with reason and evidence.

The basic logical problem with the *ad populum* fallacy is that the weight of popular opinion in favor of an argument isn't relevant to whether an argument is reasonable and true. Feelings and sentiment are an important part of being human, but arguments must be buttressed with evidence.

To summarize, what makes the *ad populum* erroneous is it attempts to gain acceptance of an argument by arousing emotion rather than by offering rational justification for the argument. The *ad populum* is, thus, a fallacy of emotional appeal.

### *Fallacy Varieties and Examples*

This common and troublesome fallacy comes in four varieties. The first is the bandwagon variety. This appeal to popular sentiment can have dramatic results, especially when exploiting the enthusiasm of a crowd. The bandwagon version of *ad populum* appeals to the gallery, the multitude, and even to the mob. The majority claim of "everybody is doing it, so you should too" is intended to arouse the enthusiasm and passion of the crowd of listeners.

*Example 1:* "The patriotic speeches of our Führer Adolf Hitler are attracting throngs of Germans in the public square. The massive crowds respond to him with the salute: 'Heil Hitler!' The approval of National Socialism by 40 million German citizens can't be wrong!"

*Example 2:* "Since more and more people are using illegal 'street drugs,' there's really nothing wrong with using the drugs. Everyone's doing it."

In both examples the justification is mere popular appeal. (Chapter 11 addresses the bandwagon effect on cognitive bias.)

The second variety is an appeal to *tradition*. It can take the form of an appeal to the people if one defines tradition as merely a practice that many or most people have done in a particular way over a long period of time.

*Example:* "The Pledge of Allegiance has been recited in American schools for many decades accompanied by the student placing his or her right hand over the heart. Given that so many students have done it that way in the past is good reason for it to remain the practice."

There may be many legitimate reasons for keeping the Pledge ceremony as is, but in this example, long-practiced tradition is the *only* reason given.

In the third variety, one appeals to *vanity*, using flattery or leveraging pride to get a person to accept a position. Because all people have psychological needs this approach can be quite effective. For instance, appeals to celebrity status play on people's vanity and pride.

*Example:* "Take a stand on the environment! Lighten your carbon footprint and 'go green' like celebrity actors Leonardo DiCaprio and George Clooney who drive one of Tesla's elite electric cars."

The appeal here is the flattery of being associated with a celebrity. This is why promotional campaigns often use a famous spokesperson.

The fourth variety of *ad populum* is snobbery. Instead of using reason, appeal to snobbery plays on the human psychological need to feel special, elite, or superior to get a person to adopt a viewpoint. Consider two examples—one religious and one secular—demonstrating how people sometimes view their minority beliefs.

*Example 1:* "To be theologically Reformed (a Calvinist) a person must be both spiritually reflective and courageous enough to challenge certain doctrinal positions that most other Christians hold dear. Therefore, Reformed theology will always be a select minority view."

*Example 2:* "Atheism has never been a popular belief among the masses. To be an atheist a person must be a fiercely independent intellectual. It takes both brains and guts to challenge the consensus concerning the biggest philosophical question of life."

While there may be a lot of truth in both examples, these statements reflect a certain appeal to elitism. In its basic logical form, the *ad populum* fallacy proceeds as follows: Most people believe or do X (premise). Therefore, you should believe or do X (conclusion).

*Exceptions, Considerations, and Advice*
Regarding the bandwagon variety, sometimes there's good reason to think that if a lot of critically minded sources all affirm something, then they're likely correct.

*Example*: Most financial advisors strongly recommend maintaining a diversified financial portfolio. Therefore, it is a good investment practice to adopt.

The advisors know that this practice of diversification has been shown over many decades to help mitigate the risk and volatility in one's investment portfolio. It's not a mere appeal to the numbers of advisors who recommend it. However, the judgment must be more than just a mere appeal to numbers. Appealing to tradition, pride, and the desire for distinctiveness are not wrong in and of themselves, but one should be able to offer good reasons for following these appeals.

Be on guard for raw emotional manipulative appeals to passions and prejudices. One can't justifiably infer the merit or truth of a claim or belief based solely on the number of people who happen to affirm it. Opinion polls are not the arbiters of truth.

If someone makes a bandwagon appeal, then ask the person why the number of people who hold a view is relevant to its reasonableness and truthfulness. If people appeal to mere tradition, ask for reasons that justify the reasonableness of that tradition. In each case, ask what *independent evidence* supports the popular view.

Do an *ad populum* check on your argument. Ask yourself, Does my argument involve emotional manipulative appeals to passions and prejudices (bandwagon, tradition, vanity, or snobbery)? Is my appeal to persuasion based on arousing emotion or offering rational justification for the argument? If my argument does involve appealing to people's psychological needs, have I buttressed my argument with good evidence?

Interestingly, history shows that sometimes being willing to challenge the consensus position does indeed end up benefiting everyone.

## *Ad Verecundiam*: Appeal to an Unqualified Authority
All of us, in one way or another, have to trust authorities in our lives. We regularly appeal to various experts for specialized guidance and advice in fields like medicine, science, and law. Appealing to authorities may also include customs, tradition, institutions, etc.[7] Trusting authorities is a necessary part of life and there is nothing wrong with it. Appealing to a genuine authority can serve to buttress the conclusion of a logical argument. As we saw in chapter 5, appeals

to authority are part of inductive reasoning that, when done properly, produce arguments with probable or likely true conclusions. However, trusting authority shouldn't be an excuse for failing to develop solid reasoning.

The *ad verecundiam* (Latin: appeal to authority or veneration[8]) fallacy takes place when an *unqualified* or *untrustworthy* authority is cited in support of an argument. Alleged authorities may be unqualified in various ways. In their judgment they may lack requisite expertise, they may be inclined to bias or prejudice, or they may lack the necessary abilities to perceive or recall. Appealed-to authorities may also be anonymous. This fallacy is often committed when the authority cited speaks outside of his or her specialized field so there is a type of illicit transfer of the authority's competence from one area to another.

To summarize, what makes the *ad verecundiam* erroneous is that it appeals to an irrelevant or questionable authority. The *ad verecundiam* is, thus, a fallacy of insufficient grounds.

*Fallacy Varieties and Examples*
This common and controversial fallacy comes in three varieties. In the first variety there is a *lack of requisite expertise*, such as appealing to an authority speaking outside his or her field.

*Example:* "The world's most famous theoretical physicist, the late Stephen Hawking, says that philosophy is dead. And Hawking was brilliant!"

This claim commits the *ad verecundiam* fallacy because, though Hawking was a physicist, he was not a philosopher. Being a brilliant physicist doesn't qualify him to speak authoritatively on philosophy, a field he wasn't trained in.

The second variety occurs as *inclined to bias or prejudice*. Bias is having a predilection, prejudice, or predisposition in favor of or against one thing, person, or group compared with another, usually in a way considered to be unfair. The two following examples illustrate authorities that assert such strong positions about race in American society that one may reasonably question whether they can be fair-minded and avoid bias or prejudice in their authoritative assessment:

*Example 1:* "The Proud Boys argue that police forces in the US should not be defunded."

*Example 2:* "Black Lives Matter argues that the police forces in the US should be defunded."

Both organizations may be able to act in an evenhanded and nonpartisan manner as true authorities are expected to, but their record raises questions about their fundamental fairness and objectivity.

The third *ad verecundiam* variety occurs when the appealed-to authority can be disqualified because he or she lacks the necessary abilities to perceive or recall.

*Example:* An elderly woman with serious vision problems standing one hundred yards away says that she saw a man behind the picket fence on the grassy knoll take a shot at President Kennedy.

In its basic logical form, the *ad verecundiam* fallacy proceeds as follows: X says you should do or believe Z (premise). X may be an expert—though not about Z (premise). Therefore, you should do or believe Z (conclusion).

*Exceptions, Considerations, and Advice*
In evaluating authoritative testimony, it's important to recognize that people can be authorities in more than one field. Also, in terms of weighing possible bias and prejudice, be careful and deliberate; don't disqualify a source too quickly. Some people can be fair-minded and reasonable and avoid excessive dogmatism. Though sources with well-known deep roots in bias and prejudice need to be analyzed critically.

We should be deliberate in evaluating both the authorities' qualifications and judgment. When we receive contradictory testimony from what appear to be equally qualified and unbiased authorities, then we may want to reserve judgment.

Do an authority check on your argument. Ask yourself, Are the authorities cited genuine specialists in the subject under discussion? Do the authorities explain their reasoning for arriving at their judgment? Do the authorities give signs of being fair-minded or biased?

A significant amount of what we know has been learned from trusting authorities (parents, teachers, textbooks, the Bible, etc.) In fact, we never get away from the need to trust authorities and, therefore, it's necessary to know how to evaluate authorities.

## *Petitio Principii*: Begging the Question

It's usually better to reason linearly rather than circularly. However, when we hold a strong position on a given topic it's easy to give in to the temptation to start with one's conclusion rather than to allow reason to move us toward it.

Instead of supporting an argument with reason, facts, and evidence, the *begging the question fallacy* (also called "circular reasoning") assumes the conclusion, which has yet to be proved. Put another way, begging the question occurs when the premises presume, covertly or openly, the very conclusion that is to be demonstrated. In effect, one of the premises is really only a reformulation of the conclusion.

*Example*: There is nothing more powerful than love because all the other emotions are far weaker than love itself.

The premise, which starts at *because*, just repeats the preceding conclusion. The reasoning error with begging the question is that the conclusion is disguised (usually in other words or presented in a different logical form) and smuggled into the argument through presumption. Because of this stealth operation the fallacious circularity of the argument is not always easy to detect but it is easy to commit.

To summarize, what makes begging the question a reasoning error is that in various ways a statement is used both as a premise and as a conclusion. Begging the question is thus a fallacy of obscurity and presumption.

*Fallacy Varieties and Examples*
This fallacy occurs in at least three ways, either explicitly or implicitly. The first occurs by concealing an essential premise.

*Example:* "Murder is a great ethical violation. In light of this, we can then conclude that abortion is a great ethical violation." The claim *presumes* that abortion does indeed constitute murder.

The second variety is assuming what should be proved. Such fallacious reasoning often includes a *fait accompli* ("something that's already done").

*Example:* "I assure you that the perpetrator will be granted a fair and judicious trial before he is given the lethal injection." In this statement, the *fait accompli* is the lethal injection; the presumption is that the trial will justify it.

The third variety is reasoning in a circle. Consider two examples of circular reasoning:

*Example 1:* "The death penalty for murder is moral because it's morally right to punish those who kill innocent people by taking their lives in turn."

*Example 2:* "All the great philosophers are atheists. If they believed in God, they wouldn't be great philosophers. If they weren't atheists, they wouldn't be great philosophers."

To put it in its logical form, begging the question is stating X is true (premise) therefore X is true (conclusion).

*Exceptions, Considerations, and Advice*
Consider this qualification: It is not circular reasoning if you present arguments

for a conclusion that you already happen to believe. An argument is not an adventure of exploration of the truth of the conclusion by the one who presents it; in fact, that person may assume its truth without having reflected about the premises. For example, many people believe in God without being able to make a logical case for that belief. Then they discover the argument from design and now are able to give an argument for a belief they already held. That's not begging the question.[9]

Remember, begging the question is a complicated fallacy that comes in several forms and is easy to commit and, at times, quite a challenge to detect. Further, there is sometimes debate even among specialists as to whether an argument has genuinely begged the question (see table 9.1).

It's easy to beg the question especially if the person first assumes the truth of their conclusion and then goes looking for evidence to support it. Investment in one's conclusion may cause a person to unknowingly engage in logical smuggling by making their premises dependent on their conclusion instead of the other way around. Be especially careful to see that a premise is not merely a restatement of the conclusion. One way to counteract the strong begging-the-question tendency is to get in the habit of writing out your premises and conclusion in a brief, outline-like form (such as the logical forms presented throughout this book). Also, please recognize that to *beg the question* is to engage in the fallacy of circular reasoning. It doesn't mean, as it's often used in discourse, to *prompt* or to *raise* a question.

Do a circular reasoning check on your argument. Ask yourself, Do any of my premises assume the truth of the conclusion? Are any of my premises merely an equivalent form of the conclusion? Do any of my premises merely restate the conclusion in different words?

Philosopher Peter Kreeft says of begging the question: It's a "very common fallacy, and even great philosophers occasionally commit it."[10] So, to be forewarned is to be forearmed.

## Equivocation Fallacy

Have you ever noticed how much of humor trades on linguistic confusion? For example, a little piece of logician humor goes like this: "Space aliens have their own preferred form of reasoning. It is called abduction." The *pun* in a joke like this one makes use of the various meanings of a word or the fact that some words sound alike but have different meanings. Well, linguistic confusion is good for humor, but not for logic.

As we saw in chapter 6, clarity is crucial in logical arguments. A lack of

> **Table 9.1 Clarifying Definitions**
>
> Since this common fallacy is tricky and thus hard to identify and easy to do, consider some additional brief definitions. Begging the question is:
>
> - When an argument presumes the very thing it's supposed to establish.
> - Drawing a conclusion that's already assumed true.
> - Relying on a premise that conveys the very same thing as the conclusion.

clarity causes confusion in first being able to understand an argument and then being able to evaluate its rational merit. The logical error of the equivocation fallacy involves linguistic confusion. This fallacy occurs when the conclusion of an argument depends on the ambiguity of a key word, term, or phrase. Inevitably employing a word or a phrase in two or more different senses in an argument misleads the reader or listener into drawing a faulty conclusion. The equivocation is, thus, a fallacy of obscurity and presumption.

*Example 1:* Logicians say the study of logic significantly improves people's ability to argue. That being the case it'll only increase the number of argumentative people we have in the world. Therefore, the study of logic is certainly not good for the world.

*Example 2:* Sardines are better than nothing. Nothing is better than logic. Therefore, sardines are better than logic.

Each of these examples involves words or terms that are used or implied in two different senses. To put it in its basic logical form, *equivocation* proceeds as follows: Claim A is made (premise). B is concluded based on an ambiguous reading of A (conclusion).

*Exceptions, Considerations, and Advice*
In chapter 2 we saw that thinking and language go together. We express our thoughts through language—the use of words. We must be careful and consistent in reasoning to not allow an important word to change in meaning within our argument. Careful arguments use words or phrases that retain the same meaning throughout the argument.

There's a considerable number of ambiguous words and terms found in such fields as theology, philosophy, and apologetics. Therefore, the equivocation fallacy is easy to commit, and it contributes to people with different worldviews misunderstanding each other and talking past one another.

Equivocation may be both the simplest and most common informal fallacy. Many key words and phrases have the potential to carry multiple meanings. Equivocation is also probably the most common fallacy involving ambiguity, though there are others including amphiboly, division, and composition. Do a clarity-consistency check on your argument. Ask yourself, Are all the key terms I'm using in my argument clear, unambiguous, and consistent? In cases of suspected equivocation, if you replace the ambiguous word with another word with the exact same meaning for all uses does the argument then make logical sense?

Remember to precisely define your key words and phrases and then use the same meaning consistently throughout your argument.

## False Alternatives Fallacy

In logic it's important to know the range of options available for careful consideration of truth. If the range of choices concerning an argument is truly an either-or deliberation, then the range of possibilities is limited and narrowly set. But what happens if viable options have been unreasonably excluded or overlooked?

The fallacy of false alternatives is known by other names: false dichotomy (an untrue division of two), false bifurcation (separating into two), and black-and-white reasoning (illegitimately eliminating middle points). This fallacy consists of assuming *too few* alternatives and then accepting one of the proposed alternatives as being true. It can take place when a person claims that there are only two legitimate options when there are actually more than two. And out of the too few alternatives, one is asserted as being true or correct. The error in reasoning caused by a lack of full inquiry creates a false scenario that the course of action for consideration has been exhausted and the choices are mutually exclusive (either-or: X or Y).

Not only are there logical *dilemmas* (false reduction to two options), but there are also *trilemmas* (false reduction to three options). In a trilemma, the actual number of viable options extends beyond three alternatives, and so forth. Moreover, there may be even a spectrum of options on a scale.

To summarize, what makes the false alternatives erroneous is that one option has been accepted as true when not all viable or plausible choices, outcomes, and views have been identified and considered. False alternatives is, thus, a fallacy of obscurity and presumption.

*Examples*
- Either increase military spending dramatically or allow Russia to rule the world.
- Either we let every immigrant enter our country or we close the borders entirely.
- Either provide safe abortion on demand in hospitals or leave no choice except back-alley abortions with coat hangers.
- America: Love it or leave it.
- Either you support affirmative action or you don't care about equity.

Each example assumes too few alternatives and/or oversimplifies the issues and exaggerates the proposed solutions. In its basic logical form, *false alternatives* proceeds as follows:

False dilemma form:
Either A or B is true (ignoring C and D).
A is not true.
Therefore, B must be true.

False trilemma form:
Either A, B, or C is true (ignoring D and E).
A and B are not true.
Therefore, C must be true.

*Exceptions, Considerations, and Advice*
There are clear cases in life and in thought where the number of viable options for one's choices, outcomes, and views is legitimately limited. For example, either-or relations are always found in statements that stand in a contradictory relationship (see chapter 4). For example, Jesus is God incarnate or he is not.

While legitimate either-or cases do emerge, they're still somewhat rare. Therefore, when they present themselves, examine them critically especially with controversial issues. Force yourself to ask what it would take to convince you that the positions you see are the *only* positions there are. Work to intentionally expand your thinking. Consider looking through the prism of alternative worldviews. Especially consider choices, outcomes, and views that differ from your own. Then proceed according to the criteria of what is the most reasonable perspective.

Do an alternatives check on your argument. Ask yourself, Have I endeavored to identify all reasonable alternatives? What is the spectrum of choices I haven't seen? Can I reasonably reduce the options to two or three? Can I leave the question of options open and consider others that may arise?

When you get into the regular habit of questioning alternatives, your thinking skills will inevitably sharpen.

**False Cause Fallacy**
Determining the likely cause of an effect can be problematic. In fact, understanding the idea of causal relationships is a challenging one in both philosophy and logic. The reason is that cause-and-effect connections can be difficult to determine. The false cause fallacy reflects a breakdown between an effect and its antecedent cause. This causal disconnect results when the link between an argument's premises and conclusion depends on a causal connection that's either weak or nonexistent.

To summarize, the error is that the proposed cause is too uncertain to justify the conclusion. The false cause is thus a fallacy of insufficient grounds.

*Fallacy Varieties and Examples*
This fallacy occurs in four specific ways. The first, called *post hoc ergo propter hoc* (Latin: "after this, therefore, because of this"), insists that because X precedes Y in time, then X must have caused Y. Temporal succession alone does not mean that X actually caused Y. The connection in time may be merely coincidental and thus a confusion of succession with causation.

*Example*: A baseball player gets two base hits whenever he eats two McDonalds Filet-O-Fish sandwiches before a game. Therefore, if the manager requires the rest of the players to adopt the same pregame meal regimen, then the team will have a more successful season.

The reasoning reflected here is that since the baseball player got two hits *after* eating two Filet-O-Fish sandwiches, therefore he got the hits *because* of the two Filet-O-Fish sandwiches. Causal explanations may range from fish protein to superstition.

The second false cause variety is called *non causa pro causa* (Latin: "not the cause for the cause"). This fallacious form of causal reasoning simply misidentifies the actual cause of an effect.

*Example*: "America's largest cities all have high percentages of homeless persons living on the streets. They also have lots of libraries. To slow down the homeless rate, the cities may want to shut down some of those libraries."

There are many reasons that likely contribute to the problem of homelessness in American cities, but it's safe to say that an abundance of libraries would not likely be one of them. The argument mentioned here provides no reason to assume the cause claimed produced the effect concluded.

The third variety is the *oversimplified cause* (reductive or selective cause). This fallacy occurs when an effect has multiple or complex causes, but only one cause is identified. Oversimplified causes are common. So a little more analysis is offered.

*Example:* America won World War II! While it is true that the United States of America and US armed forces played a crucial role in the Allied victory over the Axis powers, there are many complex factors that actually contributed to the Allied victory. Let's consider briefly just the notion of an "allied" victory itself. The victors of World War II included the US along with many allies. While the chief allied countries involved in the war included Great Britain, France, the Soviet Union, and the US, there were over two dozen countries that were wartime members of the Allied coalition.

Also, some war historians would suggest that the Allied victory was made possible by shared sacrifices and contributions: namely Soviet combat deaths (extremely high casualty rate), British intelligence (success in breaking Axis secret codes), and US industry (producing and sharing an abundance of military vehicles and weapons). To put it bluntly, some suggest World War II was won especially by "British brains, American brawn, and Russian blood."[11] Ironically, though, this last statement may also be an oversimplification.

The fourth and final variety of the false cause is known as the *gambler's fallacy*. It reasons that since a chance event has had a consistent run of luck previously, the odds of its happening in the future are greatly changed. This form of magical thinking is common among gamblers.

*Example:* "I've flipped my brand-new JFK half dollar 12 times and it's landed on heads each time. Therefore, the thirteenth flip is almost guaranteed to be tails." In reality, if the coin is flipped fairly without interference, the chance of each coin flip remains 50/50. (See chapter 13 for more details on this fallacy.)

Some philosophers think that those who propose a multiverse[12] (the view that our universe is just one among many) to explain the extraordinary fine-tuning in the observable universe may commit the *inverse gambler's fallacy*. This fallacy reasons that a highly unlikely outcome indicates that an event or process must have occurred many times before. (For example, one assumes that a lottery winner must have bought numerous tickets before the winning ticket.) A 2021 article in *Scientific American* makes this point:

> Philosopher Ian Hacking was the first to connect the inverse gambler's fallacy to arguments for the multiverse.... Just as the casino-visitor says, "Wow, that person must've been playing for a long time, as it's unlikely they'd have such good luck just from one roll," so the multiverse theorist says "Wow, there must be many other universes before this one, as it's unlikely the right numbers would have come up if there'd only been one."[13]

In its basic logical form, the *post hoc ergo propter hoc* fallacy proceeds as follows: X causes Y simply because X occurs before Y. And, in its basic logical form, the *non causa pro causa* fallacy proceeds as follows: X is regularly connected with Y. Therefore, X causes Y.

*Exceptions, Considerations, and Advice*
An exception to consider is that when strong evidence is marshalled for the causation of an effect in an argument, then there is no causal fallacy. Always look for evidence of a causal connection.

Given the challenges posed by causal relationships in philosophy and logic, pay special attention to cause-effect relationships in arguments. Look specifically for breakdowns and weaknesses in the cause-effect connection. Ensure that your arguments involving causal relationships have solid connections.

Do a causal check on your argument. Ask yourself, What weaknesses are there in my argument's causal claims? Do the causal connections in my argument show any sign of oversimplification? Are the causal connections in my argument in any way imaginary? Get in the habit of examining all cause-and-effect relationships.

**Hasty Generalization Fallacy**
As we saw in chapter 5, inductive arguments usually progress from the particular to the general or from the individual to the universal. So, generalizations move logically from the knowledge or awareness of a selected sample set to a claim about the whole group. Solid generalizations are based on abundant data that is fairly and carefully examined.

The logical error of the hasty generalization (see also forgetful and slothful generalizations in chapter 5) is drawing a general conclusion from an unrepresentative sample. In other words, a weak generalization is made based on an inadequate collection. Inadequate sample size and/or a failure to randomize the selection results in inadequate support for the generalized conclusion.

To summarize, what makes the hasty generalization logically erroneous is reaching a conclusion about a target group, based on an inadequate sample size. (For further discussion of hasty generalizations in terms of cognitive bias, see chapter 11.)

*Examples*
- I've met three redheads, and they were all hard to get along with; so all redheads are hard to get along with.
- I've known several evangelical Christians personally and they were all judgmental and unkind; so all Christians must be that way.
- Scientists Richard Dawkins, Peter Atkins, Lawrence Krauss, and Sean Carroll are all outspoken atheists. All scientists these days are atheists.
- I've interacted with seven Muslims on the web. All seven agreed that killing people in the name of God was justifiable against non-Muslims. All Muslims are radical jihadists.

In all these examples, the numbers are obviously far too small and/or not randomly selected. They do not adequately support the generalized conclusion. Nevertheless, it's easy to allow our personal encounters, maybe especially when they're negative, to color our view of a whole group.

*Hasty generalization*, in its basic logical form, proceeds as follows: Sample #1 is taken from population S (premise). Sample #1, which is a very small portion of population S, has quality P (premise). Therefore, population S has quality P (conclusion). Another example is as follows: These X's (which are in fact atypical cases) are Y (premise). So all X's are Y (conclusion).

*Exceptions, Considerations, and Advice*
Sometimes a sample from a larger and more representative collection is not available. So, depending on the issue and circumstance, some may think even an atypical sample may have some marginal value.

There are times when it's reasonable to generalize from a small sample size. This is the case when one thing is representative of all other things in that class (for example, all automobiles use energy). Everyone generalizes every day. It's a valued and necessary way of reasoning, but when done poorly it can lead to false conclusions and can serve as a source for many unfortunate stereotypes.

Philosopher Peter Kreeft described the hasty generalization as "the commonest and simplest fallacy of induction."[14] Therefore, get in the habit of examining your generalized conclusions carefully. Since hasty generalizations come from nonrepresentative samples, avoid generalizing from small and/or unrepresentative samples. Remember, a large sample size is important, but it also needs to be random and representative.

Do a generalization check on your argument. Ask yourself, Is my generalization drawn from a large sample size? Is my generalization drawn from a random and representative sample? Do my generalizations about people groups involve stereotypes?

**Red Herring Fallacy**
In chapter 6, we discussed the critical issue of staying on point in both constructing and evaluating an argument. Knowing the point is absolutely crucial in thinking through an argument; losing sight of it can be logically catastrophic. We also noted that one of the biggest obstacles to careful thinking is *distraction*. Premises that are logically unrelated to the central point of the argument provide no support for that conclusion.

The *red herring fallacy* attempts to divert or shift attention to an irrelevant side issue rather than to directly address the central issue at hand. It directs the debate away from the real issue by changing the subject to extraneous or secondary matters. Thus, it never meets its logical obligation to stay on point and meet the authentic conclusion head on. The name comes from stories of escaped prisoners using pungent herring to try to throw bloodhounds off their trail.

To summarize, what makes the red herring logically erroneous is that it draws attention away from the actual point of the argument. The red herring is, thus, a fallacy of relevance.

*Example 1:* Arguer 1 claims, "If a divine mind exists beyond and in the creation of the universe, then the intelligible features of the cosmos would have a rational ground or justification." Arguer 2 responds, "Yeah, but religious people are greedy hypocrites." In this scenario, the charge of greed and hypocrisy is a complete distraction from the issue of God being a ground for reason. It is possible, in some cases for a red herring to be related to the topic at hand and yet still take focus off the relevant issue.

*Example 2:* Arguer 1 claims, "Pro-life people often identify abortion as the death of the innocents, but what about the other issues that take life? Disease, starvation, and warfare cause countless deaths every year throughout the planet. Where's your pro-life protest about those issues?" Though similar in addressing the issue of death, there's an obvious change of subject in this example.

In its basic logical form, the red herring fallacy proceeds as follows: Argument X is presented by arguer #1. Arguer #2 introduces argument Y. Argument X is forsaken.

In a formal debate, it may not always be a red herring to respond to an argument by introducing another argument that meets the challenger's point head-to-head, but get in the habit of listening to other people's arguments and acknowledge them and respond to them accordingly.

*Exceptions, Considerations, and Advice*

The red herring fallacy serves as a diversionary tactic. In arguments, be mindful to avoid tangents and unproductive side trails. When others engage in them, respectfully direct them back to the central issue of the argument. In engaging in logical arguments with others, listen carefully to opposing arguments. Strive to prize the virtue of truth along with humility and emotional maturity higher than just winning a debate.

Do a diversionary check on your argument. Ask yourself, What's the central point of the argument? Can you repeat your opponent's argument? Is my argument or my critique of another's argument focused properly? If the argument does get off track, can I identify where and how?

T. Edward Damer rightly says staying on point "requires constant surveillance."[15]

## Slanting Fallacy

As discussed in chapter 3, the best argument is informed by both evidence for and evidence against its conclusion. In other words, a person hasn't examined all the evidence if they haven't considered the evidence against their view. There's a natural tendency, unfortunately, to examine only the evidence that supports one's conclusion. Worse still is the tendency to go looking only for support for one's position (see chapter 12 for a discussion of confirmation bias).

The *fallacy of slanting*[16] takes place when someone intentionally skews or taints something on behalf of their position in an argument. Slanting misrepresents the evidence because some data is either deliberately deemphasized or overemphasized to support one's own point of view in opposition to another. The goal is to make a position look like something it isn't by failing to present all the facts in an unbiased and fair-minded fashion. Sometimes this fallacy is identified under other names such as suppressed evidence, ignoring the counterevidence, cherry-picking, or stacking the deck.

In summary, what makes slanting logically erroneous is that it's one-sided in presenting only evidence supporting its conclusion while ignoring or downplaying counterevidence. Slanting is, therefore, a fallacy of ineffectual rebuttal.

*Example 1:* Sometimes slanting can be simply framing language to put a view in a favorable or unfavorable light. For instance, framing the abortion debate as "pro-life vs. anti-life" or "pro-choice vs. anti-choice" paints the opposing position in negative light.[17]

*Example 2:* People with strong views are sometimes tempted to slant the evidence for their own purposes. This can happen to people who hold both secular and religious worldviews:

- "As secular defenders of Darwinian evolution, we know our biological theory has its weaknesses such as a lack of clear and viable biochemical pathways, the problem of repeated evolution, the sudden emergence of complex life-forms and ecosystems, narrow time constraints, etc. But we dare not straightforwardly admit these challenges lest the creationists seize on them and replace science with theology."
- "As apologists of historic Christianity, we know aspects of the problem of evil, pain, and suffering remain an enduring challenge to faith convictions. But we dare not straightforwardly admit these challenges lest the new atheists seize on them and convince more young people to leave the church and give up their faith."

In its basic logical form, *slanting* proceeds as follows: Arguer presents selected evidence in favor of argument X while ignoring or suppressing counterevidence anti-X. Observer is oblivious of counterevidence anti-X. X conclusion is accepted.

*Exceptions, Considerations, and Advice*
There are occasions when the presentation of a one-sided case is both expected and acceptable. Attorneys in a courtroom take an adversarial stance. Politicians are expected to be partisan in debates. Advertising is another area where a one-sided presentation is expected. Yet one-sidedness is clearly unacceptable and fallacious in situations where we have a right to expect objectivity—such as in journalism, science, medicine, education, etc.

Consider this powerful comment in a day where adversarial journalism, instead of objective journalism (see chapter 8), seems at times to run rampant:

> Slanting can be one of the most insidiously deceptive booby-traps, because simply leaving out relevant information can lead people seriously astray. In order to do this, dictatorships and totalitarian governments have always attempted to monopolize the news media and education, in order to control what information people receive. It's almost impossible to detect such one-sidedness if you lack other sources for the relevant facts, which is what makes a free press so important.[18]

The rules of logic and reasonable inference call all people of truth and honor to be honest and transparent when it comes to reason, facts, and evidence. A frank acknowledgment of uncertainty about one's own view can reflect an invigorating and attractive intellectual honesty. When the evidence points in your opponent's direction, it is far better to concede a formidable argument than to slant the truth or engage in intellectual duplicity. Remember, for Aristotle *persuasion* began with ethos (character) even ahead of pathos and logos.

Do a slanting check on your argument. Ask yourself, In examining the evidence have I avoided suppressing, cherry-picking, or stacking the deck? Have I endeavored to be fair-minded and objective in setting forth the data in my argument? Have I presented the facts of my opponent's argument in an unbiased and fair-minded fashion?

When it comes to the importance of evaluating evidence, take time to reflect on the words of the great philosopher John Stuart Mill:

> He who knows only his own side of the case, knows little of that. His reasons may be good, and no one may have been able to refute them. But if he is equally unable to refute the reasons on the opposite side; if he does not so much as know what they are, he has no ground for preferring either opinion.[19]

Waiting to decide until one knows all the evidence—if one can ever truly have access to all the evidence—may be impractical. Still, one can always inquire about the best argument against one's position. Challenge yourself to consider alternative viewpoints.

**Straw Man Fallacy**

In chapter 6 we discussed the importance of asking yourself, What's the point? Ask that question and keep on asking it both for your argument and of your opponent's argument. To succeed in the logical enterprise a person must keep a close eye on both their argument as well as the argument of their opponent. When distraction strikes—straw man fallacies emerge.

Physically, it's much easier to knock down a straw man than it is to knock down a real man of firm muscle and bone. The same is true of arguments. When one arguer distorts the argument of his or her opponent and then proceeds to criticize that misrepresentation (whether in speaking or in writing), the arguer commits the informal logical fallacy known as the straw man. As a form of distortion, a straw man is often either an exaggeration or oversimplification of another's position or ideas. It's a mere caricature, weakened substitute, or an inferior version of the real argument. In a straw man fallacy, the authentic argument hasn't even been considered.

To summarize, what makes the straw man logically erroneous is that it misrepresents (through distortion) the original argument to evade answering it. The straw man is, thus, a fallacy of relevance.

Christian doctrine and values are sometimes misrepresented via straw man fallacies.

*Example 1:* "The Trinity doctrine of historic Christianity constitutes tritheism—three gods." Various critics of the Trinity often allege that this doctrine is unbiblical because it teaches three Gods. However, this objection constitutes a straw man because it ignores the nuance and actual trinitarian theology. In fact, the doctrine of the Trinity affirms the existence of only one God who subsists as three distinct persons.[20]

*Example 2:* "Christians are racists! And the Christian religion is racist as well! All Christians in colonial America used the Bible to justify slavery. It's supposed to be a holy book, but it supports racial discrimination. How could any black person be a biblical Christian?"

It's true that, as forgiven sinners, Christians are not immune from faulty thinking and immoral actions. However, the argument given here creates a straw man by failing to recognize that Christian abolitionists used the biblical teaching that all people are made in the image of God (Genesis 1:26-28) as the principal argument to bring an end to slavery in the Western world. Those Christians who attempted to use the Bible to promote slavery promoted a profound misinterpretation of the biblical text that even some secular scholars acknowledge.[21]

In its basic form, the straw man fallacy proceeds as follows: Arguer #1 makes claim X. Arguer #2 restates X in distorted manner. Arguer #2 then proceeds to critique the distorted version of X. Conclusion is drawn that X is faulty.

Intentionally distorting another's argument is logically fallacious, deceptive, and uncharitable. It can also happen *unintentionally*, though. In either case, take the time to focus attention back on the true argument.

*Exceptions, Considerations, and Advice*
The straw man is one of the most frequent informal fallacies. It's very easy to fall into, especially when one is engaged in a face-to-face argument. Amid a truly heated debate, a person might struggle to concentrate on understanding their opponent's argument and remain dispassionate and objective. Rather, he or she is probably thinking about what to say next in order to stay ahead in the debate.

We have a suggestion that often helps people stay on track instead of ending up speaking past one another. We suggest that each debater stop, take a deep breath, and a person can say something like the following, "Your central claim seems to be _____ and your support for it seems to consist of _____. Now, have I understood your argument correctly? If not, please help me get it right."

Being able to repeat your opponent's argument clearly and carefully usually produces four direct benefits. First, it helps ensure that you're not committing the straw man fallacy. It also shows that you respect truth and your opponent enough to fully consider their case. Second, all people like to know that they've been heard and that their argument has been correctly stated. Given this honest and respectful approach, they may even be more open to critique of their argument when they know you've endeavored to understand their position correctly. A charitable attitude and a gracious demeanor tend to have a direct effect on personal persuasion.

Third, you can effectively critique an argument only when you have a correct understanding of it. By first seeking truth and understanding you inevitably help your subsequent logical and apologetic critique. Fourth, this mature and honorable practice helps illustrate to your opponent (as well as to others who may be listening) that you care more about understanding truth than you do about merely winning an intellectual argument.

The straw man fallacy is commonly committed largely because people fail to stop and listen carefully to the people they're engaged in reasoning with. Philosopher Louis Pojman seems to capture the human condition in saying, "There is a tendency in all of us to attack a weaker, less plausible version of our opponent's position."[22]

To avoid this fallacy, do a misrepresentation check on your argument.

Ask yourself, have I exaggerated or oversimplified my opponent's argument? If so, how? Have I asked my opponent to ensure that I have understood their argument correctly? Have I presented the strongest version of my opponent's argument?

**Weak Analogy Fallacy**

Analogical reasoning is a highly common line of thought (see chapter 5). An analogy attempts to argue that because two things or objects share some similarities, then they likely have other characteristics in common as well. For example, if entities #1 and #2 share qualities A, B, C, and D, and entity #1 also has quality E, then it is likely that entity #2 has that distinctive quality as well. Again, according to logician Patrick Hurley: "Analogical reasoning may be the most fundamental and most common of all rational processes."[23]

Analogies break down or become fallacious, however, when the objects compared are superficial or trivial to the issue at hand—namely the conclusion. A weak analogy then consists of an argument in which the two things being compared are not sufficiently similar enough in relevant ways to carry the truth of the conclusion. For example, the objects being compared may have only peripheral commonalities and/or may have substantive differences.

To summarize, what makes the weak analogy logically erroneous is that the two things being compared are more dissimilar than similar in relationship to the conclusion. The weak analogy is, thus, a fallacy of insufficient grounds.

*Example 1:* The brain is nothing more than a computer. It takes in information, processes it, then has an output. So, we're not much more than computer-driven biological machines.

*Example 2:* Many insects are socially cooperative and engage in collaborative interactions. People are socially cooperative and engage in collaborative interactions. People are not much more than insects, but bigger.

In contrast here is a strong analogy on a controversial topic: The material cosmos resembles the intelligent productions of human beings in that it exhibits profound design. The design in any human artifact is the effect of having been made by an intelligent being. Therefore, it is reasonable to conclude that the cosmos is the product of an intelligent creator.

In its basic logical form, weak analogy proceeds as follows: Object or entity #1 is similar to object or entity #2. Object or entity #1 has characteristic X. Therefore, object or entity #2 probably has attribute X, too—but the two objects or entities being compared do not have enough in common to carry the conclusion.

Keep in mind that analogies are not good or bad, nor are they correct or incorrect. Rather analogies are *strong* or *weak*. Moreover, the persuasion of analogies carries with it an element of subjectivity.

*Exceptions, Considerations, and Advice*
Peter Kreeft notes, "Analogies are extremely useful, even essential to human thinking."[24]

Strong analogies compare objects or entities that have solid connections, directly related to the claim made by the conclusion. Such analogies also pay attention to the significance of dissimilarities. Arguments from analogy are inductive, making them suggestive at best rather than conclusive.

If you have serious doubts about a given analogy, then develop a counter analogy that highlights dissimilarities and intends to undermine the given analogy. In an analogical context, that is equivalent to asking for the best argument on the other side.

Careful thinkers therefore must give critical reflection to the common arguments derived from analogical reasoning. Do an analogical check on your argument. Ask yourself, Have I weighed the similarities carefully? Have I weighed the dissimilarities carefully? Have I considered a further way of checking through a counter analogy?

These dozen most precarious fallacies are dangerous because they are very easy to commit and hard to detect. In the next chapter we will explore other informal fallacies that are commonly found in discourse.

## Questions for Reflection
1. Of the 12 fallacies, which do you think are the three most challenging? Why?
2. Why is the begging question fallacy so easy to commit and yet also hard to detect?
3. Discuss the challenge that ambiguous words present in an argument.
4. Explain the strategy for addressing the straw man fallacy.
5. How does a strong analogy differ from a weak one?

Chapter 10

# Fifteen More Common Informal Fallacies

> The line that Plato drew to distinguish the sophist from the philosopher, both equally skilled in argument, put the philosopher on the side of those who, devoted to the truth, would not misuse logic or rhetoric to win an argument by means of deception, misrepresentation, or other trickery.[1]
> —Mortimer J. Adler, *How to Speak, How to Listen*

Remember a fallacy in logic consists of a major mistake or error in the reasoning process that causes an argument to break down and thus fail to adequately support the conclusion (see the early part of chapter 9). Because fallacies by their very nature tend to be evasive and elusive, it isn't always easy to discover whether an argument actually involves a fallacy. Fallacious arguments tend to be quite common and can be easily and unfortunately affirmed by the undiscriminating listener or reader.

Let's now look at 15 additional common fallacies.

**Accident Fallacy**

In chapter 5, we saw that inductive reasoning usually moves from the particular to the general or from the individual to the universal. In fact, we can say that a generalization is when a specific instance is applied more broadly. A general rule then may be popularly defined as a usual way things are done or applied.

The *accident fallacy* is the misapplication of a general rule in a specific case. Another way of putting it is that an arguer brings to bear a general principle to a circumstance it was never intended for. The error is failing to differentiate a general rule from a universal rule. Aristotle described this fallacy and categorized it as an "unqualified generalization."[2]

To summarize, what makes the accident logically erroneous is that there is a general principle applied to a particular instance whose situation doesn't allow its proper application. The accident is, thus, a fallacy of relevance.

*Examples*
- "Lying is always morally wrong. Therefore, it's wrong to lie to the Nazis about where the Jews are hiding."
- "Thou shall not kill. Therefore, one can't kill in self-defense, in defense of the innocent, or in defense of one's country when invaded."
- "Cutting people with knives is a criminal act. Surgeons cut people with knives. Therefore, surgeons carry on criminal activity."

All these examples seek to apply an important general rule in specific cases where they don't apply. Some Christians may balk at excusing lying. But most Christian ethicists would affirm a hierarchy of values that gives protecting human life higher importance than the offense of lying. Moreover, it makes the intentional communication of misinformation a moral good. Biblically speaking, this very scenario takes place in Exodus 1. The Hebrew midwives, Shiphrah and Puah, disobey and then lie to Pharaoh to protect the Hebrew baby boys. Scripture states that God rewarded these women for their actions.

In its basic logical form, the accident fallacy proceeds as follows: Generally, X are P (premise). So, this X (which is in fact an atypical case) is P (conclusion).

*Exceptions, Considerations, and Advice*
Be cautious of assuming that general rules or principles have no exceptions. Think carefully about general rules as opposed to universal rules.

It's easy to confuse general rules (usual application) with universal rules (all-inclusive application). In fact, there seems to be a common unwarranted assumption that a good general principle can be applied in every single case. Remember, rules of thumb are very helpful guidelines, but they shouldn't be mistaken for unconditional rules.

Do a general application check on your argument. Ask yourself, Have I mistaken a general rule for a universal one? Are there reasonable exceptions to the general rule or principle I have used in my argument? Are there reasonable exceptions to the general rule or principle my opponent has used in their argument?

English clergyman Richard Burton declared, "No rule is so general, which admits not some exception."³

## *Ad Baculum*: Appeal to Force, Threat, or the Stick

Logical arguments seek to persuade people of a given claim based on reason. When the mind tracks the inference or entailment of a conclusion that flows from the supporting premises, there is a powerful sense of rational persuasion. Of Earth's occupants, only human beings construct arguments, and they alone know the power of reason.

The *ad baculum* fallacy replaces reason with *force* to get its conclusion accepted. Reason is powerful, but so is *fear*. The threat can be either physical or psychological, delivered in the form of pressure and intimidation. It can also come either in an explicit or an implicit manner. Nonetheless, the message is clear: "Accept my conclusion or else!" Of course, threats have no logical relevance whatsoever, but they carry deep psychological relevance. And threats are often successful even if the argument itself is logically poor.

To summarize, what makes the *ad baculum* logically erroneous is that it replaces rational support for a given conclusion with a threat. The *ad baculum* is, thus, a fallacy of emotional appeal (logically irrelevant).

### *Examples*

Gary N. Curtis of Fallacy Files defines the *ad baculum* fallacy, "Appeal to force refers to the use of force and, by extension, the use of threats of force, or intimidation, to 'win' an argument by preventing the other side from presenting its case."⁴ Considering this description, examine the following examples and think of how force may be used to respond to arguments:

- "The United States should endorse the People's Republic of China's historical argument that Taiwan is part of China. If not, there will be severe political, economic, and military repercussions."
- "You're one of the most scholarly and skilled philosophy professors at our school, but you must accept and abide by our new position at the university on matters of race, gender, and class. If not, you'll be 'canceled'."
- "If we can't persuade you to accept our political views through debate in the Congress, then when we see members of your party in public, we'll call on our followers to create a crowd and make it known that your views make you very unwelcome in our society."

- "If you don't wholeheartedly accept the spiritual convictions and rules of our family, then I'll have no recourse but to send you to Jesus Camp for the summer."

All four of our examples commit the *ad baculum* fallacy. Instead of appealing to reason to support the argument, each example resorts to force, threat, pressure, or intimidation.

In its basic logical form, the *ad baculum* fallacy proceeds as follows: If you don't do/believe Y, then I'll harm you (premise). So, you should do/believe Y (conclusion).

*Exceptions, Considerations, and Advice*
Don't be surprised that appeals to force are common or that they actually work in getting people to accept even bad arguments. People know when they've been threatened and for various reasons some are unwilling (or unable) to appropriately challenge the logically irrelevant threat.

Stay away from any form of intimidation in setting forth your argument. Don't trade in fear. Work hard in the development of your argument and then let the power of reason do its persuasive work.

When threatened, consider exposing the illogical irrelevancy. As Peter A. Angeles put it, "When reasoning is replaced by force, the result is termination of logical argument."[5] So, when facing this fallacy, challenge your opponent with the following: Other than the brutish threat, do you actually have any logical reasons for accepting your argument?

Do a threat assessment check on your argument. Ask yourself, Does my argument or discourse concerning my argument involve any form of force, threat, pressure, or intimidation? Does my argument use irrelevant emotional appeals? Do I have confidence that I've done my logical due diligence so I can trust the power of reason to make the case?

## *Ad Ignorantiam*: Appeal to Ignorance
Valid and strong arguments possess substantive support for the claims they make. These evidence-rich premises reflect genuine *knowledge claims* about reality that means things are actually known (in epistemological terms *knowledge* reflects justified or warranted, true belief).

The *ad ignorantiam* fallacy occurs when the premises of an argument fail to prove anything definite about the conclusion—neither true nor false—yet a specific conclusion is still drawn. Such an error of "appealing to ignorance" typically takes two forms: (1) arguing for the truth of an assertion on the basis that it hasn't been falsified, or (2) claiming that it's false solely because it hasn't been proven. The basic problem with such reasoning is that nothing has been established about the conclusion and yet "nothing" is appealed to as somehow being "something"—namely evidence. Ignorance on a particular point proves only a lack of knowledge on that very point. Ignorance can't serve as evidence for a conclusion.

To summarize, what makes the *ad ignorantiam* logically erroneous is that it argues that a lack of evidence actually proves something definitive. The *ad ignorantiam* is, thus, a fallacy of insufficient grounds.

*Examples*
Consider these two examples where the truth of the claim rests on a lack of evidence to the contrary:

- "Your inability to prove that God doesn't exist is actually evidence that God does exist." This is an affirmative case because the conclusion is considered correct since there is no evidence *against* it.
- "Your inability to prove that God exists is actually evidence that God doesn't exist." This is a negative case because the conclusion is considered incorrect since there is no evidence *for* it.

The question of the correct epistemological starting point, burden of proof, as well as what proof means when it comes to arguing about God's existence is debated in the field of the philosophy of religion. Atheists who claim that no evidence exists for God's existence are potentially susceptible to the *ad ignorantiam* fallacy. Concluding God's existence to be unproven, at least some atheists go further by concluding that God does not actually exist.

But assuming, for the sake of argument, that God's existence can't be *proven* doesn't mean his existence has actually been *disproved*. Some atheists argue that atheism should be presumed until convincing evidence for God is set forth. This presumption of atheism strikes some theistic philosophers as being little more than an "arbitrary intellectual imperialism."[6]

In its basic logical form, *ad ignorantiam* proceeds as follows:

Premise: There's no proof that A is not true.
Conclusion: Therefore, A is true.

Premise: Statement not-P is unproved.
Conclusion: Therefore, P is true.

Premise: There is no proof that A is true.
Conclusion: Therefore, A is not true.

Premise: Statement P is unproved.
Conclusion: Therefore, not-P is true.

*Exceptions, Considerations, and Advice*
There's an important area of inquiry where nothing proven actually does equate to something proven. In many countries and legal systems (the US included), a defendant is assumed innocent until proven guilty. So, if the prosecution can't prove the defendant's guilt (either beyond reasonable doubt in a criminal case or by the preponderance of evidence in a civil case), then the lack of proof is viewed as equating to the defendant being not guilty.

Generally speaking, the reasonable position to hold when nothing is proven is to reserve intellectual judgment on the matter. Drawing definite conclusions from premises that fail to prove anything—an appeal to ignorance (or no knowledge)—proves nothing. From a logical standpoint, nothing comes from no-knowledge claims.[7] Peter Kreeft states, "Ignorance can never be a premise or reason. Premises must express knowledge claims."[8]

Do an appeal to ignorance check on your argument. Ask yourself, Has anything definitive been proven or established by my argument? If not, have I nevertheless drawn a definitive conclusion? Is this, then, a case in which one should reserve judgment?

### *Ad Misericordiam*: Appeal to Pity or Misery
One of the main ways that premises can go wrong is when they lack logical relevance to the conclusion. Only relevant premises can inferentially support and produce a logically acceptable conclusion. Thus, as we saw earlier, logically relevant premises, by definition, are pertinent, applicable, and solidly linked to the conclusion.

The fallacy of *ad misericordiam* attempts to persuade others of one's viewpoint, not with evidence, but by arousing pity and sympathy. The problem is that the appeal to emotional sentiment, even if true, is not logically relevant to the conclusion of the argument. Replacing evidence with feelings of pity lacks logical relevance. In other words, the pitiful consequences have no logical bearing on the truth or falsity of the conclusion itself.

We've acknowledged throughout this book that feelings, passion, and especially sympathy are important parts of being human. And, therefore, while appeals to pity are logically irrelevant, they nevertheless sometimes succeed because people relate to the appeal psychologically.

To summarize, what makes the *ad misericordiam* logically erroneous is that it replaces rational support for a given conclusion with pity. The *ad misericordiam* is thus a fallacy of emotional appeal (logically irrelevant).

*Examples*
- "It's true that I cheated on my business receipts, and I know that such an act is worthy of termination. But if I'm fired from my job my children will go without food. Thus, you can't let me go."
- "God can't possibly exist. Look at all the pain and suffering in the world!"
- "If you oppose raising taxes regardless of your reasons, then you just don't care about the poor."
- "Regardless of what the data shows, if you open the borders to immigrants, then you don't care about the working poor in our own country."

In its basic logical form, the *ad misericordiam* fallacy proceeds as follows: Pitiable people deserve special treatment (premise). I am pitiable (premise). Therefore, my self-serving conclusion is justified (conclusion).

*Exceptions, Considerations, and Advice*
Having compassion (sympathy and empathy) toward people with genuine sorrows and troubles is part of the Christian ethic of love. So, while recognizing that the appeal to pity isn't logically relevant to the argument, you may still want to think about how you might help the person in need.

It's important for people to recognize that emotional appeals can't replace genuine relevant evidence for the truth of a conclusion. Yet when one evokes pity, it's difficult as the hearer or listener to not let that cloud one's judgment of the situation. It's also true that on occasion some people use pity to seek to manipulate the audience to get their way.

We recommend that you always acknowledge the feelings being expressed whether sincere or not. But then address both the emotion and its logical irrelevance at hand. Peter Kreeft points out that, "Pity is usually a good thing, often appropriate and sometimes necessary; but it cannot be a substitute for argument."[9] Head (logic) and heart (compassion) can and should go together.

Do an appeal to sympathy check on your argument. Ask yourself, Does the appeal I'm making involve emotional sentiment that is irrelevant to the conclusion? Does my opponent's appeal involve the same? If there is an irrelevant appeal to sympathy, how can I effectively address both issues?

**Amphiboly Fallacy**
As we saw in chapter 6, clarity is crucial in logical arguments. Clarity of thought, speech, and writing promote understanding, persuasion, and truth. Ambiguity or inexactness can result from the multiple meaning of words or from problems with grammatical structure and punctuation.

In an *amphiboly*, the conclusion of the argument depends on an ambiguous statement (improper grammar or syntax) that causes the reader or listener to draw an incorrect conclusion. Usually there's a problem of sentence structure where dangling participles lead to misinterpretations.

To summarize, what makes the amphiboly logically erroneous is that a syntactical ambiguity allows one meaning to be used in the premise and another meaning to be used in the conclusion. The amphiboly is, thus, a fallacy of obscurity and presumption.

*Example 1:* "The president loves politics more than his wife. Wow! What a political obsession!" Does the president love politics more than his wife loves politics? Or does the president love politics more than he loves his wife? The wording obscures the intended meaning.

*Example 2:* "Don't let life beat you up—let God do it!" Again, linguistic confusion leads to a faulty conclusion.

In its basic logical form, amphiboly proceeds as follows: Claim Y is made. X is concluded based on an ambiguous understanding of Y.

*Exceptions, Considerations, and Advice*
The English language alone contains various ambiguous phrases and sentences. As long as these phrases retain the same meaning in all parts of the argument, then they can avoid the amphiboly fallacy. There are, of course, humorous examples of the amphiboly: As Groucho Marx once stated: "One morning I shot an elephant in my pajamas. How he got in my pajamas, I don't know."

Yet on the serious side, the fallacies of amphiboly illustrate the logical challenges that arise when words are ambiguous or when sentences violate grammatical rules within an argument. Don't allow the clarity of your argument to be compromised by the inexactness of words and grammar. If your opponent's argument appears to suffer from ambiguity, then ask for appropriate clarification. This request for clarity is especially important if your opponent appears to be unreasonable or deceptive.

Do a grammar check on your argument. Ask yourself, Is the sentence structure in my argument clear and unambiguous? Is the sentence structure in my opponent's argument clear and unambiguous?

Gary Curtis succinctly summarizes the amphiboly this way: "Logically, the fallacy of amphiboly occurs when a bad argument trades upon grammatical ambiguity to create an illusion of cogency."[10] Clarity in thought and word carries persuasion.

**Category Mistake Fallacy**

The word *category* refers to a class or division within a broad model or system of classification. Things that have shared qualities or similar characteristics are viewed as the same type or kind of being or reality. Thus, they're placed within a common grouping.

The *category mistake* in reasoning consists of a semantic (language) or ontological (relating to being) error in which things belonging to one category are placed within a fundamentally different grouping. It also consists of ascribing qualities or properties to a thing that only members of a different category have or could do. To put it philosophically, it's when a statement about something belonging to one category is only intelligible of something belonging to a different category. In other words, it's an extreme case of apples being compared with oranges. Philosopher J. P. Moreland offers this definition:

> A category fallacy is the mistake of ascribing the wrong feature to the wrong thing. For example, asking, "How many inches long is the smell of a rose?" or "What does the note C taste like?" seems to assume that smells have length and sounds have taste. Both assumptions commit a category fallacy.[11]

To summarize, what makes the category mistake logically erroneous is that in the argument it mixes ideas and qualities that do not belong together. The category mistake is thus a fallacy of obscurity and presumption.

*Examples*
- "Why can't God (an invisible, transcendent spiritual being) be seen?"

- "If God created all, then who created God?"
- "The mindless, impersonal universe produced creatures with minds."

In its basic logical form, the *category mistake* proceeds as follows: Thing A has property P (but A is not even the kind of thing that could have a property like P).

*Exceptions, Considerations, and Advice*
The challenge with the category mistake is that categories are sometimes difficult to define. It's also not always easy to know if a thing fits a particular category. Give categories careful thought and be aware of the difficulty in defining them. The best examples of the category mistake reflect a category that isn't merely wrong but one in which it's unintelligible. In other words, the thing is not even the *kind* of thing that could have a property like that ascribed to it.

Do a category check on your argument. Ask yourself, Is the category comparison in my argument clearly wrong? Is the category comparison in my opponent's argument clearly wrong? Do the category comparisons reflect unintelligibility?

Christian philosopher Norman Geisler stated, "It is a category mistake to ask, 'Who made the Unmade?' or 'Who created the Uncreated?' One may as well ask, 'Where is the bachelor's wife?'"[12] Logic helps a person to think carefully about categories.

**Complex Question Fallacy**
The fallacy of the *complex question* (Latin: *Plurium Interrogationum*, "many questions") raises multiple questions that carry built-in, unproved assumptions on an issue. The question usually disguises an unproven prior assumption of guilt or transgression on the part of the person being asked the question. In other words, it's a loaded question.

The classic example of the complex question is, Have you stopped beating your wife?

The complexity of the question means it can't be effectively answered with a mere yes or no response. A loaded question is often used as a debater's trick. The opponent, even if innocent, is usually left speechless or stammering. A complex question becomes an argument, and therefore a fallacious one, when a conclusion is drawn from the opponent's inability to respond effectively to the question. Usually, this conclusion goes unstated but is understood in the minds of the readers and listeners.

To summarize, what makes the complex question an error in reasoning is that it formulates questions that a respondent can't answer with a simple affirmative or negative answer without incriminating themselves. The complex question is, thus, a fallacy of obscurity and presumption.

*Example 1:* "How many children must die senselessly in school shootings before gun control legislation is reasonably enacted?" The assumption is that changes to gun legislation will end terrible public shootings. That may or may not work, but the so-called solution is disguised in the form of a complex question.

*Example 2:* Religious and secular people are both capable of complex questions:

- "Are you still a God-hating evolutionist?"
- "Are you still a science-denying creationist?"

*Example 3:* "Did you kill that person intentionally?" In a case like this, which one could see in a police interrogation or a criminal trial, the complex question is presented as a *leading question*. Writer Paul Elsher explains, "A leading question is one that suggests the answer desired by the speaker while a loaded question includes an implicit assumption about the respondent."[13]

Not all presumptions are disguised traps. Some assumed information is publicly accepted fact. For example, one may appropriately ask, How long can one survive without oxygen? It's obvious that oxygen is essential to life. Even the wife-beating example wouldn't constitute a fallacy if the criminal behavior were a known fact.

*Exceptions, Considerations, and Advice*
The complex question can cause real harm, especially in legal or judicial settings. Depending on the assumed accusation, even with an emphatic and outright denial by the respondent, the damage may still be done. If you're the recipient of a complex question, then simply point out the disguised assumption. Let others know that the question can't be answered straightforwardly without your being guilty either way.

Rather, appropriately divide the questions and then answer each one separately. For example, to the complex question, Do you still use insulting racial epithets?, one may appropriately answer, I have never used racial epithets. Not now, not ever.

Do a complex question check on your argument. Ask yourself, Does my argument contain any disguised and unwarranted assumptions? Am I listening carefully to the questions my opponent is asking? Has my opponent asked a question based on an unwarranted assumption?

**Composition Fallacy**
One area of logical analysis has to do with the comparison of the parts of a whole to the whole itself. The focus has to do with whether parts (aspects, attributes, properties) of a whole can be properly attributed to the whole. Sometimes the whole is merely the sum of its parts, but other times it is more.

The fallacy of *composition* consists in assuming that what is true of the parts of a whole is, therefore, true of the whole itself. Put another way, the composition fallacy takes place when the conclusion of an argument depends on a faulty inference that moves from parts to the whole.

Sometimes what's true of the parts is true of the whole, but not always. The reality is that the way the parts relate to the whole may change the nature of the whole. Therefore, a general assumption of what's true of the parts must be true of the whole is false.

To summarize, what makes the composition logically erroneous is that it argues that what is true of the parts is *necessarily* true of the whole. So, composition is a fallacy of illicit transference.

*Examples*
- "All the members of the baseball team are excellent players. Therefore, the team, as a whole, is excellent." Even if the players all possess individual talent, that doesn't mean they work well *together* as a team.
- "This member of the Samples–Perez logic class is good at logic. Therefore, the whole Samples–Perez class is good at logic."

In the previous two examples, what is true of the parts isn't necessarily true of the whole.

In its basic logical form, composition fallacy proceeds in either of these ways:

1. All the parts of the object O have the property P.
2. Therefore, O has the property P.
   (Yet the property P is one which does not distribute from parts to a whole.)

1. A is part of B.
2. A has property X.
3. Therefore, B has property X.
   (Yet the property X is one which does not distribute from parts to a whole.)

*Exceptions, Considerations, and Advice*
Generally speaking, if the whole is similar in substance or character to the parts, then it's safer to assume an inference can be made from the parts to the whole. Sometimes the whole is composed simply of the sum of its parts. In that case what's true of the parts is quite likely true of the whole. However, sometimes the whole is different or more than its parts. In that case what's true of the parts is not likely true of the whole. Be on the lookout for attributes or properties that, when transferred from parts to whole, make the whole different. Also, be aware that composition (parts to whole) can seem similar to hasty generalization (specific to general).

Do a composition check on your argument. Ask yourself, Are the parts merely the sum of the whole? Do the parts change the whole?

**Division Fallacy**
One area of logical analysis has to do with the comparison of the whole to its component parts. The focus has to do with whether what's true of the whole can be properly attributed to the parts. Sometimes the whole is merely reducible to the parts, other times it's not.

The fallacy of *division* consists in assuming that what is true of the whole is therefore true of its constituent parts. Put another way, the division fallacy takes place when the conclusion of an argument depends on a faulty inference that moves from whole to parts. This is the opposite of the composition fallacy. Sometimes what's true of the whole is true of the parts, but not always. The reality is that the way the whole relates to the parts may change the nature of the parts. Therefore, a general assumption of what's true of the whole must be true of the parts is false.

To summarize, what makes the division logically erroneous is that it argues that what's true of the whole is necessarily true of the parts. Division is, thus, a fallacy of illicit transference. Consider the following examples.

*Example 1:* "The baseball team, as a whole, is excellent. Therefore, all the members on the baseball team are excellent players."

*Example 2:* "The Samples-Perez logic class, as a whole, is good at logic.

Therefore, the individual students in the Samples-Perez class are good at logic."

In these first two examples, it's possible that the overall excellence of the team or class rests on a few outstanding individuals, while the remaining team or class members are mediocre at best. Thus, it's false to assume that each individual team member or student is skilled simply because the group score, as a whole, shows excellence.

*Example 3:* "Healthy human beings are conscious entities. Therefore, the individual cells that make up a human being are conscious entities."

In this third example what is true of the whole person is obviously not true of the individual constituent parts.

In its basic logical form, *division fallacy* proceeds in either of these ways:

1. The whole of object O has the property P.
2. Therefore, the parts of O have the property P.
   (Yet the property P is one which does not distribute from whole to parts.)

1. B is the whole of A.
2. B has property X.
3. Therefore, A has property X.
   (Yet the property X is one which does not distribute from whole to parts.)

*Exceptions, Considerations, and Advice*
Generally speaking, if the parts are similar in substance or character to the whole, then it is safer to assume an inference can be made from the whole to parts. Sometimes the parts merely add up to the whole. In that case what's true of the whole is quite likely true of the parts. However, sometimes the parts themselves do not simply add up to the whole. In that case what's true of the whole is not likely true of the parts. Be on the lookout for a whole that, when transferred to the parts, makes the parts different. Also, be aware that division (whole to parts) can seem similar to accident (general to specific). Do a division check on your argument. Ask yourself: Is the whole merely reducible to the parts? Does the whole change the parts?

## Genetic Fallacy

The *genetic* fallacy evaluates a thing exclusively in terms of its origin, source, or beginning, but then brings that past appraisal into the present while disregarding subsequent and relevant changes. Often this approach equates to arguing that something is to be rejected on the basis that its beginnings are suspicious. This fallacy fails to appreciate two critical elements: (1) that things often change over time and sometimes even significantly, and (2) something can be rational and true on its own merit even if its source is questionable. To summarize, what makes the genetic fallacy logically erroneous is that it focuses on something's origin rather than its reasonableness and truthfulness. The genetic fallacy is, thus, a fallacy of insufficient grounds. (For more on this fallacy, see chapter 7.) Consider the following examples of the genetic fallacy.

*Example 1:* "The scientific disciplines of astronomy and chemistry have deep roots in occult and magical practices: astronomy to astrology and chemistry to alchemy. Therefore, modern astronomy and chemistry can't be trusted." Obviously, a lot has changed over the centuries and these scientific disciples now stand well tested on their own rational and empirical merit.

*Example 2:* "All of Christendom's major holidays (Christmas, Lent, Easter) came from pagan superstition. Therefore, they are unbiblical and ungodly practices." Scholars now question the claim that Christianity's historic celebrations are linked to paganism.[14] But even if it were true, Christian devotion changed the focus from pagan ideas to truths about Jesus Christ.

*Example 3:* "Belief in God first arose from the early humans' terror and anxiety of the natural world. God was invented to comfort man from the fear of death's inevitability. Therefore, fear and superstition were the source of humankind's belief in the divine." This Freudian projection model confuses the supposed origin of belief in God with its rational warrant (justifying reasons). Two points should be considered. First, the example view here is an unproven assumption that presumes a naturalistic perspective. This projection theory *insists* that human beings invented God. Second, even if the belief did arise through human fear, plenty of arguments exist that offer a logical justification for a rational belief in God.

In its basic logical form, the genetic fallacy proceeds as follows:

Premise: The origin of Y is suspicious or superstitious (even though Y has changed and can stand rationally apart from its questionable source).
Conclusion: Therefore, you should reject Y.

*Exceptions, Considerations, and Advice*
Remember that some people have deep emotional connections to the origin of things. Yet, as Louis Pojman notes, "It doesn't matter where the truth comes from, as long as it is true."[15] So, convincing people to disconnect the idea from its alleged origins may be quite challenging.

Focus on showing that the value and truth of something can be distinguished from its original source.

Do a genetic check on your argument. Ask yourself, Does my argument focus on the rational basis of an idea rather than on its suspicious source? Does my opponent's argument focus on the rational basis of an idea rather than on its suspicious source?

**Prejudicial Language Fallacy**
As we saw in chapter 2, language and thinking go together. Language is powerful because it can appeal to both reason and emotion. Logic can help a person to use language with wisdom and fairness.

The fallacy of *prejudicial language* takes place when a person substitutes emotive words in place of reason and evidence that attempt to emotionally manipulate another person into accepting an argument. Emotive or loaded terminology tends to arouse intense feeling and express value judgments that can predispose a person either toward or against a position without even offering evidence. Similar to the slanting fallacy, prejudicial language serves to create a preconception in the minds of the audience that maneuvers one toward a given argument.

To summarize, what makes the prejudicial language fallacy an error in reasoning is that it uses loaded language to predispose a person toward a view before evidence is considered. Prejudicial language is, thus, a fallacy of ineffectual rebuttal.

Consider these emotive arguments and notice that in both, no evidence for evolution is even offered.

*Example 1:* "People who deny the theory of evolution are just science deniers who are impossible to convince with reason. They're just intellectually stubborn like anti-vaxxers, flat earthers, and coronavirus truthers. Don't waste your arguments on people who trust in fake experts and are addicted to conspiracy theories."

*Example 2:* "People who accept the theory of evolution don't do so based on reason. They want to be considered scientifically sophisticated. They don't think for themselves; rather, they simply accept the scientific status quo. They're motivated by anything other than genuine reason and evidence."

In its basic logical form, prejudicial language proceeds as follows: Claim B is made using loaded or emotive terms (premise). Therefore, claim B is true (conclusion).

*Exceptions, Considerations, and Advice*
Emotional appeal has its place in persuasion (see chapter 6). However, the language of persuasion should be used to *accompany* arguments, evidence, and reasons. It shouldn't be used to replace them with emotional manipulation.

Be cautious of highly inflammatory language that serves a purely emotive purpose. Lead with reason instead of predisposing one with value-laden terminology. In our increasingly post-truth age, beware of euphemisms that are used to make terms appear less offensive or negative as well as derogatory terms that are used to make something seem more offensive or negative.

Do a prejudicial language check on your argument. Ask yourself, Does my argument focus on reason or on emotive language? Does my opponent's argument focus on reason or on emotive language?

**Resort to Humor or Ridicule Fallacy**
This fallacy takes place when humor or ridicule become a replacement for relevant evidence. What often happens is that amusement or derision is injected into an argument as a means of concealing an inability to respond effectively to an opponent's argument. Creating an environment of laughter and scoffing is an almost perfect diversionary tactic for sidestepping an opponent's serious argument. Humor and jokes have a unique way of attracting listeners to one's side even though they lack in themselves rational grounds.

To summarize, what makes the resort to humor or ridicule fallacy erroneous reasoning is that it presents an opponent's argument as humorous or ridiculous and therefore not worthy of serious logical consideration. The resort to humor or ridicule is, thus, a fallacy of relevance.

Everyone is capable of resorting to humor or ridicule when in a debate. Here are examples from a secular view and a religious view.

*Example 1:* "Good luck with your invisible friend in the sky. Believing in the Flying Spaghetti Monster is equally rational."

*Example 2:* "Believing human beings sprang from apes is stupid and as a creationist I'll make monkeys of the evolutionists and their theories."

In its basic logical form, the resort to humor or ridicule fallacy proceeds as follows:

Arguer #1 reasons that X is true.
Arguer #2 makes use of humor or ridicule to bypass X.
Therefore, X is rejected as false.

*Exceptions, Considerations, and Advice*
Some think that it's appropriate to use ridicule when a position is worthy of such. As Christians, we advise against it. Everyone is made in the image of God and worthy of respect even if their position is irrelevant and their comments contemptible.

When you're the recipient of diversionary humor or ridicule, do your best to keep your cool. When an opponent uses amusement or derision as a clever means of deflection, it may be helpful to first acknowledge especially the amusing statement. You may even consider using a clever response in return. But at some point, the logical issue at hand needs a serious response. As the laughter subsides, ask for a serious logical reply.

Do a humor or ridicule check on your argument. Ask yourself, Does my argument or my opponent's argument appeal to the irrelevance of humor or ridicule as a diversionary tactic? Famed defense attorney Gerry Spence offers this advice:

> Avoid sarcasm, scorn, and ridicule. Use humor cautiously. Hold back insult. No one admires the cynic, the scoffer, the mocker, the small, and the petty. Giving respect to one's opponent elevates us. Those who insult and slight do so from low places.[16]

When logic and respect for people are cojoined you have the power of persuasion.

**Slippery Slope Fallacy**
As we saw in our discussion of the false cause fallacy (see chapter 9), knowing how causal relationships affect one another can be tricky. Again, the challenge is that cause-and-effect relations are at times difficult to determine and identify, let alone predict.

The *slippery slope* fallacy (also called the domino fallacy) involves a special type of causally connected reasoning. The fallacy is committed when someone proclaims that a particular action that's usually insignificant will, nevertheless, set off a chain reaction of events leading to disastrous consequences. The difficulty is that there's no good reason to believe the domino effect, so to speak, will indeed occur as predicted.

The specific fallacious reasoning evident in the slippery slope involves a series of intermediate steps that are causally questionable and become more and more improbable at each step. The climax of the series involves the prediction that there will be an unstoppable slope sliding down to devastation.

To summarize, what makes the slippery slope an error in reasoning is dependence on a chain reaction of causes that are not reasonably likely to occur. The slippery slope is, thus, a fallacy of insufficient grounds. Consider the following examples of the slippery slope fallacy.

*Example 1:* "If Gilbert doesn't pass his philosophy test tonight, then he won't get a passing grade in philosophy and he won't get into a good university. Without getting into a good university, he can't get a good job. Then he won't be able to get married and have a family. A poor grade on the test will ruin his life!"

*Example 2:* "If same sex marriage is legalized then the next step will be polyamorous marriages, then marriage between adults and children. The final result will be humans marrying animals. Then we're back to Sodom and Gomorrah."

*Example 3:* "If abortion on demand is allowed to stand, then the next step will be legalizing abortion all the way up to birth. The next step will be parents having two years to decide if they want to commit infanticide and the lives of special needs children will be extinguished. The brave new world will be upon us all."

Concerning examples 2 and 3, the ethical standards of society can be worn down incrementally. Yet the examples above raise questions about the reasonableness of the moral chain reaction.

In its basic logical form, the slippery slope fallacy proceeds as follows:

Premise #1: If A were to happen, then by a gradual series of causal steps through B, C, D, . . . X, Y, eventually Z will happen, too.
Premise #2: Z must not be allowed to happen.
Conclusion: Therefore, A should not be allowed to happen, either.

If A, then B, then C, . . . then ultimately Z.

*Exceptions, Considerations, and Advice*
Logician Patrick J. Hurley notes, "Deciding whether a slippery slope fallacy

has been committed can be difficult when one is uncertain whether the alleged chain reaction will or will not occur."[17] Carefully check the causal strength of the connected links in the chain. Make sure that the links are causally reasonable (where you say, "if A, then likely B, and if B, then likely C," and so forth). Especially examine the later adjacent links, which tend to be more improbable as they move down the slope.

Do a slippery slope check on your argument. Ask yourself, Are the causal links in my argument reasonable? Are the causal links in my opponent's argument reasonable? Can a more modest and, thus, more reasonable prediction be made?

**Special Pleading Fallacy**
A good argument can stand on its own. It plays fairly by the laws of logic and the rules of rational inference. It doesn't need favors or privileges to make its reasoned point. Logic includes reason, consistency, and intellectual virtue.

The fallacy of *special pleading* consists of applying rules, principles, and standards to other people's arguments while exempting one's own argument from those rational criteria without adequate justification for the exception. This creates a double standard where rules apply to one arguer but not to another similarly situated. Sometimes this inconsistency is motivated by strong subjective emotional factors. The *Internet Encyclopedia of Philosophy* succinctly defines the special pleading fallacy this way: "Special pleading is a form of inconsistency in which the reasoner doesn't apply his or her principles consistently."[18]

To summarize, what makes the special pleading erroneous reasoning is that it applies rational directives to everyone else but makes a special case for oneself. The special pleading is, thus, a fallacy of insufficient grounds. Consider the following examples of special pleading.

- "I think active euthanasia is appropriate for people who suffer from advanced dementia, but my mother's case is different. It just is."
- "Human beings generally suffer from racial bias and prejudice, but racial minorities can't be racists."
- "Police officers should treat all people equally when it comes to traffic violations, but they should retain the prerogative to give other police officers exemptions."

In its basic logical form, special pleading proceeds as follows:

Premise #1: I do think that X is true.
Premise #2: But this specific case is different and special.
Conclusion: Therefore, in this case X does not apply.

If A then B, but not when it undermines my perspective.

*Exceptions, Considerations, and Advice*
If an argument is, in fact, deserving of a special exemption *and* adequate rational justification for this special case presented, then there is no fallacy. For example, patients with certain cancers and sufferers of peripheral neuropathy may receive the exemption to purchase medical marijuana because it decreases pain and discomfort.

It's critically important that rational standards of conduct be applied to all arguments fairly. Violating conventional standards of conduct, particularly equal treatment, is a compromise of intellectual consistency and integrity. Special pleading is a fallacy because it appeals to a faulty and irrelevant claim. Of course, one may simply be mistaken in applying the rules rather than being intentionally deceptive. This fallacy is often easy to detect in the arguments of others, but sometimes hard to see in one's own arguments.

Do a special pleading check on your argument. Ask yourself, Does my argument or my opponent's argument include an unjustified and, therefore, inconsistent special exemption? Is my approach to reasoning one of accuracy and fairness?

**Wishful Thinking Fallacy**
Logical arguments are intended to show that claims are either certainly true (deduction), probably true (induction), or most plausible (abduction). In logic, claims must be supported with facts, reasons, or evidence. The fallacy of *wishful thinking* consists in assuming that because one merely *wants* a particular thing to be true, it *must* be true. And vice versa, assuming that because one *does not want* something to be true, then it's *not true*. The difficulty with this approach is that the wishing is treated as support in the form of a premise of a desired conclusion. Yet mere wishing doesn't make something either true or false.

To summarize, what makes wishful thinking a reasoning error is that the desire for something to be true or false is used in place of evidence. Wishful thinking is, thus, a fallacy of obscurity and presumption (see also chapter 7). Consider the following examples of wishful thinking.

- "I don't want the biblical God to exist with his eternal hell, so for me God and hell do not exist."
- "I wish the UFO aliens from a different galaxy to exist and, therefore, I believe they do."
- "I desire to become extremely wealthy. And wishing can make it true."
- "We're ruining our planet. So, we'll find another planet and thrive there."

In its basic logical form, wishful thinking proceeds as follows: I wish A were true (premise). Therefore, A is true (conclusion).

*Exceptions, Considerations, and Advice*
Unwarranted presumption in the form of a mere wish that may come from one's feelings or emotions has no influence on the truth or falsity of a particular logical claim. Do a wishful thinking check on your argument. Ask yourself, Does my argument or my opponent's argument involve mere wishing as support for my claim? Could my argument or my opponent's argument instead involve an inference to the best explanation form of reasoning?

**On Detecting Fallacies**
When you first start studying fallacies, you'll likely think you see fallacies everywhere. That's a common experience for new students of logic. As you study more, you'll become more seasoned and discerning in your reasoning and grow in proper logical discrimination. Logician T. Edward Damer offers a caution: "Don't be a fallacymonger."[19] In other words, don't become obsessed with identifying fallacies. Realize that behind the argument is a person that you need to respect and, if possible, build a rapport with. Damer offers further wise counsel for critiquing and correcting others' thinking:

> Find ways of challenging the reasoning process of others without alienating them or causing them unnecessary embarrassment. After all, our purpose is to assist people in thinking more clearly, not to catch them in a fallacy.[20]

Of course, we must be cognizant that we ourselves can and do engage in fallacious reasoning on occasion. Take on the needed and difficult challenge of becoming aware of the possible fallacies in your own thinking and writing. Put on your critic's hat and step outside yourself—pretend to disagree with the

> **Table 10.1 Distinguishing Fallacies**
>
> What do you do when certain fallacies look quite similar? For example, is it straw man or red herring? Is it hasty generalization or composition? Is it accident or division? When you have a hard time differentiating certain fallacies because they seem similar to other types, we recommend you do four things:
>
> 1. Examine the specific commission of the given fallacy. How is the fallacy specifically committed?
> 2. Examine and compare all the examples of a given fallacy (for example, "red herring") in the guidebook.
> 3. Look for patterns in the commission of specific fallacies. Is there a pattern that all red herrings seem to follow?
> 4. Practice by reviewing examples of specific fallacies that look similar.
>
> When implemented, these steps can help a great deal.

conclusion you're affirming and defending.

Do a *fallacy check* on your thinking and arguments. Ask yourself, What fallacies do I naturally tend to gravitate toward? Then focus special attention on those areas. What fallacies are the easiest to commit and the hardest to detect?

When you engage in fallacious reasoning by committing a particular fallacy, have the intellectual humility and courage to acknowledge it, even publicly when appropriate. Discovering truth is more important than winning an argument or a debate. After recognizing your fallacious reasoning, make the needed adjustments in your thinking or writing. But then get right back into the lifelong pursuit of gaining knowledge, truth, and wisdom through critical reflection.

Next, we turn to part three of the book, which explores the intriguing topic of cognitive biases.

**Questions for Reflection**
1. Discuss how to handle the appeal to pity logically and practically.

2. Explain the genetic fallacy.
3. Expound upon the resort to humor or ridicule fallacy.
4. Delineate the slippery slope fallacy.
5. Spell out the special pleading fallacy.

# Part III

## Cognitive Bias

Mark Perez

Chapter 11

# Cognitive Biases and Critical Thinking

"Poirot," I said. "I have been thinking."
"An admirable exercise, my friend. Continue it."[1]
—Agatha Christie, *Peril at End House*

All of us have heard the term *critical thinking* and most of us have at least a general idea of what it means. Our understanding of critical thinking sometimes helps us assess the decisions or conclusions of others, and it gives us confidence in those assessments. But there's more to critical thinking than that feeling of confidence we might have when we critique the reasoning of others.

When you search for the term *critical thinking* in books or online, you find many definitions. Most are useful and orbit around crucial cognitive skills—such as rigorous evaluation, reasoning, and analysis—that presume a rational engagement with ideas. But even with highly developed cognitive abilities, our thinking processes are often unconsciously nonrational. Tendencies to nonrational thinking distort our cognitive judgments, memory, perceptions, and decisions in surprising and sometimes dangerous ways.

Recognizing this, we've included as part of our definition of *critical thinking* the need to see and understand these tendencies. Our two-part definition presumes that we think best when we think *skillfully*, free of distorted cognition: (1) The skilled selection, analysis, questioning, and application of information to answer a question, solve a problem, or make a decision; and (2) the skill of discerning cognitive biases and avoiding their adverse effects.

We use *information* in its broadest sense to include anything presented to the mind for consideration. *Selection* refers to the process of examining information for relevance to the problem. Information is relevant when it tends to prove or disprove anything being considered. In some situations, such as science or law, this information is referred to as *evidence*. Information selection is ongoing, continuing throughout the process of critical thinking as the information gets analyzed and questioned.

*Analysis* means finding the components of a problem and seeing how they affect each other and the whole problem. *Questioning* information means assessing its truth or likelihood of being true. For example, we question information we initially find relevant to see whether it's accurate or to what degree it is probable. *Applying* information means organizing it into the form of an argument whose conclusion is a responsive answer to the original question or problem. The arguments may be deductive, inductive, or abductive. Applying information may use several argument forms and can result in more than one reasonable solution. Cognitive biases are natural, usually unconscious deviations from rational thinking. Because they can affect any number of the components of critical thinking, we include the discernment of cognitive biases in our definition of *critical thinking*.

## Introduction to Cognitive Biases

Discerning the human tendencies to deviate from rational thinking in important situations helps protect the critical thinking process from failure. We know that poor thinking leads to poor decisions. What we often *don't* know is how our natural ways of thinking mislead us. Our decisions usually feel like they're well-reasoned and our intuitions feel like they're accurate. Our assessments of arguments feel correct just as our memories feel reliable. But these intuitions and feelings often conceal cognitive errors. Because people are usually unconscious of the error-prone workings of their minds, we need to learn how to detect and manage the effects of these errors to think well.

*Your Mind Is Lazy*
For the cognitive mind, every day is a weekend. The mind will not work any harder than its owner thinks it needs to. Not much is needed for most daily decisions. We do something the same way, get the same result each time, and the experience becomes intuition. The quicker and more frequent the feedback on those experiences, the stronger the intuition. Yet there are many times where our intuitions fail us because we tend to believe whatever is easiest to recall, without considering other relevant points. We tend to jump to unwarranted conclusions, decide from incomplete data, seek what confirms our beliefs, trust

our intuitions when we shouldn't, and misjudge the meanings of numbers, statements, and other facts.

These tendencies are often referred to as cognitive biases. There are many more cognitive biases than we can describe in this book. So, we present some of the most common, well-researched, and, in some cases, most dangerous cognitive biases to help you see what your intuitions often hide. We'll go deeper with some than with others to show their surprising implications. And we'll show how some cognitive biases give a few informal fallacies remarkable deceptive power to distort thinking.

An important aspect of cognitive biases is that some correlate with informal fallacies, making the fallacies more effective in misleading people. Knowing why a few of the informal fallacies are so psychologically powerful helps us appreciate the risks of missing them. The following sections exploring cognitive biases reveal that even if you select, interrogate, analyze, and apply information to solve a problem or make a decision, doing so without knowing the cognitive biases can turn rigor into error.

### *Ad Populum* Fallacy

One of the most common of all fallacies is the *ad populum*. It appears in some form in every area where someone wants to influence another person. And it can be remarkably effective. Its emotional appeal is often to the implied primacy of group wisdom or to the fear of being left out of a valued group. Both appeals can persuade people to adopt a position without testing its merits. People adopt positions without testing the merits more often than they think, especially when in groups. When in groups, they also tend to adopt positions or make statements that are clearly contrary to fact.

Being physically present in a group is a dynamic experience of interaction where we think we control what we believe or accept. However, we're often unaware that we surrender our beliefs or decisions to others where we wouldn't do so if we were alone. Research findings repeatedly confirm what many of us would find obvious: humans have a demonstrated tendency to conform to social peer pressure. For example, an individual will often conform to a group's expressed beliefs simply to be liked.[2] What isn't obvious is that group influence occurs in some conditions even where we hold strong emotional commitments. People can hold political views, for instance, with such strong emotion or belief that they seem immune to group pressure, but even their political attitudes can unconsciously succumb to group pressure.

According to one study researching political attitudes, "when people are asked their attitudes publicly, they adjust their responses to conform to those around them, and this attitude change persists privately, even weeks later."[3] The claim isn't that we automatically change our political views because people around us do—we usually don't. The point is that we *may* change beliefs, not because we've reasoned well through the arguments but *only* because group influence affected us more than we knew. We feel the decision was our own rational analysis when it really wasn't. Thinking well requires us to understand this tendency and resist it in important decisions.

One might assume that peer pressure would happen only when other people are physically present, where we're able to read body language, hear subtle tones of voice, and sense other behavioral cues that might affect our feelings or beliefs. The tendency to conform is more powerful than the mere effects of being physically present with a group. In fact, conformity to group influence appears even in experiments using virtual reality devices, agents, and avatars.[4] Even when no one's bodily present with us, even when we can hide our identities, even when we think the virtual world is a fiction we control, we're still subject to the influence of group conformity. Our beliefs are not as self-determined as we think, even where we're anonymous and hiding behind a keyboard.

*The Bandwagon Effect*
This tendency to allow the beliefs of a group to influence one's own beliefs and behaviors is often referred to as the *bandwagon effect*. The bandwagon effect can persuade an individual in a group to do or think things they wouldn't ordinarily do or think apart from the group. It's also a source of the persuasive power of the *ad populum* fallacy.

The bandwagon effect isn't the same for all people in all conditions. Researchers study questions of what conditions produce the effect, how powerful the effect is, and many other variables. Since the seminal 1956 Asch conformity experiments,[5] researchers continue to find that although many factors can alter the power and conditions of the bandwagon effect, the effect is real and it's powerful.

In the Asch experiments, for example, male students on three university campuses were the subjects of and assistants in the tests. The students were taken to a classroom and seated in two rows of adjacent seats. The proctor instructed the group to compare the line lengths printed on 17" high cards against a standard card. The proctor would present cards, one with a shorter line, the others with longer lines. As the proctor selected a new batch of cards and showed them to the group, each person was to identify comparisons and state their answer aloud.

There was only one test subject in each group—the rest of the students were confederates of the researchers and were coached to give wrong answers. The effect of the majority on the test subject was the question Asch wanted to answer.

Asch's conclusions appeared in his 70-page report. Overall, the actions of the majority distorted one-third of the test subject answers. Compared to the less than 1% error rate of the control group, this one-third error rate is astonishing. It revealed the power of the bandwagon effect to influence people in a group setting to knowingly report false observations despite clear, objective, publicly visible facts to the contrary.

The 1956 Asch experiments began the research that has since proved one thing: even in the face of objective evidence (like a comparison of clearly different line sizes) group influence can overwhelm many people's will to speak the truth or act properly on known facts, even when there's nothing to lose in speaking the truth.

The *ad populum* fallacy is an exploitation of the bandwagon effect. Because of that, it's not merely an error in reasoning, it's a persuasive force that can move an audience to a nonrational decision without them knowing it. Politicians, advertisers, governments, religious leaders, and others use it to influence people to do or think what well-reasoned thought would otherwise reject. In the most important decisions in the world, allowing the bandwagon effect to go unchecked can lead to catastrophe. The *ad populum* fallacy, as a verbal means of exploiting the bandwagon effect, is particularly important to detect and reject.

### The Lone Voice Fallacy

When a group rejects the claim or proposal of a group member merely because the proponent is the only one who holds the position, the rejection is a *lone voice* fallacy. The lone voice is a reverse of the *ad populum*. Rather than directly appealing to the popularity of the majority view, it attacks the position of the lone contrary voice. Its purpose is to convince the one holding the unpopular position to conform. In its rhetorical use, it's intended to persuade an audience that the solitary position of an opponent is wrong *merely* because the position isn't widely held. The lone voice is fallacious in much the same way the *ad populum* is. In the *ad populum*, the appeal is to accept a view *because* a majority holds it. In the lone voice, the appeal is to reject a view because only one (or a small minority) holds it. *Ad populum* and lone voice both hold to the unproved primacy of group wisdom or to conformity bias. They promote an untested confidence in a group's view instead of a rational *test* of the group's view.

The lone voice fallacy is especially powerful when used in highly cohesive groups. In such settings the fallacy becomes groupthink. *Groupthink* is the tendency of cohesive groups to press for consensus on decisions or ideas without examining alternatives. Its potential for grave consequences is well documented in the research literature.

*Dangers of Groupthink*
Groupthink has been found to be the source of historic disastrous decisions, such as the failed Bay of Pigs invasion of Cuba in 1961, the 1972 cover up of the Watergate break-in by a sitting US President and his advisers, and the deadly launches of both space shuttle *Challenger* (1986) and space shuttle *Columbia* (2003).[6] In these cases there were lone voices initially opposing the decisions, but groupthink took over.

In the *Challenger* incident, for example, engineers had warned their management groups that the launchpad temperature was below the temperature a crucial rocket booster O-ring had been tested to withstand. The engineers recommended not launching. But the launch had already been delayed three times. NASA was concerned that they would lose credibility in the eyes of the public if another launch was cancelled. The NASA management team then directed the engineers to reconsider their position. The small engineer team, rather than holding to their original position, conceded to the larger group position and withdrew their opposition to the launch. About a minute after launch, the O-ring did fail, causing a catastrophic explosion of the rocket booster, killing all seven members of the crew.

Although groupthink and the lone voice problem occur in looser groups, group cohesiveness makes it worse. When a cohesive group uses the lone voice fallacy to force consensus, the consequences can be grave.

The *ad populum* fallacy and its fraternal twin the lone voice fallacy are particularly interesting because they do more than distort an argument. They're not merely academically interesting. They appear in a vast range of settings and forms and often persuade remarkably well by exploiting human tendencies to adopt group positions instead of relying on logic. The *ad populum* and lone voice fallacies are *practically* important because they can lead to easy and unconscious decision errors with severe results.

**Hasty Generalization and Biases**
A hasty generalization fallacy occurs when we make a universal or general

conclusion from too few instances or observations. For instance, if I see two airplane crashes in the news in two days and make the general conclusion that airplane travel is unsafe, I commit the hasty generalization fallacy. Seeing just two instances of airplane crashes without considering the thousands of safe flights in the same period is a hasty generalization.

Although not identical with the hasty generalization fallacy, the *fallacy of composition* is similar in that it infers from a part of a whole that the entire whole is like the part. For example, if you meet a worker from a business that you've not been to before and that worker is especially efficient, you might infer that the entire business is efficient. That inference is a composition fallacy—and a hasty generalization.

The hasty generalization fallacy can work well to mislead an audience or to mislead yourself. Its effectiveness flows from the mind's bias to believe what's initially presented to it, to avoid exerting mental effort, to accept stories just because they're coherent, and, in some cases, to misjudge people.

*Effortless Assessment*
When we assess an idea, we start by unconsciously accepting it to understand it. For example, when you first read "The sky is yellow," you may unconsciously accept it to be true in order to understand it. You naturally form a mental representation of a yellow sky, even though you know the sky is not really yellow. To understand an idea, we must first know what it would mean if it were true. Once we understand what it means if the idea were true, we can assess whether it *is* true.[7] At the point where we assess whether the idea is true, we become vulnerable to the hasty generalization.

Falling for a hasty generalization is easy because our minds default to easy thinking. It takes conscious mental effort to *disbelieve*. To disbelieve we keep in mind different views, weigh them against each other, test them for coherence with our prior beliefs, consider whether something's missing, and do other cognitive work. This takes mental effort, something people tend to avoid unless the effort yields reward.[8] Accepting a hasty generalization is easy, and without motivation to test it, it often succeeds in misleading its audience or proponent.

A hasty generalization that concludes with a simple coherent story can be particularly easy to accept or propose. In our airplane example, the story is, "Two airplanes crashed in two days. Air travel is unsafe." That story is simple and coherent. We easily integrate the information about the two crashes into the plausible "air travel is unsafe" story. Without deliberation, our minds quickly detect simple relations, such as identifying a group of like items—airplane crashes, for example. Our minds also integrate information about a single topic—airline safety[9]—with ease.

*Stereotyping*
Stereotyping is generalizing about people groups.[10] We stereotype when we meet or hear about only a small fraction of a people group and conclude that all or nearly all members of the group have the same attributes as the few we've met. For example, if in one area of a country we meet several people who are especially good at math, we stereotype the group when we conclude that in general, the rest of the people in the region are good at math. This is a hasty generalization fallacy because it makes a general conclusion from too small a sample size.

Stereotyping occurs often in popular media. Judging an entire occupational group by the widely shown misconduct of a few members is a classic example. Police officers are often stereotyped occupationally from a few repeatedly played videos of apparent abuse by very few officers. As in the case of the plane crashes, it is a hasty generalization to claim that all or most officers are abusive based on videos of a few bad cases. The few portrayed events in the media neglect myriad helpful police interactions that occur every day with no abuse at all.

Unfortunately, the availability and emotional effect of a few events distort the expectations of their overall prevalence.[11] The more often we see a small, emotionally intense sample, the easier it is to bring it to mind and make a hasty generalization from it. We also have more confidence that the stereotype generalization is true. The tendency of the human mind to misjudge prevalence or frequency of events by the ease with which the events come to mind is known as *availability bias*.[12] Availability bias can make stereotyping even easier than it already is.

Combining the hasty generalization of stereotyping with the tendency toward availability bias gives propagandists, advertisers, politicians, and others power to manipulate those unaware of their vulnerability to cognitive bias. To think well in the endless barrage of media clips, pay attention to where biases are most likely to occur and ask more than just, "Is this as bad as it looks?" Instead, remember that a small sample is deceptive and that the emotions of stereotyping bypass cognition. Remember, too, that the more times you experience a stereotype, the more likely you are to accept as true what is in fact unfounded.

The mind is lazy, working no harder than its owner thinks is needed. When dealing with stereotyping and the availability bias, the work *is* needed to overcome them.

*Misjudging Individuals*
Another hasty generalization concerns *individual* persons rather than groups. People tend to make unjustified inferences about someone's unknown characteristics from known, often irrelevant, information about the person. When the irrelevant information influences how we perceive another person's traits or character, that is known as a "halo effect."[13]

For example, let's say I'm looking to hire for a supervisor position. A meticulously well-dressed, attractive, and articulate candidate interviews just as well as the rest of the candidates, but none of the others are as attentive to their dress or as well-spoken as the attractive one. I infer from the meticulous attention to dress and articulateness that the candidate will be attentive to work details and an outstanding communicator with subordinates. This inference, however, isn't justified, as meticulous attention to dress isn't the same behavior as attentiveness to work details; and articulateness alone doesn't tell us whether the person knows what to convey in supervisory communications. The inference is a hasty generalization from too few known features of the candidate. The halo effect contaminates judgments in situations ranging from formal employment interviews to dating relationships. Like stereotyping, it's interesting in part because it occurs so naturally and unconsciously. And like stereotyping, it can produce an intuitive, comfortable, false evaluation of another person.

The effectiveness of the hasty generalization fallacy has its root in our tendencies to make judgments from too-small samples, to believe stories just because they're coherent, to believe as true what availability bias hands us, and to believe what takes the least effort to believe.

**Hindsight Isn't Insight**
After seeing an event and its outcome, the tendency to believe that we knew it was likely or inevitable *before* it occurred—when in fact we didn't know—is called *hindsight bias*. Hindsight bias also includes the tendency to judge another person's decision based on how good or bad the *outcome* was, not on how good or bad the other's decision *process* was. Hindsight bias can be viewed as the belief that an event is more predictable after it becomes known than it was before it became known. It can even include the inability to remember the feeling of uncertainty that came before an event.[14] Hindsight bias distorts our recollections of the past, and it does so easily, without us even knowing it.

We believe the story we tell ourselves when we look back and believe that we predicted a good decision outcome—even though at the time of the decision we really didn't know how it would turn out. For example, when our favorite sports team wins a close game, we might say, "I knew they would win like that." But we had no way of knowing how or if they would win—we are telling ourselves a story. The story we tell ourselves comes from the memories selected because they're easily available and easy to assemble coherently to make the outcome seem inevitable. We hold the story as a causal explanation, and the clearer the explanation is, the stronger the hindsight bias.[15]

Because hindsight bias distorts our memories, it hinders our ability to learn from experience, making hindsight bias particularly dangerous to clear thinking. Hindsight bias is one of the most widely studied decision biases, presented in over 800 scholarly papers.[16] Research consistently finds that the bias is real, powerful, and can affect anyone.

*The Dangers of Hindsight Bias*
The ease with which we engage in hindsight bias creates problems. One of the problems is that we can acquire an unjustified self-confidence in our predictive ability and make confident decisions from only partial evidence. Since in hindsight bias we unconsciously select the information we think made the outcome inevitable, we do not remember other factors that may have produced the outcome. Not remembering these factors makes it easy to neglect them in the next decision, as we put more weight on what we (mis)remember in hindsight than on what we need to consider in foresight. Foresight comes from looking at *all* relevant information and considering its effects. Hindsight bias *removes* relevant evidence from consideration and makes poorly informed predictions feel well-informed. Being unaware of the information debt, the faulty predictions in hindsight bias make risky predictions in foresight more likely.

There are few places where hindsight bias is more dangerous than the courtroom. In certain kinds of cases, jurors are asked to judge whether a defendant "knew or should have known" that a particular death, injury, or damage would result from the defendant's acts or omissions. The evidence the jury sees in every case is the evidence of the outcome. This can include pictures of a person severely disfigured, a video of a person violently killed by accident, blood-stained clothing—all things the jurors see, hear, or touch.[17] But not all outcomes were predictable when the decisions were made beforehand. The jury's task is to focus on the defendant's decisions based on what the defendant knew *before* the culminating event. Jurors have a responsibility to assess the predictability of the harmful outcome, and where the predictability is clear, judge the defendant guilty or liable. Or, where the outcome is deemed unpredictable given the information at the time before the outcome, the jury is to exonerate the defendant. But studies show that juries do not reliably do that.[18] The results can be unjust verdicts, with the defendants suffering liability or jail for unforeseeable outcomes due solely to jurors' hindsight bias.

Many studies on hindsight bias reveal how it can affect jurors. In one study,[19] researchers gave all subjects information about a hazardous section of train tracks. One group was given only the information of the known hazards and was tasked with deciding whether the railroad should be allowed to operate trains on the hazardous tracks. This was the "foresight group." The other group—the "hindsight group"—was given additional information, including facts about a derailment on those tracks that resulted in a hazmat release into a river which harmed property and animals.

In one sample of the foresight group, 33% opposed the train's operation on the hazardous tracks. In a hindsight group, however, 67% judged the railroad's actions worthy of punitive damages. Further, the foresight group's average estimate of the likelihood of a serious accident was .34, but the hindsight group's estimate was .59.

Finally, the hindsight group rated the defendant's conscious awareness of danger far higher than did the foresight group. The study also showed that the hindsight bias influenced participants' nonprobability evaluations such as the quality of the decisions or the qualifications of the decision makers. In other words, hindsight bias altered *more* than just the judgments of liability and predictability.

*Hindsight Bias and Medical Cases*
The severity of an injury resulting from a medical decision can affect the influence of hindsight bias on a jury. A 1991 study[20] asked subjects to determine whether a psychotherapist was negligent, acted reasonably, and could foresee violent behavior of a particular patient against a third person. The subjects were placed in three groups and all received identical pre-outcome facts. One group was given an outcome scenario where there was no violence to the third person. The second group's outcome scenario was that the third person did receive violence at the hands of the patient. For the third group, the outcome was unspecified.

When asked whether the therapist was negligent, 24% of the "violent outcome" group found the therapist negligent, but only 9% of the "unspecified outcome" group found negligence; and in the "no violence outcome" group only 4% found negligence. Despite that the study participants had the same pre-outcome information, participants' knowledge of the outcomes produced *four times* more judgments of negligence in violent outcomes than nonviolent. The hindsight bias effect was profound.

The study also showed that when provided a violent outcome scenario, participants reported that the violence was more foreseeable, and that the therapist should've done more to prevent it. The research gives strong evidence that the more harmful the perceived outcome of an event, the more intense the hindsight bias in judging negligence. The harmful effects of hindsight bias on jury pools can be powerful enough to derail justice.

Medical professionals are no better than nonexperts when it comes to hindsight bias. A study involving 112 practicing anesthesiologists[21] tasked the experts with judging the appropriateness of care for certain clinical cases. The researchers presented the physicians with two scenarios in which the case history and the care given to the patients were identical. Where the scenarios differed was in outcome—one resulted in a temporary injury, the other in permanent injury. Despite the identical case histories and care, the panel of experienced anesthesiologists assessed the cases according to hindsight bias. The care in cases with a severe outcome was about 30% more likely to be assessed as below standard compared with the same case with a favorable outcome. The results of this study, and many others, show that experts are as vulnerable to hindsight bias as nonexperts.

*Hindsight Bias and Computer Animations*
Attorneys often seek to use computer animations in courtrooms to depict accidents or crimes, usually as a visual aid to expert testimony. Animations depicting events appear in news media, social media, and elsewhere. All of these can have serious consequences because computer animations can intensify the effects of hindsight bias.

In one study,[22] researchers randomized subjects into groups to assess traffic collision scenarios. The researchers provided each group with a set of facts representing some part or the entirety of serious accidents that had actually occurred. One scenario ended before any apparent driver error. Another scenario ended after the driver error occurred, but before the collision. Another scenario showed the entire sequence, including the collision. Some participants received vehicle path information only from text-and-diagram depictions. Others saw computer animations of the same information.

Comparing all the groups, some with and others without outcome information, researchers found that the hindsight bias effect was more than *doubled* when using the computer animation to depict events up to but not including the collision. This suggests that computer animations are not neutral—they carry potential to lead viewers to misjudge an event's predictability.

*Imagination as Hindsight Protection*
The extensive, consistent research findings on hindsight bias show how vulnerable we are to its influence. Especially in cases of severe outcomes, we need to assess with great care what was known *before* an event before we leap to decisions about what to do in the future. As we've seen, this is unnatural. Our lazy minds don't want to do this, but clear thinking includes thinking when it's hard. One way to motivate that hard thinking is to envision failure. Give the mind a *reason* to think hard. For example, if you're on jury duty, envision how you'd feel if later it were proved that your hindsight bias convicted the wrong person or imagine how a loved one would feel as you hold them accountable in a hindsight bias for something they really didn't foresee. Hindsight bias is like a witness whose story is never tested. One doesn't know the truth until the testimony is compared with *all* the evidence.

## Belief Bias and Invalid Logic

We've gone through a few informal fallacies that correlate with cognitive biases, but informal fallacies aren't the only areas where cognitive biases influence conclusions. In situations where people consider formal logical arguments, there is yet one more bias to consider. When we consider facts that we know about the world and use logic to deduce a conclusion from them, we expect our conclusion to be true. However, when we come up with a conclusion based on an invalid argument, we sometimes accept the conclusions as true for reasons that have nothing to do with logic. This can happen when our conclusion is something we like. Preferred conclusions can mislead us into an unjustified confidence in the soundness of an argument without us realizing we just ignored the logic. Under some conditions, people accept conclusions they produce or agree with regardless of the validity of the argument. When someone's beliefs influence a conclusion that they produce or agree with, the phenomenon is known as *belief bias*.[23]

Belief bias is also a systematic tendency to assess a syllogism (an argument with just two premises) by the credibility of its conclusion instead of by the principle of logical necessity.[24] Here's an example:

1. All birds can fly.
2. Pigeons can fly.
Conclusion: Pigeons are birds.

The conclusion "pigeons are birds" is believable. Many people look at the example and think the argument is valid because the conclusion is believable, but the argument is not valid. Not one of the premises, nor the combination of the premises, requires the conclusion. This kind of cognitive error is common, and it's the essence of belief bias. Belief bias occurs as a result of our lazy minds. The mind will not work any harder than it needs to, unless there's a strong motivation to work. In the case of a believable conclusion, the lazy mind sees no need to go beyond the believable conclusion into the harder work of analyzing the logic. It's as though the lazy mind is saying, "If the conclusion's right, so's the argument. I'm done."

Belief bias is a threat to clear thinking because it occurs without a sense of anything being wrong. It occurs not just in cases where the belief-biased person agrees with or produced the conclusion, but also in cases where the conclusion is plausibly true no matter who proposed it. In psychological research settings, for example, subjects accept believable conclusions of invalid syllogisms almost as often as they accept believable conclusions of valid ones.[25] One study found that even people passing a university-level course in logic can accept believable conclusions from invalid arguments almost as often as untrained people.[26]

**Defeating the Bias**
If even logic-trained people suffer belief bias, is learning logic a waste of time? After all, belief bias sometimes just takes over and makes the logic irrelevant. The answer is that learning logic is rescued by research. Research shows, case-by-case, that belief bias *can* be overcome.

Researchers found that the way one *approaches* a logic problem affects belief bias. Belief bias occurs most easily when people aren't prompted to consider the rules of logic. Without this prompting, people evaluate conclusions for their believability or appeal. The mind takes the path of least resistance unless given a reason to do otherwise. Presented with the easy decision to accept a believable conclusion and presume the argument made for it was sound, it unconsciously takes it no further. We believe we've done the work even when we haven't. This effect is so strong, it even happens to logic-trained people.

To overcome belief bias, shift the focus from the appeal of the conclusion to its logical relationship to the premises. Once that shift occurs, asking the right question avoids belief bias even more effectively. In research on belief bias, for example, merely asking whether one can logically infer the conclusion from the premises is dramatically more effective in preventing belief bias than not focusing on logic at all. But asking whether the premises *necessarily imply* the conclusion yields even better results. However, stressing *logical necessity* between premises and conclusion yields the best results for both logic-trained and untrained people.[27] That conscious shift in focus moves us from the bias to the logic.

**Redeeming Logic, Thinking Well**
We think clearly when we ask whether a conclusion *necessarily follows* from its premises. We think clearly when we know the rules of logic so we can answer that question. We think best about arguments when we do both.

We've spent much of this book describing the need for and the nature of logic and rationality. In the next chapter, we'll explore a field often associated with logic and rationality: the enterprise of science. But the practice of science, as we'll see, is not always logical or rational.

**Questions for Reflection**
1. What are the components of critical thinking?
2. What is cognitive bias?
3. Explain a cognitive bias you're most familiar with and how you saw or experienced its effects.
4. Explain the consequences of a society where most people failed to practice critical thinking and knew nothing of cognitive biases.

Chapter 12

# Biases in Science

The confidence we place in science deserves close inspection.[1]
—David Harker, *Creating Scientific Controversy*

Science is the organized and systematic study of physical phenomena.[2] Professionals who apply the results of scientific studies we refer to as scientists, and scientists who seek to study and publish results of their studies of science, we refer to as researchers. Both enjoy a high status in western society because the results of their work often lead to stunning discoveries and technologies.

One of the remarkable features of scientific discoveries is the process that creates them, often called the scientific method.[3] Recited here in a simple form, the scientific method is a process that starts with an idea that arises as a scientist examines some part of nature or reviews what other scientists have found. Questions arise, such as, How does that work? Can I predict anything from this? What caused this? Once a question is decided, a researcher proposes an answer. The proposed answer is known as a hypothesis, a tentative belief that can be tested by the instruments and methods of the researcher's discipline. After designing a test of the hypothesis, an experiment ensues, and observations of the results test the researcher's hypothesis to decide whether it's true.

Experiment results are often published in journals reviewed by professional peers—other scientists from the same discipline—to assess, among other things, whether the experimenter's methods, calculations, and conclusions meet the discipline's standards for research. Researchers rely on peer-reviewed journals as credible sources of knowledge. In cases of spectacular discoveries, public media also rely on peer-reviewed journals as sources for news stories.

To be useful as a source of knowledge, experimental results need to be objective and consistent. An experiment is objective when other researchers using the same instruments and methods can repeat the experiment. Experimental results are consistent when other researchers perform the same experiment and get the same results. With effective methods, peer-reviewed journals, objective study designs, and repeatable experiments, science should yield consistently reliable knowledge. But there's a problem. Research is conducted by *scientists*; journals are produced by *editors*. And scientists and editors are subject to thinking that can make published results untrustworthy.

**Finding What You Want**
When a researcher uses what's known as a positive test strategy, they look for evidence to prove the hypothesis true. This can be an excellent way of conducting certain kinds of experiments. For example, if we suspect that a particular compound corrodes another, we apply the compound to the other and find out. This commonsense method works well to test hypotheses that are easy to show true or false with a single test. But what if the hypothesis isn't so simple? If instead your hypothesis requires much more than a simple experiment, such as the analysis of a larger number of results from one or more experiments, then looking for evidence to confirm a hypothesis will often lead to an unreliable conclusion. Such unreliable conclusions do occur in science and result from what is widely known as *confirmation bias*.

Confirmation bias is the tendency to seek data to support one's own hypothesis and ignore or not see the data that does not confirm your hypothesis. Nobel Prize winner Daniel Kahneman describes the problem: "Contrary to the rules of philosophers of science, who advise testing hypotheses by trying to refute them, people (and scientists, quite often) seek data that are likely to be compatible with the beliefs they currently hold."[4]

Examples of confirmation bias in science appear in many disciplines where reliability of outcomes may mean life or death. For instance, in a study done to see whether confirmation bias affects diagnoses in obstetrics, medically trained participants were put through several scenarios. One scenario was to estimate the amount of a blood-like substance in a simulation model's perineum. The other was to estimate a patient's amniotic fluid volume based on ultrasound images. The participant group was randomized and given information on the patient's blood pressure according to variations in the scenarios.

How did confirmation bias influence the scientists' conclusions? Participants were much more likely to overestimate blood loss when told the patient had low blood pressure compared to when they were told the blood pressure was normal. They were also less likely to estimate the amniotic fluid to be normal when told the patient had high blood pressure.[5] Even though the blood pressure was irrelevant to the observed fluid volumes, the participants answered in ways confirming their beliefs that blood pressure *should* affect the volumes.

Confirmation bias can also determine the information scientists seek. And seeking only what tends to support their decisions can have serious consequences. In an experimental study of psychiatrists and psychiatric medical interns, researchers found that after having made a preliminary diagnosis, 13% of practicing psychiatrists and 25% of the medical students used a confirmation bias when searching for new information. When using a confirmation-biased search, 70% of the psychiatrists and 63% of the students made a wrong diagnosis.[6]

**Technology and Confirmation Bias**
Scientific advances in technologies bring with them expectations of success. In technologies where the subjects are humans, not machines, confirmation bias can make research results less reliable. In these cases, it's not the researchers but the human subjects whose bias undermines reliability. In one study,[7] researchers gave a group of healthy young adults two knee braces to try. Before beginning the physical tests, the researchers informed the subjects that they would be taking part in a manufacturer-funded study of a new prototype knee brace. Subjects reviewed a flyer describing the brace as "computerized," "using a state-of-the-art microprocessor, accompanied with an accelerometer" that could "measure and adjust joint stiffness in real time." The flyer also had a graph showing knee flexion angles achieved in early testing.

The two knee braces, however, were identical, except that one had a power switch, LED light, micro-USB port, and silver paint. There was no function to the cosmetic additions. Further, the graph and description given in the flyer were contrived. The subjects were using two otherwise identical braces. After the tests, the researchers determined that the subjects' post-testing increase in preference for the "computerized" knee brace arose from confirmation bias, not any improvement in gait or any functional difference in the braces.

The danger of confirmation bias in clinical studies is so widely known that there's an ethical principle known as *equipoise*. The principle of equipoise requires that patients should only be enrolled in a randomized controlled trial if there's "substantial uncertainty about which of the trial treatments might be most beneficial."[8] This helps prevent confirmation bias, among other things, from influencing the administration of such studies and harming the subjects. But even with the widely known principle of equipoise to combat confirmation bias, some studies continue without it. Confirmation bias still affects some clinical studies.

**Conflicted Interests**
One of the most interesting questions researchers ask is, Which hypothesis should be tested? It's here where conflicts of interest can arise and influence the researcher's thinking. Researchers who aim to publish have a strong motivation to produce results publishers want to see. Getting published increases one's professional status, improves career opportunities, leads to job security and promotions, helps acquire grants, and is emotionally satisfying.

The publishers typically want novel and positive results. Novelty brings readers to the journal; positive scientific findings do, too.[9] So, creating new, positive research findings takes on a significant, if not crucial, place in researchers' decisions on design and conduct of experiments.

If researchers are biased up front to seek only results that confirm a publishable hypothesis, then the experiments can be set up to confirm what they want and make it easy to see only confirming data. Further, the experimenter may conduct a number of experiments that do not confirm the desired results, thereafter suppressing them by reporting only theory-confirming results. Confirmation bias infects research at all phases, from deciding what experiments to do to selecting which results to disclose or conceal. This bias is typically invisible to those who rely on the journals.

**The Power of Expectations**
The tendency toward confirmation bias in scientific research is no secret. There are many scientists who actively and honestly seek to avoid it by seeking disconfirming evidence, too. Wise and virtuous as this is, another peril shows up. The researcher who *does* look at disconfirming evidence is still vulnerable to a different kind of bias, known as the *disconfirmation bias*. Disconfirmation bias is the tendency to scrutinize or question disconfirming data without doing the same to supporting data.

An example of this occurred in the original experiment to quantify the pressure due to light (yes—light *does* have pressure). The original researchers' findings confirmed their predictions within 1% of the theoretical expectations, but their results were almost too good to be true. Other scientists found out why when they analyzed the calculations and found four distinct kinds of calculation errors, including units and conversion factors, incorrect formula values, and incorrect mathematical functions.[10] In this case, the researchers' findings confirmed their expectations, so they had little motivation to go back and check the math. Disconfirmation bias consumed them.

The conflict of interests arising from a scientist's strong motivation to get published isn't the only thing affecting scientific findings. Findings often depend on the researcher's *expectations*. For example, in one study of errors in handwritten recordings of observations, two-thirds of the errors favored the observer's hypothesis.[11] The researchers in this case misreported some of what they saw to conform to what they *expected* to see.

Reports of disconfirmation bias in financial conflicts of interest describe accounts of arguably unethical pharmaceutical studies.[12] The ethical questions raised are beyond the scope of this book. However, what *is* in the scope of this book is that science is vulnerable to the same biases common in less rigorous enterprises. Clear thinking about science includes recognizing that scientists and editors of their peer-reviewed journals are not rule-following machines. Whether it's the researchers, their human research subjects, or the editors who seek broader readership, trustworthiness of the scientific enterprise depends on the conduct and thinking of its people whose cognitive biases affect the reliability of their findings.

**Resistance to Change in Science**
In the preceding sections we described some of the effects confirmation bias, disconfirmation bias, and expectations can have on the reliability of scientific research reports. We explored these biases to reveal that clear thinking about science includes recognizing that dangerous cognitive biases hide behind the idealized view of scientific research. However, clear thinking about science also means we must consider the human cognitive resistance to change in science.

A popular myth among nonscientists is that scientists hold their theories tentatively, ready upon the presentation of stronger alternatives to adopt them. The myth strengthens as popular media report findings that seem to overturn or confirm theories that evoke public fear, hope, or controversy. It strengthens also as media associate these celebrated findings with earlier major discoveries, as if they're part of a steady timeline of smoothly and rationally adopted positions. But scientific progress is neither smooth nor entirely rational, particularly when it comes to adopting revolutionary new theories.

We should expect resistance to a new theory where a long-established theory has succeeded in explaining or predicting important phenomena. The new theory will not only have to do better at explaining or predicting the phenomena it's applied to, but it must overcome nonrational influences among the scientific community. These influences are not trivial. At times, they halt scientific advances for years.

The first nonrational influence is emotional. Scientists who've devoted their careers researching, publishing papers on, and presuming a theory have an emotional commitment to it. Imagine spending decades teaching and writing about a scientific theory only to find that all you taught, published, and held true was wrong. Finding that it was wrong creates a cognitive dissonance not easily resolved by the rational assessment that the new theory is right. Resolving the dissonance takes time, during which theory-defensive biases intrude.[13] Defending a cherished theory often involves confirmation bias (the tendency to see only the evidence that supports your theory) and disconfirmation bias (the tendency to scrutinize evidence hostile to your theory more than you scrutinize evidence that supports it).

Another nonrational resistance to change is philosophical. Some scientific theories presume one or more philosophical positions. Some are fundamental to science, such as the philosophical presumptions that the world is orderly and knowable. Others are narrowly applied to particular disciplines. Where the narrower, discipline-specific philosophical presumptions prevail, adherents of the philosophical presumptions do not relinquish them easily. Those presumptions are often even more compelling a reason to resist a new theory than the physical evidence. One doesn't abandon a worldview simply because scientific evidence impugns it. Below, we present a few examples where philosophical commitments hindered scientific progress.

*Resistance to Saving Women*
Ignaz Semmelweis (1818–1865), a Hungarian doctor working in the Vienna General Hospital, Austria, lost a doctor friend to sepsis after his friend was cut by a scalpel used in an autopsy. Semmelweis noticed that the symptoms of his friend's death were like those of women who died in a hospital after childbirth. The hospital was a "teaching hospital," training medical students and midwives.

During one period of the hospital's history, one of the two maternity wings of the hospital was served by medical students, who, after spending part of the day dissecting human corpses, went to the maternity wards and delivered babies without sanitizing their hands. Semmelweis noticed the smell of death on the students as they went to the delivery rooms and believed that the putrefied corpses the medical students dissected carried some kind of poison. To eliminate both the foul smell of death and the hypothesized poison, he directed the students to wash their hands in a bleach solution.

The germ theories of Lister and Pasteur had not yet been developed. Semmelweis had no theoretical grounds for believing the corpses were bacterial disease vectors. His theory was unprecedented. It was also strikingly successful. The death rate among women whose deliveries were done by the student doctors with bleach-washed hands went from an average of about one-in-six before the bleach protocol to *less than one in a hundred* during the protocol.

However, Semmelweis's rescue of women from death in doctor-attended deliveries was followed not by accolades, but by the hospital administrator's refusal to renew Semmelweis's employment contract, and later by Semmelweis's rejection from the Hungarian medical corps.

Historians offer theories for his scientific community's rejection of the obvious power of Semmelweis's protocol for decades. One was that the head of the maternity department in which Semmelweis worked was reportedly averse to adopting new ideas and did not promote the Semmelweis protocol. Another is that Semmelweis was a cantankerous and somewhat insulting man, not known for gracious persuasion.

There's evidence, however, that it wasn't merely Semmelweis's personality that caused resistance to his protocol. Another doctor at another hospital, on the verge of closing its maternity ward due to its high death rate, tried Semmelweis's protocol. The death rate dropped to just one in several months. And yet prevailing explanations for the deaths of women in maternity wards resisted blaming the unclean hands of the attending doctors. One such explanation was the generally unsanitary conditions of the wards. Even when people recognized that midwives lost fewer patients than did physicians, the difference was not attributed to the physicians carrying the pathogen. Rather, a popular alternative explanation was that because physicians were men, it was more likely that they created the inflammation by harsher physical manipulations than were done by midwives, who were always women.

None of Semmelweis's contemporaries refuted his factual claims on results. The evidence was conclusive. His protocol should've been adopted quickly and broadly by the scientific community—but it wasn't. His scientist peers rejected his theory without rational appeal to evidence that Semmelweis was wrong, despite overwhelming evidence that he was right.

The Semmelweis story is studied widely, and the account here abbreviated.[14] It's so powerful an exhibition of resistance to scientific change in the face of strong contrary evidence that the tendency to resist change this way is sometimes referred to as the Semmelweis reflex.

*Deniable Einstein*

In 1905, when Albert Einstein published his special theory of relativity, many in the scientific community resisted it. His theory entailed a denial of the nineteenth century prevailing view that an undetectable entity known as the luminiferous ether (not ether the anesthetic) occupied space. This ether seemed to explain certain problems of electricity and the motion of light.

Some scientists adopted the ether theory not on empirical evidence as much as on metaphysical grounds. Metaphysical presumptions included that a vacuum could not exist; that for two bodies to influence each other, there must be some entity in space connecting them; and that all physical interactions may be explained mechanically. To reject the existence of the ether theory was to reject not only strongly held empirical inferences, but also *metaphysical* assumptions.[15]

In the United States, as late as 1911, "the tendency in America was to ridicule the theory of relativity as being totally impractical and absurd."[16] In Britain as late as 1923, physicists were disinterested in Einstein's theory because of their commitment to ether theory.[17] The history of early scientific resistance to Einstein's theories is not part of the popular knowledge of Einstein's famous $E=MC^2$ equation. Instead, the popular understanding is that science progressed smoothly from Newton to Einstein, and that scientists readily adopt new theories when the evidence is clear.

*Summary*

Scientists are as subject to nonrational decision-making as any other group. They can be resistant to change, even in the face of strong contrary evidence. They can adhere to the beliefs of eminent peers rather than adopt the evidence controverting them. Any current theory may be the next example of the Semmelweis effect, where the objective evidence won't be as important to the theory's adherents as their bias to protect their favored theories. Because scientists can mistake metaphysical positions for science, as occurred in the resistance to Einstein's theories, we need to look for metaphysical ideas masquerading as science.

We think clearly about science when we ask what theories are being resisted, and whether the resistance is rational and evidentiary or nonrational. In cases where there are political and media influences, we should be even more cautious. Scientists have political views and can exploit their status as scientists politically. For example, in an editorial in *Scientific American*,[18] the authors call on scientists to not only act politically but also engage specific partisan issues. Scientists need not be politically mute, but when they exploit current partisan politics to acquire funding for studies politicians are interested in, they enter a conflict of interests that invites confirmation bias, disconfirmation bias, bandwagon effects, and other biases that make research findings unreliable.

When these conflicts of interests become widely known, they can erode the public's trust not only in scientists but also in science as a credible enterprise.

Knowing which research articles are reliable can be daunting, but there are ways to screen for quality. First, look for conflict statements at the end of journal articles. Many scientific journals require authors to declare conflicts of interests. If a conflict is declared, then pay attention to the kind of conflict it is. For example, suppose the author of a research study on a particular drug declares he was paid or consulted by the drug's manufacturer. That study is immediately suspect. Financial conflicts of interest are the most likely to distort findings in favor of financial interest.

Next, carefully read the abstract and compare it with the body of the study, especially where the most important findings appear. If the abstract includes some of the important findings but omits others, be suspicious of the article's reliability. Many busy scientists only scan journals for abstracts. Research writers know that. So, research authors often frame abstracts to attract attention to the article, sometimes intentionally obscuring relevant information that would make the article seem less interesting. Omitting important facts from the abstract suggests the question, "What *else* did the author omit from this study?" Also, examine the abstract for phrasing or language that suggests an attempt to persuade the reader to adopt the author's position. Inappropriate attempts at persuasion are most likely to occur in scientific studies related to controversial topics, such as climate change or vaccination safety.

Compare the facts of the findings with the claims of the conclusion. A researcher who draws a conclusion that goes beyond what the facts imply undermines the reliability of the entire study. Think clearly, using logic and reason to determine whether the facts imply the author's conclusion.

Finally, examine statements based on fractions and ratios. Which statement do you think would be more attractive in an abstract: "Drug X reduces disease D by 50%" or "Drug X reduces disease D by 1%"? Imagine that the study findings show that 2% of a population will have a particular disease, but that drops to 1% when these people use a certain drug. The percentages can be reported in the study's abstract (or conclusion) as a 1% drop in disease. They can also be reported as a 50% drop (since 1 is 50% of 2). The first is the "absolute" drop. The second is the "relative" drop. If the terms *absolute* and *relative* are not used in the abstract to describe the result, be suspicious. The absolute vs. relative distinction is easy to miss, especially when the results are significant emotionally. But it's crucial to find if you want to avoid being misled.

**Saving Science**
The emphasis in this chapter has been on how cognitive biases affect scientists and researchers, and how, therefore, cognitive biases can affect the reliability of studies and theories. Nevertheless, vulnerability to cognitive biases does not ruin science. Science is still effective in making discoveries and creating technologies.

Further, even though many important scientific theories are tentative, we still must think of some as accurately depicting crucial facts about our world that we wouldn't otherwise know. It's because science develops crucial knowledge that we scrutinize its operations and the thinking of its practitioners with great care. Few human enterprises are as worthy of respect—and scrutiny—as science.

**Questions for Reflection**
1. Given that some social media platforms censor accounts of scientific claims that aren't mainstream, how would you determine whether the Semmelweis effect is suppressing an unpopular theory?
2. How would you look for confirmation bias in a scientific journal article?
3. What are the biases that can influence a researcher who produces experiments expecting particular results?

Chapter 13

# Biases in Thinking with Numbers Big and Small

> A psychiatrist reported once that practically everybody is neurotic. . . . If a man were normal, our psychiatrist would never meet him.[1]
>
> —Darrell Huff, *How to Lie with Statistics*

After hearing that "90% of dentists surveyed recommended toothpaste X over the next leading brand," would you tend to think more highly of toothpaste X than you did before hearing the claim? Most people would. That's why claims like this are made. They tend to work. They also tend to mislead. They mislead, in part, by hiding the percentage of dentists *not* surveyed. Without knowing what percentage of dentists were surveyed, you would have no idea whether the 90% of dentists referred to are a significant proportion of all dentists. For example, the "dentists surveyed" could be only the ones the toothpaste manufacturer gives free samples to. Or maybe only 1% of all dentists were surveyed—99% of dentists were not. In short, this claim's numbers are misleading and nearly meaningless for determining the quality of toothpaste X.

To think clearly about numbers, we don't merely make careful math calculations, we ask what the calculations *mean*. People are predisposed to surprising cognitive errors when thinking with or in numbers. Because of these predispositions, we can miss the *meaning* of numbers in such things as statistics, predictions, and risks. As a result, we can make bad decisions. We'll explore a few of the ways our thinking with numbers can go awry and show how clear thinking on numbers is more than doing careful math.

## Statistics

Clear thinking about statistics is difficult. It's also extremely important. Statistics are used to explain or predict, as in the case of scientific research. Other times they're used to persuade, as in advertising, politics, and courtrooms. Some of the most important decisions in the world are based on statistics. Some of your most important decisions depend on how well you think about statistics.

The difficulty in thinking clearly on statistics comes from two sources. First, some statistics are complicated, requiring specialized training to understand, which few of us have. Second, we're prone to intuitive errors about the meaning and proper use of numbers to make decisions. The first problem is beyond the scope of this book, but the intuitive errors are more easily learned, so to those we turn now.

*Sample Size Neglect*

A common intuitive error people make in deciding from statistics is overestimating the reliability of a small statistical sample to represent a broader statistical sample. This error is not only prevalent in untrained people, but it occurs even among researchers in many scientific disciplines.[2] This tendency is known as *sample size neglect*. When significant differences between the results of small statistical samples and large ones occur, we neglect that the smaller sample is likely to have more extreme variations from the average than a large one. Let's look at an example of sample size neglect.

There are over 300 million people in the US. If you measured the weight of every American in the US, you'd have a perfect sample size to assess the average weight of Americans. But what if you only measured the weight of 500 Americans? How about 50? If your random sample of 50 Americans just happened to include two or three of the heaviest people in country, then the average for the 50-person sample would be dramatically higher than the broad average for all Americans. As the sample number gets smaller, a few very heavy (or very light) people could dramatically affect the average.

Because smaller samples have the greatest likelihood of dramatic variations from the average, this is where the sample size neglect shows up. Most people won't recognize that small samples are where the greatest variations from the large-sample averages occur. The sample size neglect leads people to believe that the small numbers are as reliable as the large ones. As a result, intuitions about sample size often don't match reality. This intuitive error could be expected among untrained people, but one of the earliest and often-cited studies on the problem showed that sample size neglect happens even among those trained in statistics, such as professional psychologists.[3]

*False Confidence*
Sample size neglect can suggest causes for which there is no evidence. For example, in one study[4] researchers compared two maps of age-adjusted kidney cancer rates for American men. The first map showed counties in the lowest 10% of cancer distribution. Those tended to be rural counties in the Midwest, the South, and the West. The researchers suggested that it would be easy to infer that the low cancer rates were caused by the rural lifestyle, clean air, clean water, and access to fresh foods.

The second map showed the counties in the *highest* 10% of age-adjusted kidney cancer rates for men in the same period as the other map. Those *also* tended to be rural counties in the Midwest, the South, and the West. The researchers suggested that it would be easy to infer that these high cancer rates could be caused by poor access to medical care, rural poverty, too much tobacco and alcohol, and a high-fat diet.

These two maps give us strikingly different information about small rural counties and kidney cancer in men. Sample size neglect could inspire confidence in either one, yet they can't both be true of the national picture. The difference between the statistics of the two maps isn't a fact about whether small counties are prone to kidney cancer. The statistics are an *artifact* of small sample statistics, not a fact about the world. Small sample statistics often produce artifacts, not trustworthy facts.

**Stories and Statistics**
One of the reasons the sample size neglect so often deceives us is that before we deliberate on the statistical evidence, we tend to create a coherent story about it. This story is a hasty generalization from numbers and requires almost no cognitive effort, so it comes easily. It's also why we so rarely recognize it.

In the case of the cancer rates mentioned, the researchers did the story making for us. In the low-incidence rural counties, they suggested that rural life with its clean water and air, etc., could explain the low incidence of cancer. Without much thought, that's an easy, coherent story to buy; and most people would adopt it. Yet when the researchers looked at the other small sample, they got a strikingly different story.

If only one of the samples had been used to decide on whether to start a cancer intervention program, one could no more accurately predict success based on the small sample size than one could by tossing a coin. Stories come easily from small sample sizes, but the stories are too often illusions. They lack predictive power, and as we've seen, they can lead to absurd results. When you see small sample size statistics, seek evidence *beyond* them to avoid creating stories *from* them.

**Numbers and Causes**

Numbers correlating events do not tell us with certainty what *caused* the events. We've all heard the phrase "correlation does not equal causation." The reason we so often hear it is that we often act intuitively like it's false. The urge to seek cause is natural and our minds avoid the work it takes to question our intuitions about numbers and causes. In the cancer data examples we saw how easy it would be to infer causes from the small samples. The tendency to infer cause from correlation between high rates of events and what seem to be obvious conditions producing them can also mislead us.

For instance, if we were to analyze the correlation between rising sea level rates and the drop in the rates of people using cassette players to listen to music between 1990 and 2020, we'd see that as sea levels rose, the use of cassette tapes sank. The correlation is remarkable. It's also irrelevant. This may seem like a silly example, but it's only because we know that listening to music on cassette players has no effect on sea levels.

The false cause fallacy is obvious, but where our intuitions can't so easily disconnect the events, we are vulnerable. Claims based on statistical correlations are not *necessarily* false, but they are always suspect. To think clearly on correlation numbers, we must be ready to ask, What evidence—*beyond the statistical correlation*—is there for the claim that one thing caused the other? This approach is particularly important when statistical correlations advance political, commercial, or other selfish interests. In these cases, users select only the data that serves their interests—also known as cherry-picking the data—and correlate the numbers to "prove" their cause.

The language of causation is often applied in studies where the correlation discussed is the only correlation presented. For example, if a study announced that in 75% of low speed, rear-end collisions in rush hour traffic, the parties at fault were drinking coffee on the way to work, the inference that drinking coffee on the way to work *causes* drivers to have rear-end collisions is an easy story to believe. We easily stop there without asking what *other* correlations were involved.

News and social media often report on instances of simple correlations and include language like "according to science" or "proved by researchers."

In many cases the media cite legitimate research findings but show only the simple statistical correlations with no mention of the researchers' caveats that the statistical correlations are not proof of cause. The stories thus acquire the illusion of credibility. They also appeal to the human tendency to avoid evaluative thought when a coherent causal story appears. When you see a simple correlation presented as a causal explanation, realize how easy it is to create or believe a false causal story.

**Numbers and Gambles**

In the summer of 1913, one of the most famous events in gambling entered the history books. At a roulette table in a Monte Carlo casino, gamblers watched as the ball on a roulette wheel kept landing on black (black and red pockets alternate for the ball to fall in). As the unbroken series of black pocket landings continued, gamblers bet on red, expecting that the black series had to end. They kept betting and kept losing. According to accounts of the event, millions of francs were bet and lost by gamblers as the series of black landings went 26 in a row.[5] This episode was the origin of the term *Monte Carlo fallacy*.[6] And it reveals something important about how people think about numbers in probabilities.

The Monte Carlo fallacy most often goes by the name *gambler's fallacy*. The gambler's fallacy is the belief that the probability of a random event happening is affected by past instances of the same kind of event. People are biased to believe that there is fairness in the laws of chance, and that if there is a deviation in one direction it'll soon be canceled by an opposite deviation.[7] If we flip a fair coin ten times and come up with heads, we expect the next flip to come up tails. That expectation is a gambler's fallacy.

The gambler's fallacy works inversely, too. In one of today's most important discussions on the origin of the universe, some argue that if an infinite number of big bang events occurred, then our exceedingly fine-tuned universe was inevitable. Therefore, as the argument goes, the fine-tuning of the universe is irrelevant to its origin. This argument appeals to our intuition that if a random-chance event in a series is given a limitless number of opportunities, the series *must* produce all possible outcomes. In particular, if an exceedingly rare random-chance event occurred, we intuit that there must have been many previous "coin flips" before it. The greater the number of events in the series leads us to believe the greater the chance we'll get our rare result, but this intuition is wrong.

This intuition is wrong because each independent physical event is also an independent statistical event. Every new universe has the same staggeringly remote odds of being fine-tuned for humanity as every other (physicist Lee Smolin estimated[8] the odds at 1 in $10^{229}$). So, even if these multiple universes existed, each new universe is like a flip of a coin: there's no way to say that just because you got an incredibly improbable result, an infinite number of coin tosses (or universes) went before it. Each new universe still has to overcome the 1 in $10^{229}$ odds *independently*. In other words, the 1 in $10^{229}$ odds against a human-supporting universe don't change merely because you "flipped the big bang coin" an infinite number of times before.[9] You can't know merely from the existence of a staggeringly unlikely event in a series that there must have been an infinite number (or any number) of similar random events before it. Believing that you *do* know is the inverse gambler's fallacy.

**Numbers and Framing**
Decisions based on numbers are often made due to how the numbers are presented or framed. When numbers are framed in ways that appeal to human tendencies to decide or behave in certain ways, the *framing effect* can be so powerful it makes nonrational choices seem rational. For example, in risky decisions people are more prone to be risk-averse when a problem is framed as a gain, but they're more prone to be risk-seeking when the same problem is framed as a loss.[10] In a famous fictitious disease study, researchers sought to determine how framing the numbers affected decisions.[11] Subjects were presented with two problems. The scenario for both groups included the presumption that the country is preparing for the outbreak of a disease expected to kill 600 people. Subjects were asked which of the two options they would select for each problem.

> For the first problem:
> If option A is selected, 200 people will survive.
> If option B is selected, there is a 1/3 probability that 600 people will survive and 2/3 probability that no one will survive.
>
> The second problem:
> If option C is selected, 400 people will die.
> If option D is selected, the probability is 1/3 that no one will die, and 2/3 probability that 600 people will die.

For problem one, 72% of the subjects chose option A. The safe choice of saving 200 people was more attractive than the prospect of a 1/3 chance of saving 600 people. For problem two, 78% of the subjects chose option D. The sure death of 400 people was less tolerable than the 2/3 chance of 600 deaths. Problem one was framed in terms of survivors. Problem two was framed in terms of people dying. The number of people who'd live or die would be the same in both problems. Despite this, the subjects made their choices between the two problems based on how the numbers were *framed*.

The risky-choice framing of the numbers in the fictional disease problems is one form of framing. Its complexity requires some work to understand, but its effects are real and the real-world situations it applies to are many.

A simpler form of framing is *attribute framing*. For example, store-bought beef is often described as "80% lean" instead of "20% fat." Even though 20% fat *means* 80% lean, purchase choice does not depend on the numbers—it depends on which attribute (fatness or leanness) the numbers are framed in.

Framing is also used widely in marketing to change potential customers' views on other items. Consider an automobile market where a segment of the population hasn't decided whether to buy a pickup truck, SUV, or sedan. The pickup truck seller can market truck T as a 22 MPG vehicle or they can market it as a "Best in Class Fuel Economy" vehicle. Framing it in terms of "Best in Class" *suggests* that the numbers will be good—whatever "good" means to the potential buyer. In this case, shifting the frame from a specific rate (a mere 22 miles per gallon) to a superlative phrase ("best in class") is a way of framing by shifting the focus *away* from the number.

**First-Seen Numbers**

When people make decisions where they are presented with a number as a starting point, that number often has a powerful influence on the final decision. For example, people are more likely to favorably evaluate an item on a store display if the price tag shows that the "original" price is "marked down" to a lower price than if they had only seen the "lower" price alone. The first number they see is the higher "original" price. That first number has a significant influence on the customer's evaluation of the product as a smart purchase, even though the "discount" or "sale" price would be more than the customer would likely spend on the item if the sale price were the *only* price shown.

Even though the practice of artificial markdowns is almost as widely known as it is widely used, it's still remarkably effective.

## Big Numbers Unquestioned

Imagine you live in a small town in England. One evening, you find your two-month-old baby not moving. You summon emergency help, but the baby is dead. The coroner's report finds the case to be a death of natural causes. Next year, the same thing happens to your new baby, also about two months old. This time the authorities suspect you of murder, as the police in your town have never seen other families with two crib deaths. The police arrest you and charge you in court with the murder of your own babies—murders you did not commit.

The prosecution brings in an expert witness, a former professor of pediatrics from a prestigious university. He testifies that the odds of a baby dying of crib death to nonsmoking affluent parents is about 1 in 8,543. The odds of the same parents having two babies dying of crib death is 1 in 73 million (multiplying 8,543 by 8,543). The jury convicts you of the murder of your children and you're sentenced to life in prison.

Your first three years of prison are dreadful. The public hates you as a baby-killer. Your reputation outside prison is destroyed. Your fellow inmates know your charges and antagonize you. And you live every minute with the thought you'll be imprisoned this way for life. After three years, you hear that the second of two appeals to higher courts has reversed your case. You're thankful beyond words, but you also want to know why they finally released you.

This scenario is exactly what happened in the 1996 case of the late Sally Clark,[12] who reportedly never recovered from the psychological trauma of her wrongful conviction. In the appeal, Mrs. Clark's defense presented to the higher court expert testimony showing that statistics used as evidence were erroneous. The error is known as the *prosecutor's fallacy*. It arises when a prosecutor argues that the odds against the defendant's claim are so extremely rare that the accused must be guilty.

Aren't *all* prosecutions that use circumstantial evidence arguing that the circumstances statistically prove the case? In general, yes. That's how circumstantial evidence cases work. So, what made this case special?

In Mrs. Clark's case the prosecutor's original expert witness testified that odds of two crib deaths occurring in the same family were one 1 in 73 million. However, the expert never testified to the odds that two children would be *murdered* by the parents in similar circumstances.[13] The jury, the prosecutor's expert witness, and the prosecutor all stopped their analysis at the stunningly high odds against a chance set of same-parent crib deaths. No one in trial asked the crucial question, What are the odds that the same parents, in a small town, would *murder* their two children a year apart in a crib-death setting? In this case, the correct answer would've been: at or near zero.

We present the case here to show how an argument with large statistical probabilities can be so powerful that even experts in law and medicine can be misled. The prosecutor's fallacy was effective because people naïve to the analyses of statistics had stopped asking questions about the *application* of the statistics.

In dealing with cases like these, we don't have statistical rules to follow, as we do in small samples and the gambler's fallacy. We *do* have three models of reasoning to apply: deductive, inductive, and abductive (detailed in part 2). The jurors in the Clark case evaluated the issue in exclusively inductive terms (What are the odds?). Had they also used abductive reasoning (What is the best explanation?), their use of the right models of reasoning could have avoided the prosecutor's fallacy and saved Sally Clark from prison.

Knowing how cognitive biases work and how profoundly they can affect decisions leads to the question, How do I deal with these biases now that I know about them? We present an answer in the next chapter.

**Questions for Reflection:**
1. What are a few biases that can occur in the use of statistics?
2. Describe a circumstance in which you've seen framing used in your own experience.
3. How could you avoid the effects of anchoring in shopping or bargaining?
4. Imagine you are a juror in a criminal case where the prosecutor presents this argument: "Given the facts, ladies and gentlemen of the jury, even though this is a circumstantial evidence case—we have no eyewitnesses to the murder—the odds of these events happening by chance are extremely small. It is therefore likely beyond a reasonable doubt that the defendant committed the murder." What questions would you bring up during your jury deliberations to avoid the errors made in the Sally Clarke case?

Chapter 14

# Mitigating the Effects of Cognitive Biases

> The more you know about the way your mind works, the easier it will be to overcome cognitive biases.[1]
> —Daniel Kahneman, *Thinking Fast and Slow*

In chapters 11–13, we presented a survey of cognitive biases that distort our thinking and the consequences biases can have. As helpful as this information may be, resisting or mitigating biases is not intuitive. Likewise, the conditions where one should slow down and look for biases may not be obvious. Cognitive biases are often invisible when you most need to see them. In this chapter, we present some methods to recognize when biases are most likely a threat and how to make them more obvious. We also offer advice on mitigating them.

**When Biases Are a Threat**
When to invest time in self-reflective bias seeking is a crucial question. Most daily decisions and problems don't demand much thought. We even have mental shortcuts to help us through them. There are times, however, when those usually helpful mental shortcuts can also become or conceal distorted thinking. Here are some situations where clear thinking means slowing down, doing the hard mental work, and avoiding shortcuts.

*When a poor decision will result in a high cost (whether that cost is financial, personal, social, etc.).*

*When you feel rushed to decide* – The more rushed we feel, the more invisible the biases. The sense of urgency to decide overcomes the priority of deciding well.

*When thinking about the important decision evokes a strong emotional response* – Emotions naturally focus our attention on the experience of the moment rather than the quality of our thinking. We can work to avoid the effects of biases *and* feel strong emotions at the same time, but only with conscious effort.

*When you've had little experience (or success) with a similar important decision in the past* – Although many people would naturally slow down and think through novel problems carefully, the temptation to use "intuition" or "gut instinct" to solve such problems is real. Intuition, which is basically insight through pattern recognition, doesn't work when there's no relevant pattern. Where there's little or no relevant experience with a particular problem, the patterns of experience one has with other problems may be irrelevant. The insights we believe we gain from intuition, or gut feeling, in novel situations are often illusions.

Once we've decided to reduce the risks of cognitive biases, there are two basic principles to operate from. The first is to do the hard work of thinking. As previously stated, the mind is lazy and clear thinking requires effort. If we violate the principle of exerting cognitive effort, the risk of suffering distorted thinking rises dramatically. The second principle is to slow down our thinking. Fast thinking is where mental shortcuts take over and cognitive biases occur invisibly. Think slow on what matters; think fast on what's trivial.

**Mitigating Cognitive Errors**
To help you mitigate the effects of cognitive errors, we've listed here the cognitive biases discussed in this book and we offer a brief strategy to consider for each one.

*Ad Populum*
When confronted with an attempt to influence you by a popular appeal, reject the appeal until research proves that your position or behavior should change. When you feel the emotional urge to conform, realize that's a perilous cognitive bias. Slow down and think rationally. The emotional urge to conform distorts thinking and hurries decisions that should be made thoughtfully.

*Anchoring*
Reject first prices, proposals, or ideas presented to you. The anchoring bias is strong enough to make you believe a first proposal, idea, or price is the worthiest of consideration. However, the worthiest option is unknown until *all*

relevant options are evaluated, not just the first.

Demand other options. Anchoring bias shortcuts full-course thinking. It distracts you from a complete evaluation of all courses of action. Defeat anchoring by forcing the evaluation of other options. For example, in the case of purchase price, ask yourself what you'd offer if there were no "discounted" or other price tag on the item.

*Availability Bias*
When making an important decision, realize that factors coming first to mind often are what your memory finds most easily available, not necessarily what's most important to the decision. Statements that you've heard many times, emotionally powerful events, and lazy-mindedness will shortcut full-course analysis. Ask what *else* is involved.

*Bandwagon Effect*
When confronted with statements like "most other people believe" or "this is widely held," etc., look for alternative explanations. Make group ideas compete with others. Make the acceptance of an idea the result of intellectual competition, not emotional submission.

Recognize that group pressure influences you, even if you're anonymous and unaccountable to the group. The bandwagon effect is astoundingly powerful because people *don't recognize its power*. They just succumb to it, much like a snorkeler carried along by the ocean current. When a snorkeler is in the water, head down and watching the marine life, he doesn't notice that the current is carrying him down the coast. It's only when he surfaces and looks outside of the water that he can see how far he's traveled.

Likewise, when considering ideas, you need to look outside the group-influence current to see that you're being carried along without knowing it. *In the current is comfort, out of it is truth.*

When you see statistics like "90% of mechanics use brand A oil for their customers" or "95% of doctors recommend drug X," recognize this as a bandwagon play. The statistics may be true, but they don't prove that the oil the mechanics use is actually good oil or that you really do need drug X. Challenge statistical assertions by demanding that proponents show the product, service, or concept is *better* than its competitors, not just more popular.

*Belief Bias*
When evaluating the conclusion of an argument, determine *first* whether the

premises *necessarily imply* the conclusion. If they don't, then reject the conclusion. Belief bias arises when you accept a conclusion because it makes sense without verifying the logic before it.

*Confirmation Bias (and Disconfirmation Bias)*
Prepare to endure discomfort with information you *don't* want to know. Our confirmation bias seeks what we're comfortable knowing. You want comfort *and* you want truth, but sometimes you can't have both. The search for truth is often the uncomfortable confrontation with reality. Confirmation bias conceals reality.

Look for information that is *contrary* to what you've found. This is especially important when using popular Internet search engines, which, through algorithms, bias to sites concordant with user attitudes. Presume for a moment the contrary data is true. Get really uncomfortable with them. Feel the tension. Ask yourself why the data makes you feel so uncomfortable. Emotions are not the problem—submission to them is. This is the decision point where you overcome confirmation bias by seeing what you may not want to and analyzing the data objectively—while *still* feeling the tension.

Recognizing an episode of confirmation bias hands control of your inquiry and decision back to your *conscious* mind, instead of losing it to thoughtless filtering.

*Framing Effect*
To avoid succumbing to the framing effect, focus on *what* the numbers or qualities being presented are, not *how* they're presented. The essence of framing is that we emotionally respond to *how* something is conveyed rather than analyzing *what* is conveyed. For example, when told a car is "best in class mileage," ask, "what is the mileage?"

When someone presents "facts" to induce you to buy something or make a decision they have an interest in, presume the facts are framed. Evaluate how adjectives affect your emotions. (Superlatives, like "best," "top valued," "industry-leading," etc., are especially powerful.) The seller or proponent of the idea is attempting to bypass your evaluation of the item or idea by supplying *their* self-interested evaluation. Understand that manipulation, then reject the offer or decision until you find specific numbers or qualities that *you* can evaluate for yourself.

*Gambler's Fallacy*
Realize that the likelihood of an independent chance event occurring has nothing to do with how many times in the past it occurred. The chance for heads on a coin flip is 50/50 no matter how many billions of times heads showed up before the next flip.

Think of the term *random* as another word for *unpredictable*. If the flip of a coin, the timing of a particular proton's decay, or the final drop of a roulette ball is random, you can't predict in any instance the outcome. Expect the same uncertainty and probability for each random event as if it were the only one that ever happened, because in the world of probabilities, each one really exists as if no others ever happened.

*Halo Effect*
When assessing someone's character or readiness for a task, ignore factors that do not *directly* reveal the character traits or tasks you want the person to meet. For example, attention to detail in clothing is not *directly* relevant to attention to detail in reviewing reports. One can be detail-attentive to clothing but detail-indifferent to reports.

Have clear standards for what you're assessing. For example, the term "attention to detail" is vague. Does that mean *all* details of *all* things under *all* conditions? What details are relevant to your needs and what are not? Specify *what* details you want attention to, when those need attention, and whether the person displays the behaviors or traits so well you could predict they will display them when they're relevant to you.

*Hasty Generalization*
If you're going to make a generalized judgment, be sure your sample size is so large that the judgment will be reliable. A single episode or incident almost never justifies a generalization.

If you feel emotion about the event, check your reaction. If it's to generalize, you're *very* vulnerable to hasty generalization. Stop and ask whether that one evocative event is a large enough sample to prove to an objective third person that your generalization is *statistically* justified. In evocative cases where you leap to a hasty generalization, your emotions bypass your rational mind. Many cases deserve emotional responses, but emotional responses never deserve cognitive priority.

## Hindsight Bias

Do not believe the first facts you remember about the cause of an event. People easily and unknowingly tend to distort their memories about what led to an outcome. We seek simple, storylike explanations, which often suppress memories of other relevant facts that don't fit the story. "I knew it all along" is that kind of simplistic story that is often factually wrong. Ask, What *else* happened that I'm not remembering?

When judging another person's ability to have foreseen an outcome, remember that the more severe the outcome, the greater the tendency you will have to *mis*judge the foreseeability of the event. Ask first, What did the person actually *know* when they made the decision? Then ask, Have I completely considered *all* the facts the decision-maker considered? Research shows that when people know the outcome of another's decision, they tend to discount or forget event facts that are *not* consistent with the outcome, while being more likely to remember facts that *are* consistent with the outcome.[2] This distortion of memory is much of what you have to avoid. You can do that by reviewing and considering all the information the decision-maker knew. The more severe the outcome, the stronger the tendency to miss the existence and importance of facts the decision-maker was faced with.

It's easier to blame another for a severe outcome they couldn't foresee than it is to be rigorous in finding what they *could* foresee. Come to terms with your moral duty to *rigorously* judge the foreseeability of an outcome. You don't have the right to be lazy minded in these cases. Slow down and do the mental work. You may be guilty of producing injustice if you don't.

## Prosecutor's Fallacy

The prosecutor's fallacy works because it presents the extreme odds against an extremely unlikely event as "obvious proof" that it didn't happen. Presenting the one in a million odds of winning a particular game of chance as obvious proof that the winner cheated is an example of this. The obvious proof is a fallacy because it ignores alternative explanations that may be equally or more likely true.

When confronted with extreme odds as an explanation against something, always consider what other facts could account for it. *Improbable* doesn't mean *impossible*. Finally, consider supplementing the odds against a *particular* event with more general odds. For example, in the Sally Clark case, the odds of two babies from the same family and family profile dying of crib death in two years was extreme. But more generally, the odds of two babies from the same family and profile being *murdered* in two years was many times *less* likely. Look for alternatives when faced with obvious long-odds arguments.

*Semmelweis Effect*
The Semmelweis effect arises from a person's or group's belief that a widely or long-accepted practice or theory should be protected from revision, even when evidence suggests the revision is prudent. Because the power of the Semmelweis effect is the ease with which adherents of theories or practices devalue contrary evidence, there are helpful steps in neutralizing the Semmelweis.

First, see your (or another's) emotional resistance to the evidence as an obstacle to rational action. Our emotions are good signals of what we value, but they're poor signals of what is rational. If you value the comfort of preserving a theory more than you value the truth, expect emotional reactions when your theory is challenged. Your reactions aren't just telling you you're uncomfortable, they're subverting your thinking.

Recognize that the strong emotional reactions are blinding you. Your first step is to remove the emotional blinders. This is the point where the Semmelweis effect takes over: You feel the emotional resistance to challenge or change without knowing the resistance is hindering your rational thought.

Second, tentatively presume that the contrary evidence is true. If the evidence contrary to your theory were true, would the new theory necessarily (or probably) be true? If yes, then the rational decision is to revise or abandon your theory and accept the new one. If the new theory's evidence, if true, doesn't imply or make probable the new theory's argument, it fails the argument test.

Failing the argument test doesn't necessarily end the process. The new theory may still be worthy of further consideration if some of the variables were different. The argument test tells us only whether to accept or reject an argument *as presented*. It doesn't tell us whether the argument, *if improved*, might succeed. Resist not only the emotional impulse to preserve your theory, but resist the impulse to end your inquiry into competing theories merely because they're imperfect. Yours may be, too.

*Stereotyping*
See stereotyping as a hasty generalization fallacy often driven by emotion. When your emotions are strong—anger, fear, affection, indignation, etc.—you're far more likely to stereotype. When you feel the emotions, they are your signal to slow down your thinking. Your emotions easily jump to stereotyping unless you stop them.

Comparing the sample size with the group size will help reduce the emotional influences. Seeking larger-group statistics is a way to let your rational cognition slow down enough to withhold judgment until the best evidence opens your mind to facts your emotions obscure. Since stereotyping is assessing a larger group by experiencing only one or a few of the group, ask whether the group you have *not* seen would believe your stereotype of them. This thought experiment moves you from your perspective to another's, a technique that helps motivate fact-checking.

In this chapter, we've explored principles and strategies for knowing when to be most vigilant for cognitive biases and how to mitigate their effects. In the next chapter, we venture into broader territory where we explore not just techniques for avoiding bias, but even ideas that question what it means to be wrong.

**Questions for Reflection**
1. Name two situations where shortcut thinking is a threat or likely to fail.
2. Explain some ways of improving your thinking in conditions where shortcut thinking is a threat.
3. Pick two of the cognitive biases listed in the book. Explain the conditions when they may occur and how you would avoid their influence.

Chapter 15

# Integrating Thoughts on Clear Thinking

> The greatest obstacle to discovery is not ignorance—it is the illusion of knowledge.[1]
> —Daniel J. Boorstin, Historian and 12th Librarian of Congress

Most of us grew up in a culture where school systems rewarded fast, correct answers to problems, not slow, deliberate *questions* about problems. Some of that was expedient to learning. For instance, we learn the times tables by memorizing them and responding fast to simple tests. But as we mature, we face more complicated problems—problems that aren't tests of memorized facts.

These complex problems often require the discovery and deliberation of thoughtful questions to understand or solve. Yet the urge to provide a fast answer lurks in the background. Our well-rewarded childhood habit to answer fast still affects us.

We also learn from an early age many useful shortcuts in our thinking (*heuristics*, they're often called) that allow us to live normally. When we see similar events and their outcomes repeatedly, for example, we don't have to think through them every time the same way we did the first time. These shortcuts from experience allow us more time and energy for other decisions.

The problem with our childhood rewards for fast answers and our many useful mental shortcuts is that they contribute to our vulnerability to dozens of cognitive biases, some of which we've talked about in this book. Since cognitive biases distract us from asking important questions, we need to know where cognitive biases are likely to occur and what questions they may hide.

What follows are some simple practices that help avoid bias and fast-answer habit traps. They can also help create or identify questions that our biases and habits won't naturally seek. These methods may at first feel unnatural or even somewhat artificial. We should expect that feeling because our minds often resist the discipline and work needed to overcome our natural mental laziness.

*If the decision has a high value, it deserves the work. The most arduous work is overcoming the resistance to seeking questions whose answers solve your problem.*

**Suggested Practices in High-Value Decisions**
*Write alternatives* to your conclusion or decision, even if you think your initial option is right. Then write the best arguments for the alternatives below each one. The act of writing, among other things, slows your thinking and presents facts in a way that's more difficult to ignore. Biases make facts easier to ignore, but writing alternatives to your (likely biased) conclusions weakens your biases and strengthens your thinking.

*Ask others* you trust to critique your conclusion. However, don't explain to your critics how you arrived at your conclusion to avoid framing or anchoring your reasoning and, thus, distorting your helpers' thinking.

*Look for cases* like the one you're dealing with, especially on large projects. One of the easiest traps to fall into is the *planning fallacy*, where our estimates are unrealistically close to best-case scenarios. In these situations, reviewing statistics would be informative.[2] Compare your estimates with the statistics of similar situations.

In long group projects, do a *pre-mortem* (sometimes called *prospective hindsight*). Assemble the team in a room together. Tell everyone to imagine that the project has been completed, and that it's such an utter disaster that everyone outside your team knows about it and is shocked at how bad it is. Let your team think on that for a minute in silence, then have them write down what they think caused the disaster. This needs to be done individually without people talking with each other. After everyone's done writing, go one-by-one around the table and have them recite their lists. You'll discover insights and dangers to act on now before the things they thought of come to pass. Part of the reason this works is that it enables everyone to view the project from a perspective devoid of optimism bias and groupthink.

*Reduce reliance* on your memory. Where you can find data independent of your personal recollection, use it.

*After the Fact: Do Results Tell Us the Truth about Our Thinking?*
The results of a decision often do not prove whether we have or haven't thought clearly. Some successes occur because forces beyond our control or foreknowledge caused them; some failures occur the same way.

Further, our hindsight bias makes events look inevitable, even when they weren't. Under the influence of hindsight bias, we are particularly susceptible to thinking poorly after and about a decision. We're also emotionally biased to accept credit for success and to evade blame for failure, an effect sometimes referred to as *self-serving bias*.[3] These influences erode our long-term learning and thinking by making it easy to judge a decision by its outcome, not by the quality of our thinking that contributed to it. We could, for example, look back on a success and in a similar situation in the future, take the same actions, only to fail because the factor that *really* caused the earlier success was missing in our failed case. We didn't know it because we enjoyed the emotional illusion that success proved we thought clearly. The tendency to judge decisions by their outcome is often referred to as *outcome bias*.

## Long-Term Improved Thinking
The power in working to eliminate outcome bias is significantly improved decision-making and problem-solving over the long term. The disciplined questioning that comes after an important outcome applies equally to "successful" and "failed" outcomes. This is a crucial point. In the long term, *the outcome isn't as important as the process that produced it.* That's why you ask at least these five questions no matter what outcome you're reviewing:

- What factors beyond our control contributed to this outcome?
- What factors within our control contributed to this outcome?
- What cognitive biases were likely at play?
- What will we do next time?
- In response to every question, ask: How do we know that?

These questions seem obvious, but our biases often blind us from asking them when we need to. The very best teams in the world use these questions to sharpen their performance to extraordinary levels. This is especially true of those whose lives depend on continually improving their thinking and actions (like Navy SEALS, elite SWAT teams, astronauts in training). Individuals like top-tier Olympic athletes ask them, too. They do the work of negating outcome bias because their decisions matter—and they thrive on continually higher levels of performance.

If you want to think clearly over the long term, improve your performance over the long term, or need to make important decisions over the long term, then you need to review your decisions after-the-fact with at least the answers to these listed questions.

## Rethinking "Failure" and "Wrong"

In the previous paragraph, I (Mark) put quotes around "successful" and "failed." The reason was to prompt consideration about layered or alternative meanings of these terms. Here I suggest some answers and some ways of thinking about them that can improve your thinking and decision-making. I don't take credit for inventing them. Many others have written on these concepts, and I merely pass on their wisdom here because it's relevant to long-term thinking.

First, when we conceive of an outcome as a failure, we may have entered a faulty dilemma. A faulty dilemma is a claim that there are only two possible answers to a question—*only* A or *only* B—when there really are other options available. In many cases an outcome needn't be either a success or a failure. It could be something else.

What is that something else?

Many important decisions, made under conditions of uncertainty, are complex. We may have incomplete data, unpredictable variables, or face conditions beyond our control. We make do with what we have even though we don't have it all. Because we don't have all the data, we're trying to decide what's *most likely* to work. The decision thus becomes a *probability estimate*. Framing a decision as a probability estimate has some advantages. One of them is that when the outcome occurs, you're no longer determining whether the outcome was a success or failure. You're recognizing that, given the probabilities, the outcome was within them.

Here's how that could look. If you assess an 80% probability for your desired outcome and the desired outcome doesn't happen, the outcome isn't a failure. It fell within the 20% of outcome possibilities you stated up front. Your prediction was *accurate* or *right* or *true* because the outcome fell within the 20% that you said was possible. If you predicted the probability was 100%, and the prediction didn't come true, *that* would be a failed prediction. When we understand that we won't have 100% predictive power in complex decisions in conditions of uncertainty, then we can finally avoid the faulty dilemma of "failure or success." Instead, we conceive of complex decisions in conditions of uncertainty as what they are: probability estimates that can often be improved now when we ask the right questions about the past.

Another way of looking at it comes from science. Let's consider an idealized scientist. If they conduct an experiment to test a hypothesis, is the experiment a failure if it doesn't prove the hypothesis? The answer, in the practice of science, is no. The experiment showed that under given conditions a specific outcome occurred. The experiment added new data to the broader body of knowledge. In that regard, every experiment rigorously testing a previously untested hypothesis is a success no matter what the outcome.

A decision you make is like a scientific hypothesis, tested not in a controlled lab, but in the wild. Our idealized scientist has the advantage of controlling the variables. In your decision experiments, you can't. You usually don't know them all. You know you face uncertainties the idealized scientist does not. But the outcome you hypothesize is still a hypothesis, tempered by probabilities you estimate without knowing all the variables. And when the result is in, your outcome review is the search for variables you didn't know before. Your experiment is a success *when you learn from your predictions*. When you see your decisions as experiments that afterwards inform your future decisions, you've escaped the faulty success-failure dilemma.

**Probabilities and Beliefs**

The use of probability estimates is remarkably useful for describing empirical beliefs that aren't necessarily decisions. For example, if I believe Earth is about 4.6 billion years old, I can estimate a probability that my belief is accurate. It may not be precise, but it doesn't have to be. I could, for instance, say about the age-of-the-earth claim, "I wasn't there when Earth was made, so my belief about its age isn't 100%. But I've seen a lot of indirect measurements, each of which had its own probability below 100%. So, I give my belief about an 80% probability of accuracy. Since I'm not 100%, I'm open to what new measurements could do to move my estimate."

An advantage of using probability estimates in empirical beliefs is that doing so corresponds to the real world. We rarely have exhaustive knowledge about anything nontrivial. Most people know that, but few act as if they do.

*Cherished Beliefs*

Our beliefs about deeply meaningful empirical claims—such as whether Jesus rose from the dead or whether the origin of life is divine or naturalistic—rely on facts no one has exhaustive knowledge about. No one alive today saw Jesus crucified and resurrected. No one alive today saw life created. Nor does anyone have all and only indisputable facts that would offer 100% certainty either way. The best we can hope for is evidence of things not seen, and from that, a degree of *probability* that our belief is true. Belief is based on evidence available to us *at the moment*. Thus, we are intellectually honest when we use a probability estimate like, "I give this a 95% probability because of the evidence," instead of saying, "This is just true."

Even in the face of contrary evidence, it's emotionally difficult to admit that deeply held beliefs about empirical claims are wrong. A benefit of using rough probability estimates in describing one's beliefs is that we need not fear being wrong. Any expressed probability under 100% is a correct statement if it roughly depicts your state of knowledge. If overwhelming evidence reduces your previous 95% probability estimate to 10%, it makes adjusting your stance easier. You weren't "wrong." In the face of new evidence, you merely adjusted your probability estimate to conform to the evidence. And you may do it in either direction later as you encounter new evidence.

*Probabilities Encouraging Conversations*
Using probability estimates in your conversations about your beliefs can also make it easier for people to help you learn new things. They don't have to worry about calling you "wrong." They can easily see that you're open to other possibilities, encouraging them to offer you alternatives to your ideas.

Using probability estimates, you can go from being shunned as dogmatic to being welcomed as open to hearing and learning. You encourage the same openness in those who speak to you. You can even hand it back by asking them what *they* think the probability of their belief is, encouraging the back-and-forth inquiry into the *evidence*, not a battle to prove who's "right." You create in yourself—and others—the intellectual humility characteristic of the greatest thinkers in the world. You give answers to anyone who asks you reasons for your belief in a way that is gracious and respectful, with the clear conscience of intellectual humility.

## Concluding Remarks: Faith, Science, and Clear Thinking
*Faith*, as we use it here, is the exercise of belief in something nontrivial, based on evidence to support the belief. We distinguish this from *blind faith*, which is holding belief based merely on feelings in the absence of evidence. Blind faith is often wishful thinking.

Both the scientist and the religious believer operate in faith. Both make empirical claims, have evidence to believe them, but lack exhaustive knowledge to certify them. Both can make probability estimates for their beliefs, then test them against rival theories or contrary evidence, and adjust if needed. They can do this with each other. When the scientist and the Christian realize that both operate in probability estimates, and thus in faith, both can more easily adopt the intellectual humility to hear the other out.

They can also move from empirical faith to philosophy, enriching their thinking as they apply logic and rigorous reasoning, sensitive to cognitive bias, to explore the philosophical implications of the empirical claims. Their work together invites a search for meaning, even as it opens them to thoughtful learning, including learning to decide what really matters.

May we humbly follow Christ—the supreme model of clear thinking in a messy world—in his flawless logic, skillful reasoning, and unbiased cognition, while speaking and seeking only the truth in love.

**Questions for Reflection**
1. Think of an important problem you worked on recently. Which of the "Suggested Practices in High-Value Decisions" could you have used more effectively?
2. How could the self-serving bias affect your ability to develop as a thinker?
3. How could rethinking your use of the terms *failure* or *success* improve the quality of your thinking?
4. How could conveying your beliefs as probabilities, rather than as "true" or "false," improve your discourse with those who disagree with you?

# Bibliography

Adler, Mortimer J. *A Guidebook to Learning: For the Lifelong Pursuit of Wisdom*. New York: Macmillan, 1986.
———. *How to Speak How to Listen*. New York: Collier Books, Macmillan, 1983.
———. *How to Think about the Great Ideas: From the Great Books of Western Civilization*. Edited by Max Weismann. Chicago: Open Court, 2000.
———. *Intellect: Mind over Matter*. New York: Macmillan, 1990.
———. *Reforming Education: The Opening of the American Mind*. Edited by Geraldine Van Doren. New York: Macmillan, 1977.
Adler, Mortimer J. and Charles Van Doren. *How to Read a Book: The Classic Guide to Intelligent Reading*. New York: Simon and Schuster, 1972.
Angeles, Peter A. *The HarperCollins Dictionary of Philosophy*. 2nd ed. New York: HarperCollins, 1992.
Aristotle. *The Organon*. Translated by Octavius Frere Owen. Augsburg, Bavaria, Germany: Jazzybee Verlag, 2015.
Augustine. *Confessions*. Translated by Pine-Coffin. New York: Penguin Books, 1961.
Baird, Forrest E. *How Do We Reason? An Introduction to Logic*. Downers Grove, IL: InterVarsity Press, 2021.
Blamires, Harry. *The Christian Mind: How Should a Christian Think?* Vancouver, B.C. Canada: Regent College Publishing, 2005.
Boice, James Montgomery. *Renewing Your Mind in a Mindless World: Learning to Think and Act Biblically*. Grand Rapids, MI: Kregel, 2009.
Breshears, Jefrey D. *C. S. Lewis on Politics, Government, and the Good Society: Relevant Insights and Sage Wisdom for Contemporary Christians*. Knox, ME: Centre Pointe Publishing, 2020.
Clark, Gordon. *Logic*. Unicoi, TN: Trinity, 2004.
Copi, Irving, M. and Carl Cohen. *Introduction to Logic*. 10th ed. Upper Saddle River, NJ: Prentice Hall, 1998.
Craig, William Lane. *Learning Logic*. Illustrated by Marli Renee. Spartanburg, SC: CreateSpace, 2014.
Damer, T. Edward. *Attacking Faulty Reasoning: A Practical Guide to Fallacy-Free Arguments*. 4th ed. Belmont, CA: Wadsworth, 1995.
Davis, John Jefferson. *Handbook of Basic Bible Texts: Every Key Passage for the Study of Doctrine*

*and Theology*. Grand Rapids, MI: Zondervan, 1984.
Dickinson, Travis. *Logic and the Way of Jesus: Thinking Critically and Christianly*. Nashville, TN: B&H, 2022.
Dienar, David. *Plato: The Great Philosopher-Educator*. Camp Hill, PA: Classic Academic Press, 2015.
Gamble, Richard M., ed. *The Great Tradition: Classic Readings on What It Means to Be an Educated Human Being*. Wilmington, DE: ISI Books, 2007.
Geisler, Norman L. and Ronald M. Brooks. *Come, Let Us Reason: An Introduction to Logical Thinking*. Grand Rapids, MI: Baker Books, 1990.
Groothuis, Douglas. *On Jesus*. Belmont, CA: Thomson Wadsworth, 2003.
Guinness, Os. *Fit Bodies Fat Minds: Why Evangelicals Don't Think and What to Do about It*. Grand Rapids, MI: Baker Books, 1994.
Hannam, James. *The Genesis of Science: How the Christian Middle Ages Launched the Scientific Revolution*. Washington, DC: Regnery, 2011.
Hirsch. E. D. Jr., Joseph F. Kett, and James Trefil. *The New Dictionary of Cultural Literacy: What Every American Needs to Know*. Revised and updated, 3rd ed. Boston: Houghton Mifflin, 2002.
Hitz, Zena. *Lost in Thought: The Hidden Pleasures of an Intellectual Life*. Princeton, NJ: Princeton University Press, 2020.
Holland, Tom. *Dominion: How the Christian Revolution Remade the World*. New York: Basic Books, 2019.
Hooykaas, R. *Religion and the Rise of Modern Science*. Grand Rapids, MI: Eerdmans, 1972.
Horner, Grant. *John Milton: Classical Learning and the Progress of Virtue*. Camp Hill, PA: Classic Academic Press, 2015.
Hudson, Deal W. *How to Keep from Losing Your Mind: Educating Yourself Classically to Survive Cultural Indoctrination*. Charlotte, NC: Tan Books, 2019.
———. *365 Days of Catholic Wisdom: A Treasury of Truth, Goodness, and Beauty*. Gastonia, NC: Tan Books, 2020.
Hurley, Patrick J. *A Concise Introduction to Logic*. 12th ed. Stamford, CT: Centage Learning, 2015.
———. *Logic: The Essentials*. Stamford, CT: Centage Learning, 2016.
Josephson, John R. and Susan G. Josephson, eds. *Abductive Inference: Computation, Philosophy, Technology*. New York: Cambridge University Press, 1996.
Kahneman, D. *Thinking, Fast and Slow*. New York: Farrar, Straus and Giroux, 2011.
Kirby, Gary and Jeffery R. Goodpaster. *Thinking*. Englewood Cliffs, NJ: Prentice Hall, 1995.
Kreeft, Peter. *Socratic Logic: A Logic Text Using Socratic Method, Platonic Questions, and Aristotelian Principles*. 2nd ed. Edited by Trent Dougherty. South Bend, IN: St. Augustine's Press, 2005.
Kreeft, Peter. *Wisdom of the Heart: The Good, the True, and the Beautiful at the Center of Us All*. Gastonia, NC: Tan Books, 2020.
Lee, Zach. *Logic for Christians: Critical Thinking for the People of God*. Houston, TX: Lucid Books, 2021.
Lehman, Jeffrey S. *Augustine: Rejoicing in the Truth*. Camp Hill, PA: Classic Academic Press, 2018.
Lehner, Ulrich L. *Think Better: Unlocking the Power of Reason*. Grand Rapids, MI: Baker Academic, 2021.
Lewis, C. S. *The Abolition of Man: How Education Develops Man's Sense of Morality*. New York:

Macmillan, 1978.
Markos, Louis. *C. S. Lewis: An Apologist for Education*. Camp Hill, PA: Classic Academic Press, 2015.
McAdams, John. *JFK Assassination Logic: How to Think about Claims of Conspiracy*. Sterling, VA: Potomac Books, 2011.
McGrath, Alister E. *Surprised by Meaning: Science, Faith, and How We Make Sense of Things*. Louisville, KY: Westminster John Knox Press, 2011.
Miller, Ed L. *God and Reason: An Invitation to Philosophical Theology*. 2nd ed. Saddle River, NJ: Prentice Hall, 1995.
Miller, Ed L. and Jon Jensen. *Questions That Matter: An Invitation to Philosophy*. 6th ed. New York: McGraw-Hill, 2004.
Moore, Brook Noel and Richard Parker. *Critical Thinking*. 7th ed. New York: McGraw-Hill, 2004.
Moreland, J. P. *Love Your God with All Your Mind: The Role of Reason in the Life of the Soul*. Revised. Colorado Springs, CO: NavPress, 2012.
Moreland, J. P. and Mark Matlock. *Smart Faith: Loving Your God with All Your Mind*. Colorado Springs, CO: Think, 2005.
Nance, James B. and Douglas J. Wilson. *Introductory Logic: For Christian and Home Schools*. 4th ed. Revised and Expanded. Moscow, ID: Canon Press, 2006.
Nash, Ronald H. *Life's Ultimate Questions: An Introduction to Philosophy*. Grand Rapids, MI: Zondervan, 1999.
Naugle, David K. *Philosophy: A Student's Guide*. Wheaton, IL: Crossway, 2012.
Noll, Mark A. *Jesus Christ and the Life of the Mind*. Grand Rapids, MI: Eerdmans, 2011.
———. *The Scandal of the Evangelical Mind*. Grand Rapids, MI: Eerdmans, 1994.
Pascal, Blaise. *Pensées*. New York: Penguin Books, 1966.
Pearcy, Nancy and Charles B. Thaxton. *The Soul of Science: Christian Faith & Natural Philosophy*. Wheaton, IL: Crossway, 1994.
Pennington, Jonathan T. *Jesus the Great Philosopher: Rediscovering the Wisdom Needed for the Good Life*. Grand Rapids, MI: Brazos Press, 2020.
Perrin, Christopher A. *An Introduction to Classical Education*. Camp Hill, PA: Classic Academic Press, 2004.
Plantinga, Alvin. *Knowledge and Christian Belief*. Grand Rapids, MI: Eerdmans, 2015.
Plantinga, Alvin and Nicholas Wolterstorff, eds. *Faith and Rationality: Reason and Belief in God*. Notre Dame, IN: University of Notre Dame Press, 1983.
Plato, *The Republic*. Translated by Desmond Lee. New York: Penguin Books, 2007.
Pojman, Louis P. *Philosophy: The Quest for Truth*. 4th ed. Belmont, CA: Wadsworth, 1999.
Poythress, Vern Sheridan. *Logic: A God Centered Approach to the Foundation of Western Thought*. Wheaton, IL: Crossway, 2013.
Priest, Graham. *Logic: A Very Short Introduction*. 2nd ed. Oxford, UK: Oxford University Press, 2017.
Rana, Fazale with Hugh Ross. *Who Was Adam? A Creation Model Approach to the Origin of Humanity*. 2nd ed. Covina, CA: RTB Press, 2015.
Rana, Fazale R. with Kenneth R. Samples. *Humans 2.0: Scientific, Philosophical, and Theological Perspectives on Transhumanism*. Covina, CA: RTB Press, 2019.
Reynolds, John Mark. *When Athens Met Jerusalem: An Introduction to Classical and Christian Thought*. Downers Grove, IL: InterVarsity, 2009.
Ryken, Leland and Glenda Faye Mathes. *Recovering the Lost Art of Reading: A Quest for the True, the Good, and the Beautiful*. Wheaton, IL: Crossway, 2021.

Samples, Kenneth Richard. *A World of Difference: Putting Christian Truth Claims to the Worldview Test*. Grand Rapids, MI: Baker Books, 2007.
———. *Christian Endgame: Careful Thinking about the End Times*. Covina, CA: RTB Press, 2013.
———. *Christianity Cross-Examined: Is It Rational, Relevant, and Good?* Covina, CA: RTB Press, 2021.
———. *Classic Christian Thinkers: An Introduction*. Covina, CA: RTB Press, 2019.
———. *God among Sages: Why Jesus Is Not Just Another Religious Leader*. Grand Rapids, MI: Baker Books, 2019.
———. *7 Truths That Changed the World: Discovering Christianity's Most Dangerous Ideas*. Grand Rapids, MI: Baker Books, 2012.
———. *Without a Doubt: Answering the 20 Toughest Faith Questions*. Grand Rapids, MI: Baker Books, 2004.
Schall, James V. *A Students Guide to Liberal Learning: Liberal Learning Guide*. Wilmington, DE: Intercollegiate Studies Institute, 2019.
———. *The Life of the Mind: On the Joys and Travails of Thinking*. Wilmington, DE: Intercollegiate Studies Institute, 2008.
Sire, James W. *Habits of the Mind: Intellectual Life as a Christian Calling*. Downers Grove, IL: InterVarsity, 2022.
Smith, David L. *John Amos Comenius: A Visionary Reformer of Schools*. Camp Hill, PA: Classic Academic Press, 2015.
Spence, Gerry. *How to Argue and Win Every Time: At Home, at Work, in Court, Everywhere*. New York: Macmillan, 1995.
Spitzer, Robert J. *Ten Universal Principles: A Brief Philosophy of the Life Issues*. San Francisco, CA: Ignatius Press, 2011.
Stott, John. *Your Mind Matters*. Downers Grove, IL: InterVarsity, 1972.
Turley, Stephen R. *Awakening Wonder: A Classical Guide to Truth, Goodness & Beauty*. Camp Hill, PA: Classical Academic Press, 2014.
Vaughn, Lewis. *The Power of Critical Thinking: Effective Reasoning about Ordinary and Extraordinary Claims*. 3rd ed. Oxford, UK: University Press, 2010.
Weaver, Richard M. *In Defense of Tradition: Collected Shorter Writings of Richard M. Weaver, 1929–1963*. Edited by Ted J. Smith III. Indianapolis, IN: Liberty Fund, 2000.
Woods. Robert M. *Mortimer Adler: The Paideia Way of Classical Education*. Camp Hill, PA: Classical Academic Press, 2019.

# Notes

**Acknowledgments**
1. Francis Bacon, *The Essays of Francis Bacon: The Fifty-Nine Essays* (Le Verguier, France: Adansonia Press, 2018), "Of Studies," 88.

**Introduction: Why Christians Need to Be Clear Thinkers**
1. Mark A. Noll, *The Scandal of the Evangelical Mind* (Grand Rapids, MI: Eerdmans, 1994); Os Guinness, *Fit Bodies Fat Minds: Why Evangelicals Don't Think and What to Do about It* (Grand Rapids, MI: Baker, 1994); Mark A. Noll, *Jesus Christ and the Life of the Mind* (Grand Rapids, MI: Eerdmans, 2011); J. P. Moreland, *Love Your God with All Your Mind: The Role of Reason in the Life of the Soul*, revised (Colorado Springs, CO: NavPress, 2012).
2. C. S. Lewis, *Mere Christianity* (New York: Macmillan, 1952), 75.
3. Lewis, *Mere Christianity*, 75.

**Chapter 1: Christianity and the Life of the Mind**
1. Ronald H. Nash, *Worldviews in Conflict: Choosing Christianity in a World of Ideas* (Grand Rapids, MI: Zondervan, 1992), 74.
2. I'm influenced here by Dallas Willard, "Jesus the Logician," *Christian Scholar's Review* 28, no. 4 (1999): 605–614, dwillard.org/articles/jesus-the-logician; Travis Dickinson, "Jesus the Logician," chap. 2 in *Logic and the Way of Jesus: Thinking Critically and Christianly* (Nashville, TN: B & H, 2022); and Douglas Groothuis, "Jesus' Use of Argument," chap. 3 in *On Jesus* (Belmont, CA: Thomson Wadsworth, 2003).
3. For a broad comparison of Jesus with Krishna, Buddha, Confucius, and Muhammad, see Kenneth Richard Samples, *God among Sages: Why Jesus Is Not Just Another Religious Leader* (Grand Rapids, MI: Baker Books, 2017).
4. Willard, "Jesus the Logician."
5. Grant R. Osborne, *The Hermeneutical Spiral: A Comprehensive Introduction to Biblical Interpretation* (Downers Grove, IL: InterVarsity Press, 2006), 291–302.
6. Dickinson, *Logic and the Way of Jesus*, 41.
7. Groothuis, *On Jesus*, 32.
8. Dickinson, *Logic and the Way of Jesus*, 37.
9. R. C. Sproul, "Thinking Like Jesus," Ligonier, October 1, 2012, ligonier.org/learn/articles/thinking-like-jesus.
10. See Kenneth Richard Samples, *A World of Difference: Putting Christian Truth-Claims to the*

*Worldview Test* (Grand Rapids, MI: Baker Books, 2007), 80–81.
11. For many within the historic Christian tradition saving faith is viewed distinctly as the gift of God (Acts 13:48; 1 Corinthians 12:3; Ephesians. 2:8–9; Hebrews 12:2). For a helpful biblical discussion of how faith is a sovereign gift of God, see Anthony A. Hoekema, *Saved by Grace* (Grand Rapids, MI: Eerdmans, 1989), 143–145.
12. Greg Koukl, "Are Faith and Reason Compatible?," Stand to Reason, December 13, 2011, str.org/w/are-faith-and-reason-compatible.
13. Larry Hurtado, "Early Christianity: A 'Bookish' Religion," *Larry Hurtado's Blog*, January 15, 2016, larryhurtado.wordpress.com/2016/01/15/early-christianity-a-bookish-religion/.
14. Mark A. Noll, *The Scandal of the Evangelical Mind* (Grand Rapids, MI: Eerdmans, 1994); Os Guinness, *Fit Bodies Fat Minds: Why Evangelicals Don't Think and What to Do about It* (Grand Rapids, MI: Baker, 1994); Mark A. Noll, *Jesus Christ and the Life of the Mind* (Grand Rapids, MI: Eerdmans, 2011); J. P. Moreland, *Love Your God with All Your Mind: The Role of Reason in the Life of the Soul*, revised (Colorado Springs, CO: NavPress, 2012).
15. "Six Reasons Young Christians Leave Church," *Barna*, September 27, 2011, barna.com/research/six-reasons-young-christians-leave-church/.
16. Jaroslav Pelikan, *The Christian Tradition: A History of the Development of Doctrine*, vol. 1, *The Emergence of the Catholic Tradition: 100–600* (Chicago: University of Chicago Press, 1971), 1.
17. See Kenneth Richard Samples, *Classic Christian Thinkers: An Introduction* (Covina, CA: RTB Press, 2019) for an introduction to the lives and beliefs of Irenaeus, Athanasius, Augustine, Anselm, Aquinas, Luther, Calvin, Pascal, and C. S. Lewis.
18. Mark A. Noll, *Jesus Christ and the Life of the Mind* (Grand Rapids, MI: Eerdmans, 2011), x.
19. C. S. Lewis, *Mere Christianity* (New York: Macmillan, 1952), 75.

**Chapter 2: Why Study Logic?**
1. Thomas Jefferson, *The Life and Selected Writings of Thomas Jefferson: Including the Autobiography, The Declaration of Independence & His Public and Private Letters* (Modern Library Classics) (New York: Random House, 2004), 651.
2. For a detailed discussion of the Christian views concerning the *imago Dei* and the intellectual endowments connected with it, see Kenneth Richard Samples, *7 Truths That Changed the World: Discovering Christianity's Most Dangerous Ideas* (Grand Rapids, MI: Baker Books, 2012), chaps. 11 and 12.
3. Mortimer J. Adler, "The Confusion of the Animalists," Radical Academy, accessed October 12, 2023, radicalacademy.org/adleranimalists.html; see also Mortimer J. Adler, *The Difference of Man and the Difference It Makes* (New York: Fordham University Press, 1993).
4. See the discussion of human exceptionalism and science in Kenneth Richard Samples, *Christianity Cross-Examined: Is It Rational, Relevant, and Good?* (Covina, CA: RTB Press, 2021), 32–34.
5. For a discussion of the human capacity for symbolism and its relationship to human exceptionalism, see James R. Hurford, "Human Uniqueness, Learned Symbols and Recursive Thought," *European Review* 12, no. 4 (2004): 551–565, lel.ed.ac.uk/~jim/europeanreview.html.
6. See Mortimer J. Adler, *Intellect: Mind over Matter* (New York: Macmillan, 1990).
7. Hugh Ross, "Five Best Scientific Evidences for the God of the Bible," *Today's New Reason to Believe* (blog), Reasons to Believe, June 4, 2018, reasons.org/explore/blogs/todays-new-reason-to-believe/read/todays-new-reason-to-believe/2018/06/04/five-best-scientific-

evidences-for-the-god-of-the-bible. For more about human exceptionalism, see Fazale Rana with Hugh Ross, *Who Was Adam? A Creation Model Approach to the Origin of Humanity*, 2nd ed. (Covina, CA: RTB Press, 2015), 313–325.

8. Peter Kreeft, *Socratic Logic: A Logic Text Using Socratic Method, Platonic Questions, and Aristotelian Principles*, 2nd ed., ed. Trent Dougherty (South Bend, IN: St. Augustine's Press, 2005), 1.
9. Ed L. Miller, *Questions That Matter: An Invitation to Philosophy*, 4th ed. (New York: McGraw-Hill, 1996), 31.
10. Gary R. Kirby and Jeffery R. Goodpaster, *Thinking* (Englewood Cliffs, NJ: Prentice Hall, 1995), xiii.
11. Kenneth Richard Samples "The 3 Transcendentals: Truth, Goodness, & Beauty," *Reflections* (blog), Reasons to Believe, February 2, 2021, reasons.org/explore/blogs/reflections/the-3-transcendentals-truth-goodness-beauty.
12. Robert P. George (@McCormickProf), "Why can't people understand the difference—and the importance of the difference—between education (good) and indoctrination (bad)? This is NOT hard. It is not a 'fine line.' Teaching young people HOW to think (carefully, critically) is different from telling them WHAT to think," Twitter, March 18, 2018, 8:44 a.m., twitter.com/McCormickProf/status/975367345773391872.
13. Lewis Vaughn, *The Power of Critical Thinking: Effective Reasoning about Ordinary and Extraordinary Claims*, 3rd ed. (Oxford, UK: Oxford University Press, 2009), 4.
14. T. Edward Damer, *Attacking Faulty Reasoning: A Practical Guide to Fallacy-Free Arguments*, 3rd ed. (Belmont, CA: Wadsworth, 1995), 3. We use Damer's excellent book as one of our required textbooks when we teach college courses in logic and critical thinking.
15. Nathan Harden, "2020 College Free Speech Rankings Reveal Crisis on Campus," Real Clear Education, September 29, 2020, realcleareducation.com/articles/2020/09/29/2020_college_free_speech_rankings_reveal_crisis_on_campus_110476.html.
16. John "Jay" Ellison, Dean of Students, The University of Chicago, news.uchicago.edu/sites/default/files/attachments/Dear_Class_of_2020_Students.pdf.
17. Ulrich L. Lehner, *Think Better: Unlocking the Power of Reason* (Grand Rapids, MI: Baker Academic, 2021), 5.
18. The Committee on Freedom of Expression, University of Chicago, "Report of the Committee on Freedom of Expression," provost.uchicago.edu/sites/default/files/documents/reports/FOECommitteeReport.pdf.
19. Vaughn, *Power of Critical Thinking*, 8.
20. Zach Lee, *Logic for Christians: Critical Thinking for the People of God* (Houston, TX: Lucid Books, 2021), 6.
21. See Peter A. Angeles, s.v. "Laws of Thought, The Three," in *The HarperCollins Dictionary of Philosophy*, 2nd ed. (New York: HarperCollins, 1992), 167; Ronald H. Nash, *Life's Ultimate Questions: An Introduction to Philosophy* (Grand Rapids, MI: Zondervan, 1999) 193–208.
22. Angeles, s.v. "Laws of Thought, The Three."
23. Mortimer J. Adler, *Intellect: Mind over Matter* (New York: Macmillan, 1990), 185.
24. Wikiquote, s.v. "Meditations" by Marcus Aurelius, Book IV, (3), last modified March 15, 2023, 08:57, en.wikiquote.org/wiki/Marcus_Aurelius#Meditations (c._AD_121–180).
25. Kreeft, *Socratic Logic*, 1.
26. Robert P. George (@McCormickProf), "Students: May I suggest a couple of New Year's resolutions? 1) If you don't have a smart friend who disagrees with you about important things that you deeply care about, make one. 2) Resist groupthink and self-censorship. Think for

yourself; seek the truth; speak your mind," Twitter, January 1, 2022, 3:54 p.m., twitter.com/McCormickProf/status/1477427962400157700. Robert P. George is McCormick Professor of Jurisprudence and Director of the James Madison Program in American Ideals and Institutions at Princeton University.
27. For a discussion of postmodernism, see Kenneth Richard Samples, *A World of Difference: Putting Christian Truth-Claims to the Worldview Test* (Grand Rapids, MI: Baker Books, 2007), chap. 13. For a critique of identity politics and critical race theory, see Jefrey D. Breshears, *American Crisis: Cultural Marxism and The Culture War: A Christian Response* (Knox, ME: Centre-Pointe, 2020); For a case for identity politics and critical race theory, see Robin DiAngelo, *White Fragility: Why It's So Hard for White People to Talk about Racism* (Boston: Beacon Press, 2018).
28. T. Edward Damer, *Attacking Faulty Reasoning*, 1.
29. Centre for Clinical Psychology, "Basic Emotions," ccp.net.au/basic-emotions/.
30. Damer, *Attacking Faulty Reasoning*, 2.
31. Kreeft, *Socratic Logic*, 5.
32. Ed L. Miller, *God and Reason: An Invitation to Philosophical Theology*, 2nd ed. (Saddle River: NJ, Prentice Hall, 1995), 2.
33. Lehner, *Think Better*, 5.

**Chapter 3: The Basic Elements of Logical Arguments**
1. Peter Kreeft, *Socratic Logic: A Logic Text Using Socratic Method, Platonic Questions, and Aristotelian Principles*, 2nd ed., ed Trent Dougherty (South Bend, IN: St. Augustine's Press, 2005), 8.
2. Peter A. Angeles, s.v. "argument" in *The HarperCollins Dictionary of Philosophy*, 2nd ed. (New York: HarperCollins Publisher, 1992), 20.
3. Ed L. Miller, *Questions That Matter: An Invitation to Philosophy*, 4th ed. (New York: McGraw-Hill, 1996), 51.
4. Patrick J. Hurley, *A Concise Introduction to Logic*, 8th ed. (Belmont, CA: Wadsworth, 2003), 1. We use Hurley's excellent book as one of the required textbooks when we teach college courses in logic and critical thinking.
5. Damer, *Attacking Faulty Reasoning: A Practical Guide to Fallacy-Free Arguments*, 4th ed. (Belmont, CA: Wadsworth, 2001), 4.
6. Damer, *Attacking Faulty Reasoning*, 12.
7. Miller, *Questions That Matter*, 31.
8. Miller, *Questions That Matter*, 46–51; Damer, *Attacking Faulty Reasoning*, 6.
9. The construction of our "TRACKS" acrostic was first influenced by Damer, *Attacking Faulty Reasoning*, 12–23. This topic is an expansion of what is found in Kenneth Richard Samples, *A World of Difference: Putting Christian Truth-Claims to the Worldview Test* (Grand Rapids, MI: Baker Books, 2007), 48.
10. Damer, *Attacking Faulty Reasoning*, 6.
11. Kreeft, *Socratic Logic*, 29.
12. Damer, *Attacking Faulty Reasoning*, 13.
13. Our term "adequate support" generally covers what T. Edward Damer refers to as the acceptability and sufficient grounds criteria. See Damer, *Attacking Faulty Reasoning*, 14–16.
14. Damer, *Attacking Faulty Reasoning*, 28.
15. See President's Commission on the Assassination of President Kennedy, "Chapter 3: The Shots from the Texas School Book Depository," in *Report of the President's Commission on*

the Assassination of President John F. Kennedy, vol. 1, National Archives, Record Group 272, Washington, DC: GPO, 1964, archives.gov/research/jfk/warren-commission-report/chapter-3.html, accessed November 17, 2023; see Kenneth Samples, "New Evidence for a JFK Conspiracy?," *Reflections* (blog), Reasons to Believe, October 31, 2023, reasons.org/explore/blogs/reflections/new-evidence-for-a-jfk-conspiracy.

16. Louis P. Pojman, *Philosophy: The Quest for Truth*, 4th ed. (Belmont, CA: Wadsworth, 1999), 31.
17. Pojman, *Quest for Truth*, 16.
18. Wikipedia, s.v. "Lee Harvey Oswald," last modified November 25, 2023, 09:12 (UTC), en.wikipedia.org/wiki/Lee_Harvey_Oswald; President's Commission on the Assassination of President Kennedy, "Appendix 13: Biography of Lee Harvey Oswald," in *Report of the President's Commission on the Assassination of President John F. Kennedy*, vol. 1, National Archives, Record Group 272, Washington, DC: GPO, 1964, archives.gov/research/jfk/warren-commission-report/appendix-13.html, accessed November 17, 2023; and Samples, "New Evidence."
19. Max Holland, "The Zapruder Film Reconsidered," Roosevelt House Public Policy Institute at Hunter College, presented December 3, 2015, YouTube video, 1:19:49, posted December 11, 2015, youtube.com/watch?v=t8Hp9ZqVxGA; see also Samples, "New Evidence?"
20. See Wikipedia, s.v. "Single-bullet theory," last modified November 23, 2023, 15:12 (UTC), en.wikipedia.org/wiki/Single-bullet_theory; and Samples, "New Evidence?"
21. Eric Bland, "Tech Puts JFK Conspiracy Theories to Rest," NBC News, November 13, 2008, nbcnews.com/id/wbna27705829; Samples, "New Evidence?"
22. See "Appendix 16: A Biography of Jack Ruby," National Archives, JFK Assassination Records, last reviewed August 15, 2016; Samples, "New Evidence?"

**Chapter 4: The Laws of Logic**
1. Aristotle, *Metaphysics*, Book IV, Part 3, trans. W. D. Ross, classicallibrary.org/Aristotle/metaphysics/book04.htm.
2. Wikipedia, s.v. "Law of Thought," last modified February 5, 2023, 22:16, en.wikipedia.org/wiki/Law_of_thought.
3. See Peter A. Angeles, s.v. "Laws of Thought, The Three," in *The HarperCollins Dictionary of Philosophy*, 2nd ed. (New York: HarperCollins, 1992); Ed L. Miller, *Questions That Matter: An Invitation to Philosophy*, 4th ed. (New York: McGraw-Hill, 1996), 32–33.
4. Kenneth Richard Samples, *Christianity Cross-Examined: Is It Rational, Relevant, and Good?* (Covina, CA: RTB Press, 2021), 53–54; Kenneth Richard Samples, *A World of Difference: Putting Christian Truth-Claims to the Worldview Test* (Grand Rapids, MI: Baker Books, 2007), 42–44.
5. Aristotle, *Metaphysics*, Book IV, Part 4.
6. Aristotle, *Metaphysics*, Book IV, Part 4.
7. Aristotle, *Metaphysics*, Book IV, Part 7.
8. In reviewing this work in manuscript form Winfried Corduan offered this comment: "I'm not sure this explanation works as it stands. Using two different sentences to express the law of identity seems to get confusing. It might be more helpful to say that for the Christian 'Jesus' and 'Son of God' are identical, viz. J=S because they share all of the same predicates and do not differ. For the Muslim you could say that Jesus is identical to the last prophet to the Jews, thereby claiming that J=L. For the other two laws, 2 'opposite' sentences are, of course, necessary."

9. Douglas Groothuis, *Truth Decay: Defending Christianity against the Challenges of Postmodernism* (Downers Grove, IL: InterVarsity, 2000), 166.
10. Ronald H. Nash, *Life's Ultimate Questions: An Introduction to Philosophy* (Grand Rapids, MI: Zondervan, 1999), 194.
11. See Angeles, s.v. "Laws of Thought, the Three"; Nash, *Life's Ultimate Questions*, 193–208.
12. Wikipedia, "Law of Thought."
13. Douglas Groothuis, *Christian Apologetics: A Comprehensive Case for Biblical Faith* (Downers Grove, IL: InterVarsity, 2011), 48.
14. The chart was produced by the Smithsonian Museum but was later removed because of the controversy it engendered. The chart can be viewed at miamiherald.com/news/nation-world/national/article244309587.html.
15. Douglas Groothuis, *Christian Apologetics*, 48.
16. See Angeles, s.v. "Laws of Thought, The Three"; Nash, *Life's Ultimate Questions*, 193–208.
17. Peter Kreeft, *Socratic Logic: A Logic Text Using Socratic Methods, Platonic Questions, and Aristotelian Principles*, 2nd ed., ed. Trent Dougherty (South Bend, IN: St. Augustine's Press, 2005), 6–7.
18. Zach Lee, *Logic for Christians: Critical Thinking for the People of God* (Houston, TX: Lucid Books, 2021), 15.
19. Ulrich L. Lehner, *Think Better: Unlocking the Power of Reason* (Grand Rapids, MI: Baker Academic, 2021), 6.
20. C. Stephen Evans, s.v. "Antithesis" in *Pocket Dictionary of Apologetics & Philosophy of Religion* (Downers Grove, IL: InterVarsity, 2002).
21. Aristotle, *Metaphysics* IV, 61011b13–20.
22. Angeles, *HarperCollins Dictionary*, s.v. "Logic, Dialectic."
23. Angeles, *HarperCollins Dictionary*, s.v. "Logic, Dialectic."
24. Angeles, *HarperCollins Dictionary*, s.v. "Logic, Dialectic."
25. In reviewing this work in manuscript form Winfried Corduan offered this explanation: "I know that you know that things are more complex than that. 'Eastern' formal logics usually take into account different perspectives in order not to get into contradictions. However, Madhyamaka Buddhism would be a good case in your point." Corduan then recommended the following article, Sonam Thakchoe, "The Theory of Two Truths in India," *The Standard Encyclopedia of Philosophy*, ed. Edward N. Zalta (Summer 2022), accessed October 13, 2023, plato.stanford.edu/entries/twotruths-india/.
26. Wikipedia, s.v. "Tetralemma," last modified November 28, 2023, 14:45 (UTC), en.wikipedia.org/wiki/Tetralemma.
27. Nishanth Arulappan, "Logic in the East and the West: Does It Differ?," Reflections on Biblical and Christian Philosophy, accessed November 19, 2023, biblicalphilosophy.org/logic-in-the-east-and-the-west-does-it-differ/.
28. Arulappan, "Logic in the East and West."
29. Samples, *Christianity Cross-Examined*, 57.
30. Lehner, *Think Better*, 105.
31. In reviewing this work in manuscript form RTB staff member Jacob Rodriguez offered this explanation: "For those who are not instructed in metaphysics and might have trouble considering the connection to logic, the laws of thought might be akin to the idea, or form, of 'Beauty' as Plato conceives of it. For Plato, beauty exists, and it is out there, even if there is no particular thing that is 'Beauty' itself. Proponents of this atheistic Platonic view would argue the laws of logic are like this."

32. Travis Dickinson, *Logic and the Way of Jesus: Thinking Critically and Christianly* (Nashville, TN: B&H, 2022), 95.
33. Kreeft, *Socratic Logic*, 29.
34. William Lane Craig, "Are There Uncreated Abstract Objects?," *The Good Book Blog*, Biola University Talbot School of Theology Faculty, August 21, 2015, biola.edu/blogs/good-book-blog/2015/are-there-uncreated-abstract-objects.
35. William Lane Craig, "Do the Laws of Logic Provide Evidence for God?," *The Good Book Blog*, Biola University Talbot School of Theology Faculty, April 7, 2017, biola.edu/blogs/good-book-blog/2017/do-the-laws-of-logic-provide-evidence-for-god.
36. J. P. Moreland, "What Are the Three Laws of Logic?" in *The Apologetics Study Bible: Understand Why You Believe*, gen. ed. Ted Cabal (Nashville, TN: Holman, 2007), 1854.
37. James N. Anderson and Greg Welty, "The Lord of Non-Contradiction: An Argument for God from Logic," *Philosophia Christi* 13, no. 2 (2011), 321–338, doi:10.5840/pc201113229.
38. Gordon Clark, *Logic* (Unicoi, TN: Trinity, 2004), 115.
39. Gavin McGrath, W. C. Campbell-Jack, and C. Stephen Evans, eds., s.v. "Contradiction and Non-Contradiction," in *New Dictionary of Christian Apologetics* (Leicester, England: InterVarsity, 2006), Nash, *Life's Ultimate Questions*, 193–207.
40. Samples, *World of Difference*, 44–46.
41. In reviewing this work in manuscript form Winfried Corduan offered this comment: "You're probably aware that ever since George Boole, the square of opposition is no longer recognized in the majority of textbooks. The reason is that the relationship between the universals (A & E) and the particulars (I & O) are considered hypothetical. Thus, A does not necessarily imply I unless the subject of A exists, and the same for E & O. We Aristotelians, who believe in 'formal causes' take exception to that restriction. Philosopher Gordon Clark led a crusade for all 25 versions of the syllogism being valid."
42. It is commonly accepted that Mark's Gospel relied upon the eyewitness testimony of Peter. See D. A. Carson and Douglas Moo, *An Introduction to the New Testament*, 2nd ed. (Grand Rapids, MI: Zondervan, 2005), 172–177.

**Chapter 5: Three Types of Logical Reasoning**
1. Butte College, "TIP Sheet: Deductive, Inductive, and Abductive Reasoning," butte.edu/departments/cas/tipsheets/thinking/reasoning.html.
2. Our discussion of the five basic forms of logical arguments was influenced by Lewis Vaughn, *The Power of Critical Thinking: Effective Reasoning about Ordinary and Extraordinary Claims*, 3rd ed. (Oxford, UK: Oxford University Press, 2009), chaps. 6–9; Ed L. Miller, *Questions That Matter: An Invitation to Philosophy*, 4th ed. (New York: McGraw-Hill, 1996), 35–45; Louis P. Pojman, "A Little Bit of Logic," chap. 2 in *Philosophy: The Quest for Truth*, 4th ed. (Belmont, CA: Wadsworth, 1999), 16–23; and Peter Kreeft, *Socratic Logic: A Logic Text Using Socratic Method, Platonic Questions, and Aristotelian Principles*, 2nd ed., ed. Trent Dougherty (South Bend, IN: St Augustine's Press, 2005), chaps. 9, 10, and 14. We use all four of these fine books as textbooks in the college courses we teach in philosophy and logic.
3. Peter A. Angeles, s.v. "Deduction," in *The HarperCollins Dictionary of Philosophy*, 2nd ed. (New York: HarperCollins, 1992).
4. This discussion is influenced by Patrick J. Hurley, *Logic: The Essentials* (Independence, KY: Cengage Learning, 2016), 32–34. We have used Hurley's text in teaching logic and critical thinking over many years.

5. For more discussion of these deductive arguments, see Pojman, *Philosophy*, 17–20; Vaughn, *Power of Critical Thinking*, 92–93.
6. For a discussion of classical Christian views of the Trinity and Christology, see Kenneth Richard Samples, *Without a Doubt: Answering the 20 Toughest Faith Questions* (Grand Rapids, MI: Baker Books, 2004), chaps. 5 and 9.
7. For three critical New Testament passages concerning the relationship between a saving faith in Christ and a subsequent Christian life of expressing that faith through works of love, see Ephesians 2:8–10, Titus 3:4–7, and Galatians 5:1–6. For a detailed discussion of the biblical and historic Christian view of salvation by grace through faith in Christ, see Kenneth Richard Samples, *7 Truths That Changed the World: Discovering Christianity's Most Dangerous Ideas* (Grand Rapids, MI: Baker Books, 2012), chaps. 9–10.
8. Classical Christianity affirms that Jesus Christ did what he did soteriologically (in terms of salvation) because he was who he was ontologically (in terms of being). For a discussion of classical Christology and soteriology, see Samples, *Without a Doubt*, chaps. 9 and 11.
9. For a discussion of the contingent versus necessary nature of the cosmos, see Kenneth Richard Samples, *Christianity Cross-Examined: Is It Rational, Relevant, and Good?* (Covina, CA: RTB Press, 2021), chap. 4.
10. *Internet Encyclopedia of Philosophy*, s.v., "Reductio ad Absurdum," accessed October 13, 2023, iep.utm.edu/reductio/.
11. Samples, *Christianity Cross-Examined*, chap. 4.
12. Vaughn, *Power of Critical Thinking*, 73.
13. Pojman, *Philosophy*, 27.
14. This discussion is influenced by Hurley, *Logic: The Essentials*, 34–35.
15. Pojman, *Philosophy*, 27.
16. Angeles, *The HarperCollins Dictionary of Philosophy*, s.v. "Induction, Problem of."
17. This brief discussion of inductive generalizations comes from our colleague Winfried Corduan.
18. Vaughn, *Power of Critical Thinking*, 302.
19. In reviewing this work in manuscript form Jacob Rodriguez offers an additional factor: "I think another useful evaluative frame for analogical reasoning is the similarity or applicability of the properties contained in the premises to the property reasoned to in the conclusion. Refuting an analogical argument often involves reasoning why it is that the analogical reasoning does not follow, given the particular nature of the properties contained in the premises and its relation to the property argued for in the conclusion."
20. Patrick J. Hurley, *A Concise Introduction to Logic*, 8th ed. (Belmont, CA: Wadsworth, 2003), 467.
21. Vaughn, *Power of Critical Thinking*, 303.
22. Distinguished philosophers of science Karl Popper and Thomas Kuhn have of course challenged this outline.
23. The five characteristics of judging scientific theories comes from Vaughn, *Power of Critical Thinking*, 400.
24. Vaughn, *Power of Critical Thinking*, 441.
25. My comparison of deductive and inductive arguments was influenced by Hurley, *Concise Introduction to Logic*, 48.
26. In reviewing this work in manuscript form Winfried Corduan offered this comment: "Some books use a negative definition that may possibly make validity easier to understand. 'An argument is valid if it is impossible for the premises to be true and the conclusion to be

false.' That definition is really behind RAA's (*reductio ad absurdum*) reasoning and is the backbone of testing expressions by way of truth tables."
27. My comparison of deductive and inductive arguments was partly influenced by Norman L. Geisler and Ronald M. Brooks, *Come, Let Us Reason: An Introduction to Logical Thinking* (Grand Rapids, MI: Baker Books, 1990), 23.
28. Pojman, *Philosophy*, 34.
29. John R. Josephson and Susan G. Josephson, eds., *Abductive Inference: Computation, Philosophy, Technology* (New York: Cambridge University Press, 1996), i.
30. Richard Swinburne, *Is There A God?* (Oxford, UK: Oxford University Press, 1996), 2.
31. An abductive case for accepting Jesus of Nazareth as the divine Messiah is in Samples, *Without A Doubt*, 109–118.

**Chapter 6: Positive Steps to Reinforce Clear Thinking**
1. Ulrich L. Lehner, *Think Better: Unlocking the Power of Reason* (Grand Rapids, MI: Baker Academic, 2021), 54.
2. Lehner, *Think Better*, 54.
3. Dennis Prager, "Clarity over Agreement," *PragerU*, prageru.com/video/ep-182-clarity-over-agreement.
4. Mortimer J. Adler and Charles Van Doren, *How to Read a Book* (New York: Simon and Schuster, 1972), 162
5. C. S. Lewis, "Christian Apologetics," in *Essay Collection: Faith, Christianity, and the Church* (New York: HarperCollins, 2002), 155.
6. T. Edward Damer, *Attacking Faulty Reasoning: A Practical Guide to Fallacy-Free Arguments*, 3rd ed. (Belmont, CA: Wadsworth, 1995), 22.
7. Damer, *Attacking Faulty Reasoning*, 2.
8. Ed L. Miller, *Questions That Matter: An Invitation to Philosophy*, 4th ed. (New York: McGraw-Hill, 1996), 51.
9. Lehner, *Think Better*, 63.
10. "About the Campaign," smokeybear.com, accessed September 6, 2023, smokeybear.com/en/smokeys-history/about-the-campaign.
11. Mortimer J. Adler, "Who Were History's Great Leaders?," *Time*, July 15, 1974, accessed October 13, 2023, content.time.com/time/subscriber/article/0,33009,879377,00.html.
12. See Kenneth Richard Samples, *Without a Doubt: Answering the 20 Toughest Faith Questions* (Grand Rapids, MI: Baker Books, 2004); Kenneth Richard Samples, *7 Truths That Changed the World: Discovering Christianity's Most Dangerous Ideas* (Grand Rapids, MI: Baker Books, 2012); Kenneth Richard Samples, *Christianity Cross-Examined: Is It Rational, Relevant, and Good?* (Covina, CA: RTB Press, 2021).
13. See Kenneth Samples, "Five Greek Words and Apologetics Persuasion," *Reflections* (blog), Reasons to Believe, August 6, 2019, reasons.org/explore/blogs/reflections/five-greek-words-and-apologetics-persuasion.
14. For more on epistemological virtues, see Linda Trinkaus Zagzebski, *Virtues of the Mind: An Inquiry into the Nature of Virtue and the Ethical Foundations of Knowledge* (Cambridge, UK: Cambridge University Press, 1996).

**Chapter 7: Overcoming Common Obstacles to Clear Thinking**
1. Brooke Noel Moore and Richard Parker, *Critical Thinking*, 7th ed. (Boston: McGraw-Hill, 2004), 3.

2. Lewis Vaughn, *The Power of Critical Thinking: Effective Reasoning about Ordinary and Extraordinary Claims*, 3rd ed. (Oxford, UK: Oxford University Press, 2008), 43.
3. See Charley Rosen, *The Pivotal Season: How the 1971–72 Los Angeles Lakers Changed the NBA* (New York: Thomas Dunn, 2005), 274–279.
4. Ed L. Miller, *God and Reason: An Invitation to Philosophical Theology*, 2nd ed. (Saddle River, NJ: Prentice Hall, 1995), 2.
5. For a discussion of Martin Luther's accomplishments and controversies, see Kenneth Richard Samples, *Classic Christian Thinkers: An Introduction* (Covina, CA: RTB Press, 2019), 110–127.
6. Vaughn, *Power of Critical Thinking*, 43.
7. Thomas Nagel, *The Last Word* (Oxford, UK: Oxford University Press, 1997), 130–131.
8. For a discussion of C. S. Lewis's argument from desire, see Samples, *Classic Christian Thinkers*, 171–172.
9. For a definition of enculturation, see merriam-webster.com/dictionary/enculturation.
10. Vaughn, *Power of Critical Thinking*, 4.
11. See Kenneth Samples, "How to Make Sense of Things We Can't Control," *Reflections* (blog), Reasons to Believe, June 15, 2016, reasons.org/explore/blogs/reflections/how-to-make-sense-of-things-we-can-t-control.

**Chapter 8: Evaluating Propaganda and Conspiracy Theories**
1. John "Jay" Ellison to class of 2020 students, letter from Dean of Students in The College, University of Chicago, news.uchicago.edu/sites/default/files/attachments/Dear_Class_of_2020_Students.pdf.
2. Dwight D. Eisenhower to George C. Marshall, April 15, 1945, eisenhowerlibrary.gov/sites/default/files/research/online-documents/holocaust/1945-04-15-dde-to-marshall.pdf.
3. Albert Speer, *Inside the Third Reich: Memoirs*, trans. Richard Winston and Clara Winston (New York: Simon & Schuster, 1970), 22.
4. Wikipedia, s.v. "Journalism," last modified April 25, 2023, 21:32 (UTC), en.wikipedia.org/wiki/Journalism.
5. Alison Hill, "Citizen Journalism vs. Traditional Journalism," *Writer's Digest*, February 27, 2022, writersdigest.com/write-better-nonfiction/citizen-journalism-vs-traditional-journalism.
6. The Aspen Institute, "The 1997 Catto Report on Journalism and Society," (1997): 55–56, aspeninstitute.org/wp-content/uploads/files/content/docs/cands/MARKETJOURNALISM.PDF.
7. Wikipedia, s.v. "Advocacy Journalism," last modified March 8, 2023, 13:06 (UTC), en.wikipedia.org/wiki/Advocacy_journalism.
8. Wikipedia, s.v. "Adversarial Journalism," last modified August 9, 2022, 16:25 (UTC), wikipedia.org/wiki/Adversarial_journalism.
9. Vitaly Kurennoy, "Philosophy of Liberal Education: The Principles," IDEAS, ideas.repec.org/a/nos/voprob/2020i1p8-39.html.
10. Richard M. Weaver, *In Defense of Tradition: Collected Shorter Writings of Richard M. Weaver, 1929–1963*, illustrated ed. (Carmel, IN: Liberty Fund, 2001), 300.
11. Wikipedia, s.v. "Chicago principles," last modified January 7, 2024, 15:50 (UTC), en.wikipedia.org/wiki/Chicago_principles.
12. Weaver, *In Defense of Tradition*, 300.
13. University of Chicago, "Identity Guidelines, Communicating UChicago: A Resource

for Communicators," news.uchicago.edu/sites/default/files/attachments/_uchicago.identity.guidelines.pdf.
14. University of Chicago, The Committee on Freedom of Expression, "Report of the Committee on Freedom of Expression," provost.uchicago.edu/sites/default/files/documents/reports/FOECommitteeReport.pdf.
15. University of Chicago, "Report."
16. Weaver, *In Defense of Tradition*, 300–311.
17. Tim Keller (@timkellernyc), "When you listen to and read one thinker, you become a clone; Two different thinkers, you become confused; Ten thinkers, you'll begin developing your own voice; Two or three hundred thinkers, you become wise," Twitter, January 7, 2022, 11:14 a.m., twitter.com/timkellernyc/status/1479531788443729926.
18. University of Chicago, "Report."
19. University of Chicago, "Report."
20. For a definition of conspiracy theory, see merriam-webster.com/dictionary/conspiracy%20theory.
21. Darren K. Carlson, "Most Americans Believe Oswald Conspired with Others to Kill JFK," Gallup, April 11, 2001, news.gallup.com/poll/1813/Most-Americans-Believe-Oswald-Conspired-Others-Kill-JFK.aspx.
22. Joseph E. Uscinski, "Almost 60 Percent of Americans Believe in Conspiracy Theories about JFK. Here's Why That Might Be a Problem," *American Politics and Policy Blog*, USApp, November 22, 2018, blogs.lse.ac.uk/usappblog/2018/11/22/almost-60-percent-of-americans-believe-in-conspiracy-theories-about-jfk-heres-why-that-might-be-a-problem/.
23. For anti-conspiracy sources on the JFK assassination, see *Reclaiming History: The Assassination of President John F. Kennedy* (2007) by Vincent Bugliosi and the Warren Commission Report (1963–1964), available at archives.gov/research/jfk/warren-commission-report. For pro-conspiracy sources, see *The Plot to Kill the President* (1981) by G. Robert Blakey and the House Select Committee on Assassinations (1976–1979), available at archives.gov/research/jfk/select-committee-report.
24. Lydia Saad, "Do Americans Believe in UFOs?," Gallup, August 20, 2021, news.gallup.com/poll/350096/americans-believe-ufos.aspx.
25. Cassie Buchman, "Poll: Many Believe Government Is Hiding What It Knows about UFOs," July 11, 2023, *NewsNation*, newsnationnow.com/space/ufo/poll-government-hiding-what-it-knows-ufos/.
26. Buchman, "Many Believe."
27. Brett Tingley, "Pentagon Has 'No Credible Evidence' of Aliens or UFOs That Defy Physics," Space.com, April 19, 2023, space.com/pentagon-aaro-ufo-hearing-april-2023.
28. Mark Clark, "Recent UAP Hearings Provide Much Ado about Nothing New," *Voices* (blog), Reasons to Believe, August 3, 2023, reasons.org/explore/blogs/voices/recent-uap-hearings-provide-much-ado-about-nothing-new.
29. Resources on UFO conspiracy theories: Hugh Ross, Kenneth Samples, and Mark Clark, *Lights in the Sky and Little Green Men* (Colorado Springs, CO: NavPress, 2002); Jerome Clark, *The UFO Book: Encyclopedia of the Extraterrestrial* (Canton, MI: Visible Ink Press, 1998); and Office of the Director of National Intelligence Preliminary Assessment: Unidentified Aerial Phenomenon (2021), available at dni.gov/files/ODNI/documents/assessments/Prelimary-Assessment-UAP-20210625.pdf.
30. Tia Ghose, "Half of Americans Believe in 9/11 Conspiracy Theories," LiveScience, October 13, 2016, livescience.com/56479-americans-believe-conspiracy-theories.html.

31. For anti-conspiracy sources on the 9/11 attacks, see the 9/11 Commission Report (2004), available at govinfo.library.unt.edu/911/report/index.htm; and "Debunking the 9/11 Conspiracy Theories: Special Report – The World Trade Center," *Popular Mechanics*, September 9, 2022, popularmechanics.com/military/a6384/debunking-911-myths-world-trade-center/. For a pro-conspiracy source on 9/11, see Wikipedia, s.v. "9/11 Truther Movement," en.wikipedia.org/wiki/9/11_truth_movement.
32. "Conspiracy Theories, Separating Fact from Fiction: Secret Societies Control the World, *Time*, November 20, 2008, content.time.com/time/specials/packages/article/0,28804,1860871_1860876_1861005,00.html.
33. For a book that provides measured and accurate information about fraternal organizations and their goals and purposes, see J. Gordon Melton, *Melton's Encyclopedia of American Religions*, 8th ed. (Farmington Hills, MI: Gale, 2009).
34. Ghose, "Half of Americans Believe in 9/11 Conspiracy Theories."
35. Katherine Schaffer, "A Look at the Americans Who Believe There Is Some Truth to the Conspiracy Theory That COVID-19 Was Planned," Pew Research Center, July 24, 2020, pewresearch.org/fact-tank/2020/07/24/a-look-at-the-americans-who-believe-there-is-some-truth-to-the-conspiracy-theory-that-covid-19-was-planned/.
36. My thinking about the causes of conspiracy theories was influenced by Steven Willing, "Christians and Conspiracies," *The Soggy Spaniel* (blog), February 5, 2021, swilling.com/christians-and-conspiracies/.
37. Wikipedia, s.v. "Assassination of Abraham Lincoln," last modified April 9, 2023, 22:40 (UTC), en.wikipedia.org/wiki/Assassination_of_Abraham_Lincoln.
38. See Gerald Posner, *Case Closed: Lee Harvey Oswald and the Assassination of JFK* (New York: Random House, 1993), 471; and Robert Dallek, *An Unfinished Life: John F. Kennedy, 1917–1963* (New York: Little, Brown and Company, 2003), 698–699.
39. Shayan Sardarizadeh, "11 September 2001: The Conspiracy Theories Still Spreading after 20 Years," BBC, September 9, 2021, bbc.com/news/58469600.
40. Willing, "Christians and Conspiracies."
41. Willing, "Christians and Conspiracies."

**Chapter 9: Twelve Precarious Informal Fallacies**
1. Peter A. Angeles, *The HarperCollins Dictionary of Philosophy*, 2nd ed. (New York: HarperCollins, 1992), 104.
2. Angeles, *HarperCollins Dictionary of Philosophy*, s.v. "Fallacy."
3. My discussion of informal fallacies was influenced by Louis P. Pojman, *Philosophy: The Quest for Truth*, 4th ed. (Belmont, CA: Wadsworth, 1999), 25–27; Lewis Vaughn, *The Power of Critical Thinking: Effective Reasoning about Ordinary and Extraordinary Claims*, 3rd ed. (Oxford, UK: Oxford University Press, 2009), 193–198; Angeles, *The HarperCollins Dictionary of Philosophy*, s.v. "Fallacy," 105–110; T. Edward Damer, *Attacking Faulty Reasoning: A Practical Guide to Fallacy-Free Arguments*, 3rd ed. (Belmont, CA: Wadsworth, 1995), chaps. 5–8; Patrick J. Hurley, *Logic: The Essentials* (Stamford, CT: Centage Learning, 2016), 63–121; and Norman L. Geisler and Ronald M. Brooks, *Come, Let Us Reason: An Introduction to Logical Thinking* (Grand Rapids, MI: Baker Academic, 1990), 90–118; Peter Kreeft, *Socratic Logic: A Logic Text Using Socratic Method, Platonic Questions, and Aristotelian Principles*, 2nd ed., ed. Trent Dougherty (South Bend, IN: St. Augustine's Press, 2005), 85–104.
4. A number of good online sources about informal fallacies have influenced this work,

including: Southern Evangelical Seminary and Bible College (website), ses.edu/?s=fallacy; Gary N. Curtis, "What Are the Fallacy Files?," Fallacy Files (website), last updated April 29, 2022, fallacyfiles.org/whatarff.html; Logically Fallacious (website), logicallyfallacious.com; Fallacy in Logic (website), fallacyinlogic.com/logical-fallacies/; Bruce Thompson's Fallacy Page (website), palomar.edu/users/bthompson/Introduction%20to%20Fallacies.html; "The Illogic Primer: Logical Fallacies Catalog," Afterall.net, accessed April 28, 2023, afterall.net/illogic/.
5. Our discussion of fallacies was influenced by, "Logical Reasoning in Humanitarian Analysis: Annex 1," Logical Fallacies, slideshare.net/ClaudiaGrigore2/logical-reasoning-in-humanitarian-analysis-71729727.
6. Angeles, *HarperCollins Dictionary of Philosophy*, s.v.v. "fallacy, types of informal," "3. fallacy of argumentum ad hominem."
7. Angeles, "8. fallacy of argumentum ad verecundiam."
8. Angeles, "8. fallacy of argumentum ad verecundiam."
9. Our colleague Winfried Corduan made this point when reviewing this work in manuscript form.
10. Kreeft, *Socratic Logic*, 94.
11. For the reasons the Allies won World War II, see Richard Overy, *Why the Allies Won* (New York: W. W. Norton and Company, 1995).
12. For a discussion of the multiverse in light of cosmology and the Christian worldview, see Kenneth Richard Samples, *Christianity Cross-Examined: Is It Rational, Relevant, and Good?* (Covina, CA: RTB Press, 2021), 87–90.
13. Philip Goff, "Our Improbable Existence Is No Evidence for a Multiverse," *Scientific American*, January 10, 2021, scientificamerican.com/article/our-improbable-existence-is-no-evidence-for-a-multiverse/?fbclid=IwAR0FA4CmKP4mkSXVjZw5YbX1EhkUALpfxILhR9zOFVZsYEUnAITOJjjhFt0.
14. Kreeft, *Socratic Logic*, 100.
15. Damer, *Attacking Faulty Reasoning*, 163.
16. Daniel, "Logical Fallacies 101: Slanting" (blog), Southern Evangelical Seminary and Bible College, January 31, 2017, ses.edu/logical-fallacies-101-slanting/.
17. Daniel, "Logical Fallacies 101: Slanting" (blog), Southern Evangelical Seminary and Bible College, January 31, 2017, ses.edu/logical-fallacies-101-slanting/.
18. Gary N. Curtis, "One-Sidedness," Fallacy Files (website), accessed April 28, 2023, fallacyfiles.org/onesided.html#Note8.
19. John Stuart Mill, *On Liberty* (London, 1859; Project Gutenberg, 2011), 67, gutenberg.org/cache/epub/34901/pg34901-images.html.
20. For a discussion of the Trinity, see Samples, *Christianity Cross-Examined*, chap. 5.
21. Samples, *Christianity Cross-Examined*, chap. 8.
22. Pojman, *Philosophy*, 33.
23. Pojman, *Philosophy*, 524; Patrick J. Hurley, *A Concise Introduction to Logic*, 12th ed. (Stamford, CT: Centage Learning, 2015).
24. Kreeft, *Socratic Logic*, 102.

**Chapter 10: Fifteen More Common Informal Fallacies**
1. Mortimer J. Adler, *How to Speak How to Listen* (New York: Simon & Schuster, 1983), 27–28.
2. Aristotle, Sophistical Refutations 5, 167a: 1–20, logoslibrary.org/aristotle/sophistical/05.html.

3. Richard Burton, *The Anatomy of Melancholy* (New York: New York Review Books, 2001).
4. Gary N. Curtis, "Appeal to Force," The Fallacy Files, accessed April 28, 2023, fallacyfiles.org/adbacula.html.
5. Peter A. Angeles, *The HarperCollins Dictionary of Philosophy*, 2nd ed. (New York: HarperCollins, 1992), s.v.v. "fallacy," "2. fallacy of argumentum baculinum."
6. Alvin Plantinga and Nicholas Wolterstorff, eds., *Faith and Rationality: Reason and Belief in God* (Notre Dame: University of Notre Dame Press, 1983), 25–28.
7. Peter Kreeft, *Socratic Logic: A Logic Text Using Socratic Method, Platonic Questions, and Aristotelian Principles*, 2nd ed., ed. Trent Dougherty (South Bend, IN: St. Augustine's Press, 2005), 86.
8. Kreeft, *Socratic Logic*, 86.
9. Kreeft, *Socratic Logic*, 84.
10. Gary N. Curtis, "Amphiboly," The Fallacy Files, accessed May 1, 2023, fallacyfiles.org/amphibol.html.
11. J. P. Moreland, "Who or What Caused God?," J. P. Moreland, originally published by Focus on the Family, 2007, jpmoreland.com/articles/who-or-what-caused-god/.
12. Norman Geisler and Ravi Zacharias, eds., *Who Made God? And Answers to Over 100 Other Tough Questions of Faith* (Grand Rapids, MI: Zondervan, 2003), 24.
13. Paul Elsher, "What Is the Loaded Question Fallacy? Definition and Examples," Fallacy in Logic, accessed May 1, 2023, fallacyinlogic.com/loaded-question-fallacy/.
14. Anthony McRoy, "Was Easter Borrowed from a Pagan Holiday?," *Christianity Today*, April 2, 2009, christianitytoday.com/history/2009/april/was-easter-borrowed-from-pagan-holiday.html.
15. Louis P. Pojman, *Philosophy: The Quest for Truth*, 4th ed. (Belmont, CA: Wadsworth, 1999), 33.
16. Gerry Spence, *How to Argue and Win Every Time* (New York: St. Martin's Griffin, 1996), 203.
17. Patrick J. Hurley, *Logic: The Essentials* (Stamford, CT: Centage Learning, 2016), 93.
18. "Fallacy," Internet Encyclopedia of Philosophy, s.v. "special pleading," accessed May 3, 2023, iep.utm.edu/fallacy/#SpecialPleading.
19. T. Edward Damer, *Attacking Faulty Reasoning: A Practical Guide to Fallacy-Free Arguments*, 3rd ed. (Belmont, CA: Wadsworth, 1995), 29.
20. Damer, *Attacking Faulty Reasoning*, 30.

**Chapter 11: Cognitive Biases and Critical Thinking**
1. Agatha Christie, *Peril at End House* (New York: HarperCollins, 1932), 14.
2. Daniel J. Mallinson and Peter K. Hatemi, "The Effects of Information and Social Conformity on Opinion Change," *PLoS ONE* 13, no. 5 (May 2, 2018): e0196600, doi:10.1371/journal.pone.0196600.
3. Lindsey C. Levitan, and Brad Verhulst, "Conformity in Groups: The Effects of Others' View on Expressed Attitudes and Attitude Change," *Political Behavior* 38, no. 2 (June 2016): 277, doi:10.1007/s11109-015-9312-x.
4. Christos Kyrlitsias and Despina Michael-Grigoriou, "Asch Conformity Experiment Using Immersive Virtual Reality: Asch Experiment Using IVR," *Computer Animation and Virtual Worlds* 29, no. 5 (2018): e1804, doi:10.1002/cav.1804.
5. Solomon E. Asch, "Studies of Independence and Conformity: A Minority of One against a Unanimous Majority," *Psychological Monographs* 70, no. 9 (1956): 1–70, doi:10.1037/

h0093718.
6. Fred C. Lunenburg, "Group Decision Making: The Potential for Groupthink," *International Journal of Management, Business, and Administration* 13, no. 1 (2010), nationalforum.com/Electronic%20Journal%20Volumes/Lunenburg,%20Fred%20C.%20Group%20Decision%20Making%20IJMBA%20V13%20N1%202010.pdf.
7. Daniel T. Gilbert, "How Mental Systems Believe," *American Psychologist* 46, no. 2 (February 1991): 107–119, doi:10.1037/0003-066X.46.2.107.
8. Wouter Kool et al., "Decision Making and the Avoidance of Cognitive Demand," *Journal of Experimental Psychology: General* 139, no. 4 (November 2010): 665–682, doi:10.1037/a0020198.
9. Daniel Kahneman, *Thinking, Fast and Slow* (New York: Farrar, Straus and Giroux, 2013).
10. C. McCauley, C. L. Stitt, and M. Segal, "Stereotyping: From Prejudice to Prediction," *Psychological Bulletin* 87, no. 1 (1980): 195–208, doi:10.1037/0033-2909.87.1.195.
11. Kahneman, *Thinking, Fast and Slow*, 138.
12. Amos Tversky and Daniel Kahneman, "Judgment under Uncertainty: Heuristics and Biases," *Science* 185, no. 4157 (September 27, 1974): 1124–1131, doi:10.1126/science.185.4157.1124.
13. Joseph P. Forgas, "She Just Doesn't Look Like a Philosopher . . . ? Affective Influences on the Halo Effect in Impression Formation," *European Journal of Social Psychology* 41, no. 7 (December 2011): 812–817, doi:10.1002/ejsp.842.
14. Neal J. Roese and Kathleen D. Vohs, "Hindsight Bias," *Perspectives on Psychological Science* 7, no. 5 (2012): 411–426, doi:10.1177/1745691612454303.
15. Roese and Vohs, "Hindsight Bias," 411–426.
16. Roese and Vohs, 411–426.
17. Judges control what juries see. Images or other evidence deemed unduly prejudicial may be withheld from the jury. Nevertheless, even where the worst may be withheld, the plaintiff must be allowed to present all relevant evidence, even when that means some, but not all, very graphic and shocking evidence will be admitted.
18. Erin M. Harley, "Hindsight Bias in Legal Decision Making," *Social Cognition* 25, no. 1 (February 2007): 48–63, doi:10.1521/soco.2007.25.1.48.
19. Reid Hastie, David A. Schkade, and John W. Payne, "Juror Judgments in Civil Cases: Hindsight Effects on Judgments of Liability for Punitive Damages," *Law and Human Behavior* 23, no. 5 (October 1999): 597–614, doi:10.1023/A:1022352330466.
20. Susan J. LaBine and Gary LaBine, "Determinations of Negligence and the Hindsight Bias," *Law and Human Behavior* 20, no. 5 (October 1996): 501–516, doi:10.1007/BF01499038.
21. R. A. Caplan, K. L. Posner, and F. W. Cheney, "Effect of Outcome on Physician Judgments of Appropriateness of Care," *Journal of the American Medical Association* 265, no. 15 (April 17, 1991): 1957–1960, doi:10.1001/jama.1991.03460150061024.
22. Neal J. Roese et al., "The Propensity Effect: When Foresight Trumps Hindsight," *Psychological Science* 17, no. 4 (April 2006): 305–309, doi:10.1111/j.1467-9280.2006.01703.x.
23. Maxwell J. Roberts and Elizabeth D. A. Sykes, "Belief Bias and Relational Reasoning," *Quarterly Journal of Experimental Psychology* 56, no. 1 (January 2003): 131–153, doi:10.1080/02724980244000233.
24. Laura Macchi et al., "How to Get Rid of the Belief Bias: Boosting Analytical Thinking via Pragmatics," *Europe's Journal of Psychology* 15, no. 3 (2019): 595–613, doi:10.5964/ejop.v15i3.1794.
25. Roberts and Sykes, "Belief Bias."
26. Macchi et al., "How to Get Rid of the Belief Bias," 605.

27. Macchi et al., 607.

**Chapter 12: Biases in Science**
1. David Harker, *Creating Scientific Controversy: Uncertainty and Bias in Science and Society* (Cambridge, UK: Cambridge University Press, 2015), 3.
2. This is a simplistic definition of "science." There are more elaborate definitions, but they are not necessary here. Among philosophers of science, an exhaustive definition of "science"—or whether there even is one—is still in debate.
3. A single, comprehensive definition of "scientific method" is elusive because one can argue that different methods apply in different sciences or approaches to science. We use a simplified definition here because it serves our purposes. We acknowledge that other definitions could be used as well.
4. Daniel Kahneman, *Thinking, Fast and Slow* (New York: Farrar, Straus and Giroux, 2013), 81.
5. Fouad Atallah et al., "Confirmation Bias Affects Estimation of Blood Loss and Amniotic Fluid Volume: A Randomized Simulation-Based Trial," *American Journal of Perinatology* 38, no. 12 (October 2020): 1277–1280, doi:10.1055/s-0040-1712167.
6. R. Mendel et al., "Confirmation Bias: Why Psychiatrists Stick to Wrong Preliminary Diagnoses," *Psychological Medicine* 41, no. 12 (December 2011): 2651–2659, doi:10.1017/S0033291711000808.
7. Brittany Balsamo et al., "Confirmation Bias Affects User Perception of Knee Braces," *Journal of Biomechanics* 75 (June 25, 2018): 164–170, doi:10.1016/j.jbiomech.2018.04.028.
8. Benjamin Djulbegovic, Alan Cantor, and Mike Clarke, "The Importance of the Preservation of the Ethical Principle of Equipoise in the Design of Clinical Trials: Relative Impact of the Methodological Quality Domains on the Treatment Effect in Randomized Controlled Trials," *Accountability in Research* 10, no. 4 (October–December 2003): 301–315, doi:10.1080/714906103.
9. Brian A. Nosek, Jeffrey R. Spies, and Matt Motyl, "Scientific Utopia: II. Restructuring Incentives and Practices to Promote Truth over Publishability," *Perspectives on Psychological Science* 7, no. 6 (November 2012): 615–631, doi:10.1177/1745691612459058.
10. Monwhea Jeng, "A Selected History of Expectation Bias in Physics," *American Journal of Physics* 74, no. 7 (July 2006): 578, doi:10.1119/1.2186333.
11. Jeng, "A Selected History," 578.
12. R. DuBroff, "Confirmation Bias, Conflicts of Interest and Cholesterol Guidance: Can We Trust Expert Opinions?," *QJM: An International Journal of Medicine* 111, no. 10 (October 2018): 687–689, doi:10.1093/qjmed/hcx213; and J. Lexchin et al., "Pharmaceutical Industry Sponsorship and Research Outcome and Quality: Systematic Review," *BMJ* 326, no. 7400 (May 29, 2003): 1167–1170, doi:10.1136/bmj.326.7400.1167.
13. The discussion here on the psychology of change aversion in science is necessarily superficial. We present just a few of the elements that connect with other concepts discussed earlier in the book. A thorough discussion on all aspects of cognitive dissonance, change aversion, etc., would take us far afield from the point of the chapter, and exceeds the scope of this book.
14. Jean-Marc Cavaillon and Fabrice Chrétien, "From Septicemia to Sepsis 3.0 – from Ignaz Semmelweis to Louis Pasteur," *Microbes and Infection* 21, nos. 5–6 (June–July 2019): 213–221, doi:10.1016/j.micinf.2019.06.005.
15. Stanley Goldberg, "In Defense of Ether: The British Response to Einstein's Special Theory of Relativity, 1905–1911," *Chymia* 2 (January 1949): 89–125, republished in *Historical Studies*

*in the Natural Sciences* (January 1, 1970), doi:10.2307/27757305.
16. Goldberg, "In Defense of Ether," 98.
17. Goldberg, 100.
18. Alyssa Shearer et al., "Yes, Science Is Political," *Scientific American*, October 8, 2020, scientificamerican.com/article/yes-science-is-political/.

**Chapter 13: Biases in Thinking with Numbers Big and Small**
1. Darrell Huff, *How to Lie with Statistics* (New York: W. W. Norton & Co., 1954), 19.
2. D. V. M. Bishop, Jackie Thompson, and Adam J. Parker, "Can We Shift Belief in the 'Law of Small Numbers'?," *Royal Society Open Science* 9, no. 3 (March 2022): 211028, doi:10.1098/rsos.211028.
3. Amos Tversky and Daniel Kahneman, "Belief in the Law of Small Numbers," *Psychological Bulletin* 76, no. 2 (August 1971): 105–110, doi:10.1037/h0031322.
4. Howard Wainer and Harris L. Zwerling, "Evidence That Smaller Schools Do Not Improve Student Achievement," *Phi Delta Kappan* 88, no. 4 (December 2006): 300–303.
5. Jonah Lehrer, *How We Decide* (Boston: Houghton Mifflin Harcourt, 2009), 66.
6. "Roulette Odds & Probabilities: Online Roulette Guide," Roulette17.com, accessed May 9, 2023, roulette17.com/resources/probabilities/. This is one of many sources on this event. It also reports the odds of getting 26 blacks in a row as 1 in 145,000.
7. Tversky and Kahneman, "Belief in the Law of Small Numbers," 105–110.
8. Roger White, "Fine-Tuning and Multiple Universes," *Noûs* 34, no. 2 (June 2000): 260–276, doi:10.1111/0029-4624.00210.
9. We use this narrow multiverse argument *merely* as a simple example of the gambler's fallacy. There are other arguments independent of the one we presented here to support or refute multiverse theories. Those arguments are beyond the scope of this book.
10. Adele Diederich, Marc Wyszynski, and Ilana Ritov, "Moderators of Framing Effects in Variations of the Asian Disease Problem: Time Constraint, Need, and Disease Type," *Judgment and Decision Making* 13, no. 6 (November 2018): 529–546, doi:10.1017/S1930297500006574.
11. Amos Tversky and Daniel Kahneman, "The Framing of Decisions and the Psychology of Choice," *Science* 211, no. 4481 (January 30, 1981): 453, doi:10.1126/science.7455683. This study is often referred to in later research studies as the "Asian Disease Problem."
12. Evidence beside the statistics was received in the court case. However, the statistics were seen as harmfully prejudicial. The appellate court's decision brief gives a more detailed account of the facts and their effects on the final decision to release Sally Clark from prison: Clark, R v [2003] EWCA Crim 1020 (11 April 2003), BAILII, netk.net.au/UK/SallyClark1.asp.
13. The Royal Statistical Society published a news release on October 23, 2001, identifying problems in the original expert's methodology: Royal Statistical Society, "Royal Statistical Society Concerned by Issues Raised in Sally Clark Case," October 23, 2001, republished on "Sally Clark," The Inference Group, last updated October 12, 2011, inference.org.uk/sallyclark/RSS.html.

**Chapter 14: Mitigating the Effects of Cognitive Biases**
1. Daniel Kahneman, *Thinking, Fast and Slow* (New York: Farrar, Straus and Giroux, 2011), 272.
2. Erin M. Harley, "Hindsight Bias in Legal Decision Making," *Social Cognition* 25, no. 1

(2007): 48–49, doi:10.1521/soco.2007.25.1.48.

## Chapter 15: Integrating Thoughts on Clear Thinking

1. Daniel J. Boorstin, interviewed by Carol Krucoff, "The 6 O'Clock Scholar," *Washington Post*, January 29, 1984, washingtonpost.com/archive/lifestyle/1984/01/29/the-6-oclock-scholar/eed58de4-2dcb-47d2-8947-b0817a18d8fe/.
2. Daniel Kahneman, *Thinking, Fast and Slow* (New York: Farrar, Straus and Giroux, 2011), 249–252; Erin M. Harley, "Hindsight Bias in Legal Decision Making," *Social Cognition* 25, no. 1 (2007): 48–49, doi:10.1521/soco.2007.25.1.48.
3. Thomas Shelley Duval and Paul J. Silvia, "Self-Awareness, Probability of Improvement, and the Self-Serving Bias," *Journal of Personality and Social Psychology* 82, no. 1 (January 2002): 49–61, doi:10.1037/0022-3514.82.1.49.

# Index

9/11 attacks, 135–136

Adams, John, 137–138
Adler, Mortimer J., 42, 48, 107, 111, 133, 169
    *How to Speak, How to Listen*, 169
ambiguity, 153–154, 176–177
Anderson, James N., 75–76
Angeles, Peter A., 48, 72–73, 85, 95, 141
anti-intellectualism, 20
apologetics, 30, 37, 44, 102–103, 111–112
Apostles' Creed, 31
Aquinas, Thomas, 111
arguments
    deductive, 57, 64, 85
    inductive, 57, 62, 64, 158
    logical, 55–66, 85, 105–109, 112–114
    nonarguments, 58, 66
Aristotle, 46, 53, 67–72, 76, 110–111, 119, 121, 163, 170
    *Art of Rhetoric*, 110
    *Metaphysics*, 67–68
*Art of Rhetoric* (Aristotle), 110
Arulappan, Nishanth, 73
Asch conformity experiments, 198–199
Augustine, Saint, 111
Aurelius, Marcus, 48

Bacon, Francis, 17
bandwagon effect, 146–148, 198–199, 233
Bay of Pigs, 200
beliefs and rational considerations, 118
bias, 149
    anchoring, 232–233
    availability, 202, 233

belief, 207–209, 233–234
   cognitive, 21, 196–197, 215, 220, 231–241
   confirmation, 212–214, 216, 234
   disconfirmation, 214–216, 234
   hindsight, 203–207, 236, 241
   optimism, 240
   outcome, 241
   self-serving, 241
Bible
   parables, 27
   verses, 19–20, 26–29, 32, 37, 38, 42, 47, 53, 59–60, 76, 112, 124, 164, 170
biblical faith, 19
Biden, Joe, 143–144
Boole, George, 257n41
Boorstin, Daniel J., 239
Boston Celtics, 116–117
Brown, Dan, 135
   *The Lost Symbol*, 135
Buddhist logic, 73, 256n25
Burton, Richard, 171
Butte College, 85

C. S. Lewis Society, 37. *See also* Lewis, C. S.
categorical propositions. *See under* fallacies
Catholicism, 37
cause-and-effect, 158
central point. *See* conclusion
Christian intellectuals, 34–38
*Christian Scholar's Review*, 26
Christian worldview, 31, 33–34, 40, 53, 76, 102–103
Christianity, historic, 19–20, 25, 30–32, 34, 75, 164, 252n11
Christie, Agatha, 195
   *Peril at End House*, 195
Christology, 78–79
Churchill, Winston, 125
clarity, 107–108, 152–154, 176–177
Clark, Gordon, 76
Clark, Sally, 228–229, 267n12
*Classic Christian Thinkers*, 36
clear thinking, 113–115, 119–120
cognitive dissonance, 216
cognitive resistance, 215–216, 266n13
coherence, 109
conclusion, 56–63, 65, 85–87, 94–95, 98, 105–109, 115, 145–147, 174–175
conditions, necessary and sufficient, 92–93
Connally, John, 64
conspiracy theories, 133–139

Corduan, Winfried, 255n8, 256n25, 257n41, 258n25
correspondence theory of truth, 61
COVID-19 pandemic, 135, 139
Craig, William Lane, 75
*Creating Scientific Controversy* (Harker), 211
*Critical Thinking*, 115
critical thinking, 44–45, 195–197, 208–209, 244–245
cumulative case approach, 102
Curtis, Gary N., 177

Damer, T. Edward, 45, 50–51, 56, 59–60, 108–109, 161, 190
decision-making, 50
dialectical thinking, 72–73
Dickinson, Travis, 27–28, 74
    *Logic and the Way of Jesus*, 28
dilemmas,
    logical, 154
    success-failure, 242–243
    trilemma, 154
discernment, 46–47, 49
distraction, 160
doctrines, 30

Eastern mysticism, 102
Eastern Orthodoxy, 37
education, 44–46, 49, 127–133
    classical, 45
Einstein, Albert, 218
Eisenhower, Dwight D., 125
either-or, 155–156
Ellison, John "Jay," 45, 125
Elsher, Paul, 179
emotions, 51, 232–238
enculturation, 123–124
epistemology, 68–69
equipoise, 213–214
ether theory, 218
*ethos*, 111, 163
evangelicalism, 34–35
extraterrestrial life, 134

faith
    and knowledge, 29–30
    and reason, 19–21, 25, 30–31
    saving faith, 29–30, 257n7
faith seeking understanding, 30
fallacies, 141–167, 169–191

accident, 169–171
*ad baculum*, 171–172
*ad hominem*, 143–146
*ad ignorantiam*, 172–174
*ad misericordiam*, 174–176
*ad populum*, 146–148, 197, 200, 232
*ad verecundiam*, 148–150
amphiboly, 107, 176–177
begging the question, 122, 150–152
category mistake, 76–79, 177–178
complex question, 178–180
composition, 180–181, 201
division, 181–182
domino. *See* slippery slope
equivocation, 107, 152–154
false alternatives, 154–155
false cause, 156–158, 224–225
formal, 141
gambler's, 157, 225–226, 235, 267n9
genetic, 117, 182–184
hasty generalization, 158–160, 200–203, 235
informal, 57, 106–107, 116–117, 121, 126, 132–133, 141–167, 169–191, 197, 207, 262n4
inverse gambler's, 157–158
lone voice, 199–200
missing the point, 106
Monte Carlo, 225
*non causa pro causa*, 156–158
oversimplified cause, 157
*petitio principii*, 122, 150–152
planning, 240
*post hoc ergo propter hoc*, 156, 158
prejudicial language, 184–185
prosecutor's, 228–229, 236–237
red herring, 106, 160–161
ridicule, 185–186
slanting, 161–163
slippery slope, 186–188
special pleading, 188–189
straw man, 106, 163–166
weak analogy, 166–167
wishful thinking, 122–123, 189–190
Franklin, Benjamin, 137

Gautama, Siddhartha, 48
Geisler, Norman, 178
George, Robert P., 44–45, 49

*Godfather, The*, 121
God's
    creation, 76
    existence, 75, 122
    image, 32, 37, 41–43, 53, 121, 186
    nature, 75, 78–79
Goodpaster, Jeffery R., 44
gospel, 33
Gray, Hanna Holborn, 46
Groothuis, Douglas, 28, 70–71
groupthink, 200, 240
Grusch, David, 134

Hacking, Ian, 158
halo effect, 203, 235
Harker, David, 211
    *Creating Scientific Controversy*, 211
*HarperCollins Dictionary of Philosophy*, 141
Hebrew Scriptures, 26–27
heuristics, 239
Hill, Alison, 127
Hitler, Adolf, 126
    *Mein Kampf*, 126
Holland, Max, 63
*How to Lie with Statistics* (Huff), 221
*How to Speak, How to Listen* (Adler), 169
Huff, Darrell, 221
    *How to Lie with Statistics*, 221
human exceptionalism, 41–43. *See also* God's image
human origins, 103
Hurley, Patrick J., 56, 97, 187–188
Hurtado, Larry, 32–33
Hutchins, Robert M., 133
hypothesis, 212, 214, 243

indoctrination, 44–46, 129
induction, problem of, 95–96
inference, 56, 58–59, 62–63, 85, 101
*Internet Encyclopedia of Philosophy*, 188

Jefferson, Thomas, 39
Jesus Christ, 20, 25–29, 258n8
Josephson, John, 100
Josephson, Susan, 100
journalism, 126–128, 162–163

Kahneman, Daniel, 212, 231

*Thinking Fast and Slow*, 231
Keller, Tim, 133
Kennedy, John F., 62–64, 134, 136–137
Kirby, Gary, 44
Kirk, Captain James T., 120–121
Koukl, Greg, 31
Kreeft, Peter, 43, 48, 51, 55, 61, 72, 152, 160, 167, 175–176

law
    of excluded middle, 68–70
    of identity, 68–69, 255n8
    of noncontradiction, 68, 70, 72–74, 76
    of rational inference, 69
laws of logic, 47–48, 67–81, 188
laws of thought, 76, 80
leading question, 179
Lee, Zach, 47, 72
    *Logic for Christians*, 47
legal proceedings, 265n17
Lehner, Ulrich L., 45, 53, 72, 105, 110
Lehrer, Jim, 127–128
Lewis, C. S., 20–21, 40, 107, 122
    *Mere Christianity*, 20–21
*lexis*, 112
life of the mind, 31–40, 46, 53
Lincoln, Abraham, 136
loaded question, 178
logic, 21, 41, 43–44, 46–53, 55, 114
    and passion, 118–120
*Logic and the Way of Jesus* (Dickinson), 28
*Logic for Christians* (Lee), 47
*logos*, 67, 112, 121, 163
long-term thinking, 241–242
Los Angeles Dodgers, 61
Los Angeles Lakers, 116–117
*Lost Symbol, The* (Brown), 135
Luther, Martin, 119

Marx, Groucho, 176
Marx, Karl, 72–73
McCoy, Leonard "Bones," 120–121
*Mein Kampf* (Hitler), 126
*Mere Christianity* (Lewis), 20–21
metaphysics, 68–69, 256n31
*Metaphysics* (Aristotle), 67–68
Mill, John Stuart, 163
Miller, Ed L., 44, 52, 55–56, 59

*modus ponens*, 27–28, 87–88, 91
*modus tollens*, 88–89, 91
Moore, Brooke Noel, 115
Moreland, J. P., 177
*Myth of the Twentieth Century* (Rosenberg), 126

Nagel, Thomas, 122
NASA, 200
Nash, Ronald H., 25, 70
    *Worldviews in Conflict*, 25
National Basketball Association (NBA), 116–117
National Museum of African American History and Culture (NMAAHC), 71
naturalism, 74
Nazi, 125–126, 136
*NewsHour with Jim Lehrer, The*, 127
Nicene Creed, 31
Nixon, Richard, 136
Noll, Mark, 38
numbers
    and causes, 224–225
    and gambles, 225–226
    and framing, 226–227, 234
    first-seen, 227

opinions, 56
Osborne, Grant B., 27
Oswald, Lee Harvey, 62–64, 136–137

Parker, Richard, 115
*pathos*, 111–112, 121, 163
peer pressure, 197–198
Pelikan, Jaroslav, 35
*Peril at End House* (Christie), 195
persuasion, 110–113, 163
philosophy, 51–52
Plato, 74, 119, 256n31
Pojman, Louis, 63, 94–95, 165
political ideology, 50
Prager, Dennis, 107
pre-mortem, 240
premise, 56–63, 65, 85–87, 94–95, 98, 105–106, 108, 145, 147, 174–175
presumption, 121–123
probability, 93–95, 98–99
    estimate, 242–245
propaganda, 44–46, 126–127, 129–133

Rana, Fazale, 42

rational inference, 46, 50
reality, 61
Reasonable Faith, 37
reasoning
    abductive, 100–101
    analogical, 96–97, 258n19
    deductive, 85–93, 98–99
    discursive, 30
    inductive reasoning, 93–99
    informal, 21
    preferential, 115–118
Reasons to Believe, 37, 42
rebuttal, 109–110
*reductio ad absurdum*, 90–91, 258n26
relevance, 106–107
revelation
    general, 32
    special, 32
rhetoric, 59, 113. *See also* persuasion
Roddenberry, Gene, 121
Rosen, Charley, 117
Rosenberg, Alfred, 126
    *Myth of the Twentieth Century*, 126
Ross, Hugh, 42
Ruby, Jack, 64

science, 211–216, 218–220, 243, 266n2
*Scientific American*, 158, 219
scientific method, 97, 211, 266n3
secret societies, 135
Semmelweiss, Ignaz, 216–218
    Semmelweiss effect, 237
Sharman, Bill, 117
Smokey Bear, 110
social construct, 71–72
Socrates, 47–49
space shuttle
    *Challenger*, 200
    *Columbia*, 200
Speer, Albert, 125–126
Spence, Gerry, 186
Spock, 120–121
Sproul, R. C., 29
*Star Trek*, 119–121
statistics, 221–223, 267n12
    sample size, 238
    sample size neglect, 222–224

stereotyping, 202–203, 237
Stone, Oliver, 137
Swinburne, Richard, 102
syllogisms, 87–90, 92, 207–208, 257n41

tautologies, 107
*taxis*, 112
*tetralemma*, 73
theology, 52–53
theory of relativity, 218
*Thinking*, 44
*Thinking Fast and Slow* (Kahneman), 23
Traditional Square of Opposition, 79–80
transitive property of equality, 69
Trinity, 30, 59–60, 164
Trump, Donald, 143
truth, 52–53

UFOs, 134
University of Chicago, 129–133
US Forest Service, 110
US government, 134–136

Vaughn, Lewis, 45, 47, 93, 96–97, 116–117, 120, 123

Warren Commission, 63–64
Watergate, 200. *See also* Nixon, Richard
Weaver, Richard M., 129, 131–133
Welty, Greg, 75–76
Willard, Dallas, 26
Willing, Steven, 136–137
*Worldviews in Conflict* (Nash), 25
World War II, 110, 125, 156–157
*Writer's Digest*, 127

# About the Authors

**Kenneth Richard Samples** serves as senior research scholar at Reasons to Believe (RTB), an organization that researches and communicates how God's revelation in the Bible harmonizes with science and philosophy.

Kenneth holds a BA in social science with an emphasis in history and philosophy from Concordia University and an MA in theological studies from Talbot School of Theology. Prior to joining RTB, he worked as senior research consultant and correspondence editor at the Christian Research Institute and regularly cohosted popular call-in radio program *The Bible Answer Man*.

Kenneth's other books include *Christianity Cross-Examined*, *Classic Christian Thinkers*, and *God among Sages*. He leads RTB's *Clear Thinking* podcast and writes *Reflections*, a weekly blog dedicated to exploring the Christian worldview. Additionally, he is currently an adjunct instructor of apologetics at Biola University and has spoken at universities and churches around the world.

Kenneth lives in Southern California with his wife, Joan. They have three grown children.

**Mark Perez** serves as chief operating officer at Reasons to Believe (RTB), an organization that researches and communicates how God's revelation in the Bible harmonizes with science and philosophy.

Mark earned a BA in philosophy and an MA focusing on analytic philosophy of science from California State University, Los Angeles, where he also acquired a California State University Certificate in Teaching Critical Thinking.

He also holds a masters in public administration from American Military University with an emphasis on organizational development.

Mark has taught critical thinking and problem solving in the government sector (primarily to managers) and has made presentations on apologetics, critical thinking, and philosophy of science to church groups and other Christian organizations. Mark is a contributing author to the RTB book *Thinking about Evolution* with coauthors Anjeanette Roberts, Fazale Rana, and Sue Dykes.

Mark lives in Southern California with his wife, Kathleen. They have two grown sons.

# About Reasons to Believe

Reasons to Believe (RTB) exists to reveal God in science. Based in Covina, California, RTB was established in 1986 and since then has taken scientific evidence for the God of the Bible across the US and around the world. Our ongoing work is providing content for all who desire to explore the connection between science and the Christian faith.

RTB is unique in its range of resources. The curious can explore articles, podcasts, and videos. Those who want to learn more can delve into books, in-person and livestreamed events, and online courses. Donors enable us to continue this important work.

**For more information, visit reasons.org.**

**For inquiries, contact us via:
818 S. Oak Park Rd.
Covina, CA 91724
(855) REASONS | (855) 732-7667
ministrycare@reasons.org**

# OVERFLOWING FROM THE BIBLE INTO HISTORY ITSELF

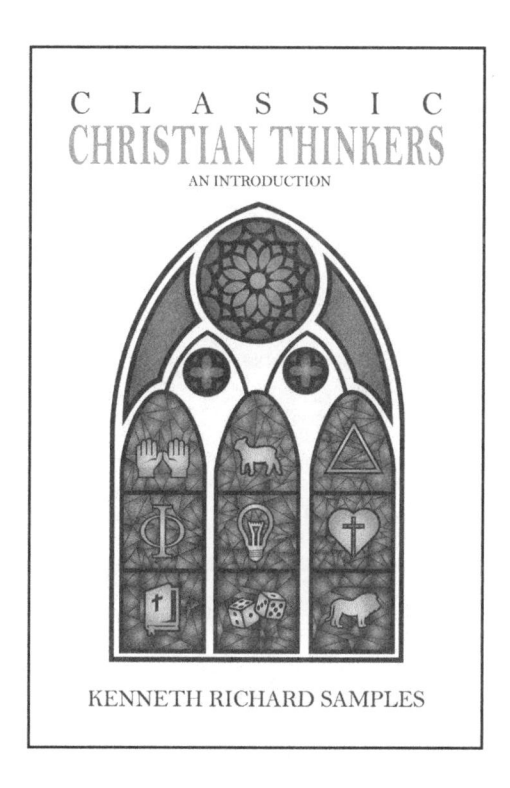

**CLASSIC CHRISTIAN THINKERS**
AN INTRODUCTION

KENNETH RICHARD SAMPLES

The history of the Christian faith continues on in the works of these nine truth-seekers. Read about the rich legacy left behind by these champions of the Christian faith.

reasons.org | @RTB_Official

# Do you still have questions about Christianity?

## WITHOUT a DOUBT
### ANSWERING THE 20 TOUGHEST FAITH QUESTIONS

**KENNETH RICHARD SAMPLES**
FOREWORD BY RONALD NASH

Unpacking topics from naturalism to God's existence, *Without a Doubt* provides clear, solid answers to tough questions about Christianity.

reasons.org | @RTB_Official